Michael Moorcock

CRITICAL EXPLORATIONS IN SCIENCE FICTION AND FANTASY
(a series edited by Donald E. Palumbo and C.W. Sullivan III)

1 *Worlds Apart? Dualism and Transgression in Contemporary Female Dystopias* (Dunja M. Mohr, 2005)

2 *Tolkien and Shakespeare: Essays on Shared Themes and Language* (ed. Janet Brennan Croft, 2007)

3 *Culture, Identities and Technology in the* Star Wars *Films: Essays on the Two Trilogies* (ed. Carl Silvio, Tony M. Vinci, 2007)

4 *The Influence of* Star Trek *on Television, Film and Culture* (ed. Lincoln Geraghty, 2008)

5 *Hugo Gernsback and the Century of Science Fiction* (Gary Westfahl, 2007)

6 *One Earth, One People: The Mythopoeic Fantasy Series of Ursula K. Le Guin, Lloyd Alexander, Madeleine L'Engle and Orson Scott Card* (Marek Oziewicz, 2008)

7 *The Evolution of Tolkien's Mythology: A Study of the History of Middle-earth* (Elizabeth A. Whittingham, 2008)

8 *H. Beam Piper: A Biography* (John F. Carr, 2008)

9 *Dreams and Nightmares: Science and Technology in Myth and Fiction* (Mordecai Roshwald, 2008)

10 Lilith *in a New Light: Essays on the George MacDonald Fantasy Novel* (ed. Lucas H. Harriman, 2008)

11 *Feminist Narrative and the Supernatural: The Function of Fantastic Devices in Seven Recent Novels* (Katherine J. Weese, 2008)

12 *The Science of Fiction and the Fiction of Science: Collected Essays on SF Storytelling and the Gnostic Imagination* (Frank McConnell, ed. Gary Westfahl, 2009)

13 *Kim Stanley Robinson Maps the Unimaginable: Critical Essays* (ed. William J. Burling, 2009)

14 *The Inter-Galactic Playground: A Critical Study of Children's and Teens' Science Fiction* (Farah Mendlesohn, 2009)

15 *Science Fiction from Québec: A Postcolonial Study* (Amy J. Ransom, 2009)

16 *Science Fiction and the Two Cultures: Essays on Bridging the Gap Between the Sciences and the Humanities* (ed. Gary Westfahl, George Slusser, 2009)

17 *Stephen R. Donaldson and the Modern Epic Vision: A Critical Study of the "Chronicles of Thomas Covenant" Novels* (Christine Barkley, 2009)

18 *Ursula K. Le Guin's Journey to Post-Feminism* (Amy M. Clarke, 2010)

19 *Portals of Power: Magical Agency and Transformation in Literary Fantasy* (Lori M. Campbell, 2010)

20 *The Animal Fable in Science Fiction and Fantasy* (Bruce Shaw, 2010)

21 *Illuminating* Torchwood: *Essays on Narrative, Character and Sexuality in the BBC Series* (ed. Andrew Ireland, 2010)

22 *Comics as a Nexus of Cultures: Essays on the Interplay of Media, Disciplines and International Perspectives* (ed. Mark Berninger, Jochen Ecke, Gideon Haberkorn, 2010)

23 *The Anatomy of Utopia: Narration, Estrangement and Ambiguity in More, Wells, Huxley and Clarke* (Károly Pintér, 2010)

24 *The Anticipation Novelists of 1950s French Science Fiction: Stepchildren of Voltaire* (Bradford Lyau, 2010)

25 *The* Twilight *Mystique: Critical Essays on the Novels and Films* (ed. Amy M. Clarke, Marijane Osborn, 2010)

26 *The Mythic Fantasy of Robert Holdstock: Critical Essays on the Fiction* (ed. Donald E. Morse, Kálmán Matolcsy, 2011)

27 *Science Fiction and the Prediction of the Future: Essays on Foresight and Fallacy* (ed. Gary Westfahl, Wong Kin Yuen, Amy Kit-sze Chan, 2011)

28 *Apocalypse in Australian Fiction and Film: A Critical Study* (Roslyn Weaver, 2011)

29 *British Science Fiction Film and Television: Critical Essays*
(ed. Tobias Hochscherf, James Leggott, 2011)

30 *Cult Telefantasy Series: A Critical Analysis of* The Prisoner, Twin Peaks, The X-Files, Buffy the Vampire Slayer, Lost, Heroes, Doctor Who *and* Star Trek (Sue Short, 2011)

31 *The Postnational Fantasy: Essays on Postcolonialism, Cosmopolitics and Science Fiction*
(ed. Masood Ashraf Raja, Jason W. Ellis and Swaralipi Nandi, 2011)

32 *Heinlein's Juvenile Novels: A Cultural Dictionary* (C.W. Sullivan III, 2011)

33 *Welsh Mythology and Folklore in Popular Culture: Essays on Adaptations in Literature, Film, Television and Digital Media* (ed. Audrey L. Becker and Kristin Noone, 2011)

34 *I See You: The Shifting Paradigms of James Cameron's* Avatar (Ellen Grabiner, 2012)

35 *Of Bread, Blood and* The Hunger Games*: Critical Essays on the Suzanne Collins Trilogy* (ed. Mary F. Pharr and Leisa A. Clark, 2012)

36 *The Sex Is Out of This World: Essays on the Carnal Side of Science Fiction* (ed. Sherry Ginn and Michael G. Cornelius, 2012)

37 *Lois McMaster Bujold: Essays on a Modern Master of Science Fiction and Fantasy* (ed. Janet Brennan Croft, 2013)

38 *Girls Transforming: Invisibility and Age-Shifting in Children's Fantasy Fiction Since the 1970s* (Sanna Lehtonen, 2013)

39 Doctor Who *in Time and Space: Essays on Themes, Characters, History and Fandom, 1963–2012* (ed. Gillian I. Leitch, 2013)

40 *The Worlds of* Farscape*: Essays on the Groundbreaking Television Series*
(ed. Sherry Ginn, 2013)

41 *Orbiting Ray Bradbury's Mars: Biographical, Anthropological, Literary, Scientific and Other Perspectives* (ed. Gloria McMillan, 2013)

42 *The Heritage of Heinlein: A Critical Reading of the Fiction Television Series* (Thomas D. Clareson and Joe Sanders, 2014)

43 *The Past That Might Have Been, the Future That May Come: Women Writing Fantastic Fiction, 1960s to the Present* (Lauren J. Lacey, 2014)

44 *Environments in Science Fiction: Essays on Alternative Spaces*
(ed. Susan M. Bernardo, 2014)

45 *Discworld and the Disciplines: Critical Approaches to the Terry Pratchett Works*
(ed. Anne Hiebert Alton and William C. Spruiell, 2014)

46 *Nature and the Numinous in Mythopoeic Fantasy Literature*
(Christopher Straw Brawley, 2014)

47 *J.R.R. Tolkien, Robert E. Howard and the Birth of Modern Fantasy* (Deke Parsons, 2014)

48 *The Monomyth in American Science Fiction Films: 28 Visions of the Hero's Journey*
(Donald E. Palumbo, 2014)

49 *The Fantastic in Holocaust Literature and Film: Critical Perspectives*
(ed. Judith B. Kerman and John Edgar Browning, 2014)

50 Star Wars *in the Public Square:* The Clone Wars *as Political Dialogue*
(Derek R. Sweet, 2016)

51 *An Asimov Companion: Characters, Places and Terms in the Robot/Empire/Foundation Metaseries* (Donald E. Palumbo, 2016)

52 *Michael Moorcock: Fiction, Fantasy and the World's Pain* (Mark Scroggins, 2016)

Michael Moorcock
Fiction, Fantasy and the World's Pain

MARK SCROGGINS

CRITICAL EXPLORATIONS IN
SCIENCE FICTION AND FANTASY, 52

Series Editors Donald E. Palumbo *and* C.W. Sullivan III

McFarland & Company, Inc., Publishers
Jefferson, North Carolina

LIBRARY OF CONGRESS CATALOGUING-IN-PUBLICATION DATA

Names: Scroggins, Mark, 1964– author.
Title: Michael Moorcock : fiction, fantasy and the
world's pain / Mark Scroggins.
Description: Jefferson, North Carolina : McFarland & Company, Inc.,
Publishers, 2016. | Series: Critical explorations in science fiction
and fantasy ; 52 | Includes bibliographical references and index.
Identifiers: LCCN 2015047827 | ISBN 9781476663074
(softcover : acid free paper) ∞
Subjects: LCSH: Moorcock, Michael, 1939—Criticism and interpretation.
Classification: LCC PR6063.O59 Z46 2016 | DDC 823/.914—dc23
LC record available at http://lccn.loc.gov/2015047827

BRITISH LIBRARY CATALOGUING DATA ARE AVAILABLE

ISBN (print) 978-1-4766-6307-4
ISBN (ebook) 978-1-4766-2417-4

© 2016 Mark Scroggins. All rights reserved

No part of this book may be reproduced or transmitted in any form
or by any means, electronic or mechanical, including photocopying
or recording, or by any information storage and retrieval system,
without permission in writing from the publisher.

Front cover painting of Elric of Melniboné: Jeffrey Catherine Jones,
White Bird (1976), © Estate of Jeffrey Catherine Jones; used by permission

Printed in the United States of America

McFarland & Company, Inc., Publishers
Box 611, Jefferson, North Carolina 28640
www.mcfarlandpub.com

For Olly and Steve, the boys in Drööd

Table of Contents

Acknowledgments   xi
Preface   1
Introduction   5

   1. The Multiverse and the Champion   15
   2. A Messiah for the Age of Entropy   35
   3. New Avatars, New Time Streams and a Farewell to Fantasy   60
   4. Reality and Its Bitter Myths   86
   5. Consolidating the Multiverse   112
   6. The Second Ether, the Moonbeam Roads and Beyond   142

Conclusion   166
Appendix: The Eternal Champion Omnibus Editions   171
Chapter Notes   175
Bibliography   191
Index   195

Acknowledgments

I have spent most of my academic career working with twentieth and twenty-first century avant-garde poetry, and many of my friends and acquaintances from that world, poets and scholars both, have been warmly supportive of this project. I especially thank Norman Finkelstein, Robert Archambeau, Peter O'Leary, Patrick Pritchett, Eric Hoffman, and Andrew Joron. In my own Department of English at Florida Atlantic University, a flourishing program in fantasy and science fiction demonstrated to me that these popular forms can be discussed with both enthusiasm and scholarly rigor, and my colleagues Carol McGuirk, Lisa Swanstrom, and the late Robert Collins provided models of that sort of work. My department chair, Eric Berlatsky, has been both a patient sounding board for ideas and a model for critical practice in his own work on Alan Moore and graphic novels more generally. I'm particularly grateful for my old friend Lisa Lynne Moore's enthusiasm and support. Eric Murphy Selinger is one of my oldest and dearest friends from the world of poetry criticism; his more recent work in romance fiction has been a particular inspiration. I have benefited from conversations and correspondences with a bunch of other folks—colleagues, graduate students, old friends, new acquaintances: I thank William Bradley, Papatya Bucak, Oliver Buckton, Skye Cervone, Dan Creed, Alex Davis, Samuel R. Delany, Stephen Engle, Taylor Hagood, Martha Hollander, Krista Kasdorf, Ben Kolstad, Rob Latham, Pollyanna Parker, and Ben Robertson. I thank the organizers of the annual International Conference on the Fantastic in the Arts, who provided a venue to present papers drawn from or related to this work in 2013, 2014, and 2015. I thank FAU's Dorothy F. Schmidt College of Arts and Letters for a sabbatical during which much of this book was drafted.

Dr. Michael Sanders made possible my acquisition of Gollancz's latest edition of Moorcock's works; those twenty-eight handsome volumes are known around this household as "The Michael Sanders Michael Moorcock Collection." I thank Julianna Jones Muth, who made an adolescent dream come true by letting me use Jeffrey Catherine Jones's "White Bird" on this book's cover. Barbara Bonn gave me the pen with which I wrote most of the book; if only it enabled me to write prose as graceful as hers!

I am grateful for the work of earlier Moorcock critics and commentators, especially Colin Greenland, Jeff Gardiner, and the incomparable John Clute. The various contributors to the website "Moorcock's Miscellany" (multiverse.org)—most notable among them Moorcock himself—have saved me hundreds of hours of research and cross-referencing, and have given me a wealth of insights into Moorcock's work; they represent the power of community crowd-sourcing at its best. John Davey, Moorcock's editor and bibliographer, has been unfailingly generous and helpful. And I thank Michael Moorcock for looking over my manuscript as a whole and making some extremely useful suggestions.

As to the dedication: Drööd is a part-time (but tenured) rock 'n' roll power trio, whose members include Oliver Buckton (guitar, vocals) and Stephen Engle (drums). We are proud to have one more umlaut than Motörhead, whose bassist and singer Lemmy used to make music with Michael Moorcock. I have named my two electric basses "Stormbringer" and "Mournblade."

My daughters Pippa and Daphne are a ceaseless fountain of pleasure only occasionally leavened with exasperation; I have high hopes of dooming at least one of them to an adolescence of geekdom. As so many times before, my wife Jennifer A. Low has been beside me every step of the way. Warmest love to all three of them.

Preface

Now well into his sixth decade as a professional writer, Michael Moorcock is a looming presence in fantasy literature and has left his mark on science fiction as well. He has won a long string of prizes for individual works—the Nebula Award for best novella, the British Fantasy Award for best short story, the John W. Campbell Award for best science fiction novel, the World Fantasy Award for best novel, and four August Derleth Awards for best novel—and a number of awards recognizing lifetime achievement: a 1993 British Fantasy Award, a 2000 World Fantasy Award, a 2004 Prix Utopiales Award, and a 2005 Bram Stoker Award; in 2002 he was inducted into the Science Fiction Hall of Fame, and in 2008 was named a Science Fiction Writers of America Grand Master. And Moorcock has achieved significant recognition outside the fields of fantasy and science fiction. His novel *The Condition of Muzak* won the *Guardian* Fiction Prize, and *Mother London* was short-listed for the Whitbread Prize. In 2008, he was named by the London *Times* as one of the fifty greatest British writers since 1945.

While the institutional and popular recognition his works have garnered is undeniable, it's challenging to get an overall sense of Moorcock's achievement, if only because the man has been so prolific. Over the course of his long career he has published at least seventy novels or collections of closely interlinked short stories, some 150 short stories, and uncounted thousands of pages of journalistic and critical prose. *Michael Moorcock: Fiction, Fantasy and the World's Pain* aims to provide an overview of Moorcock's writing career from its beginnings to his most recent departures. To some degree, I have focused on Moorcock's fantasy writings, since it is in the field of fantasy that he is perhaps best known and in which his work has had the most influence. But I hope to have done justice as well to his achievements in science fiction and in "realistic" fiction, for much of what makes Moorcock so interesting is his constant probing at the boundaries of genre writing, his insistent questioning both of the pigeonholes into which writerly and readerly communities and the publishing industry force writing, and the stances towards reality implied by the decision to write "fantasy" or "realism."

Moorcock has always viewed himself as a popular writer, one who writes to give pleasure to as large an audience as possible. Paradoxically perhaps, he has also made a name for himself (especially during his editorship of *New Worlds* magazine) as a champion of the provocative and experimental, and many of his works are written in distinctly unconventional, non-linear forms. The tension between "popular," even "formulaic" genre fiction—as in the many brief heroic fantasy novels Moorcock turned out between the mid-sixties and the mid-seventies—and his more challenging "modernist" works, is paralleled by a tension between fantasy itself and "realism," fiction which deals with twentieth-century history in a mode unleavened by the marvelous. But the two tensions cannot be mapped onto one another in any straightforward manner, for Moorcock has written both fantastic and realistic fictions in non-linear forms as well as in narrative modes inherited straight from Dickens and Wells.

One constant throughout Moorcock's work, however, is his simultaneous desire to present his readers with an entertaining story and to grapple with ideas of ethical and social consequence. If Moorcock is only intermittently a *didactic* writer, he is more or less constantly a *moral* one. In many of his fantasy novels, we are presented with an overt dialectical struggle, not between Good and Evil but between Law and Chaos: two ever-present tendencies in individual human nature and society, each necessary in moderation and each life-threatening in excess. In a very long series of his heroic fantasy novels, an "Eternal Champion" fights either Chaos or Law on behalf of a cosmic "Balance."

That struggle between Law and Chaos, fought out across the various realms of a "multiverse" which Moorcock first imagined in the early 1960s—and which has more recently become the focus of serious discussion among physicists and cosmologists—has been complicated and subtilized over the years in Moorcock's writings. What has remained constant has been his abiding concern with human unhappiness, with the individual and social sources of what he has named in one of his titles "the world's pain." Moorcock's social ideal is an anarchist, communitarian one; his ethical ideal, like Aristotle's, is a matter of a hard-won moderation, a "golden mean." In some sense, all of his books argue these ideals, and they do so in a bewildering variety of modes and registers. But Moorcock's books are never merely didactic. Horace argued that the purpose of poetry is to "instruct and delight." While there is certainly an instructional, a moral (though never *moralizing*) aspect of Moorcock's work, it never overshadows his primary desire to delight the reader, to entertain, divert, and give pleasure. *Michael Moorcock: Fiction, Fantasy and the World's Pain* aims to provide some signposts to the initially confusing sprawl of this vast, thoughtful, and entertaining fictive *œuvre*.

Introduction

How in the world did I get started with Michael Moorcock? I blame Frank Frazetta (1926–2010), the fantasy artist whose improbably kinetic paintings—muscled barbarians, busty (and usually naked) women, menacing apes, giant snakes, and demons, all knotted together in compositions of breathless energy—had by the early 1970s, on the covers of what seemed like hundreds of paperbacks, become *the* inescapable face of heroic fantasy.

The first Moorcock novel I acquired and read was *Phoenix in Obsidian*, under its U.S. title *The Silver Warriors*, in a 1977 Dell paperback. No doubt I was attracted to the book in large part because of its Frazetta cover painting. I had been collecting Frazetta covers for some time at that point, and I recognized "The Silver Warrior," the artist's portrait of Urlik Skarsol, his black sword upraised as four polar bears drew his chariot across a snow field, as one of Frazetta's best. I was primed for the book's contents, as well: not merely was I thirteen or fourteen, the ideal age for reading fantasy novels featuring hard-thewed barbarian sword-wielders, but I was already steeped in the tales of Edgar Rice Burroughs's Barsoom and Robert E. Howard's Hyborian Age, two crucial forerunners of the vast Moorcockian tapestry of worlds and heroes in which Urlik Skarsol's adventures, I would learn, formed only one vivid episode.

For of course *The Silver Warriors* was just the beginning of my explorations in Moorcock's multiverse. By the time I graduated high school I must have read over forty of his books, delighting as did so many other fans in the way he cleverly interwove the otherwise disparate worlds and quests of a whole stable of heroes: Urlik, Erekosë (the Eternal Champion), Corum Jhaelen Irsei (the Prince in the Scarlet Robe), Duke Dorian Hawkmoon of Köln, and most of all, the unforgettable doomed albino emperor, wielder of the black sword Stormbringer, Elric of Melniboné. And beyond the realms of epic fantasy, I was fascinated by the decadent dwellers of Moorcock's End of Time novels, the alternative histories of his Oswald Bastable books, and the splintered, modular narratives featuring Jerry Cornelius, a hipster messiah for the age of entropy.

I largely set aside science fiction and heroic fantasy during the first decades of my (still-continuing) sojourn in the no less fantastic worlds of literary modernism and avant-garde poetry. But I cherished a deep (though mostly concealed) affection for Moorcock's books, and tried to keep up, in however desultory a fashion, with whatever he was writing: no easy proposition, for even after Moorcock slackened the frenetic production pace he had maintained throughout the 1970s, he still seemed to produce at least three or four substantial books a year. And when I decided around ten years ago to systematically catch up with what Moorcock had been up to in the decades while I was assiduously cracking the codes of vast, polyglot modernist poems, I was delighted to discover that he had not been merely repackaging the array of novels that had made him a star in the heroic fantasy genre. Nor was he simply repeating the fictive gestures that had proved so successful in the thirty-odd novels that made up the first layer, as it were, of his "Eternal Champion" mythos.

Over the last two decades of the twentieth century, Moorcock extended the Elric franchise in new novels that subtilized and complicated his conception of the albino anti-hero. He launched an entirely new fantasy sequence, this one revolving around the von Bek family, guardians of the Holy Grail, who had distant relations and analogues in a whole range of Beks, Becks, and Beggs scattered throughout his novels and stories. In such major works as *Mother London* and the four large Pyat novels, he anatomized and memorialized both the darker and the more hopeful history of his own century. And perhaps most surprisingly, in the books of the Second Ether sequence, Moorcock set aside the sometimes histrionic tragedy of his epic fantasy mode for a quasi-comic, quasi-science fictional framework that thoroughly updates the concept of the multiverse, the framework of multiple secondary universes which had on some level underpinned most of his books since 1965's *The Sundered Worlds*. More recently, in the three long novels of the Moonbeams Roads sequence, Moorcock set a grand capstone to the whole edifice of his Eternal Champion writings, as well as to the Elric franchise, weaving it more closely, by dint of recurring characters, settings, and concepts, with the von Bek novels, the Cornelius stories, and indeed most of the books he has written.

As his writing career has passed the half-century mark, it's become clear that Moorcock for a long time has not just been writing novels, but

Introduction

with every new book has been quite self-consciously producing another thread that will lend its calibrated weight and tension to the vast web that is his fictive *œuvre* as a whole—a single, sprawling work. The new books serve to knit the old ones even more tightly together. Simultaneously, through selective revision and determined repackaging, Moorcock has continually reasserted the unity of all of his fiction. The whole business has an odd analogue in the process of the canonization of the Christian Bible, that extraordinarily heterogeneous collection of sixty-six books of varying authorship, genre, and language, which has been presented for some 1700 years as a unity, the product of a singular inspiration.

Something is gained, and something is lost, in the tightening intertextuality of Moorcock's recent work. The old DAW paperback collections of the Elric stories, for instance—the ones in which I first read about the fall of Melniboné and about the Black Sword Stormbringer—used to boast on their back covers that each volume could be read on its own, without reference to Moorcock's other works. In contrast, *The War Amongst the Angels* (1996) or *Daughter of Dreams* (2001) seem at first glance to present rather tough going for readers without a pretty solid familiarity with much of Moorcock's previous writing. But that's only one way of looking at it: conversely, every book in the Moorcock canon can be seen as an entry point, some more confusing than others, to the interlocking labyrinth of his created worlds. A certain degree of bafflement is inevitable for the first-time visitor, but any book can be the start of a reading exploration whose pleasures include the gradual grasping of the shape of the network as a whole.[1] My own entry point was *The Silver Warriors*; I have yet to emerge.

* * *

Any overall critical assessment of Moorcock's achievement has to begin with three unavoidable facts: he has written a very large amount; his writings fall into a wide and often incommensurable variety of genres; and the literary quality of his work is extremely variable. By my count, Moorcock has published something over seventy separate novels, many of them brief 60,000-word affairs, but a substantial number of them stretching over four or five hundred pages. To the novels—which are clearly at the heart of his achievement—add around 150 short stories, which have been collected and re-collected in various volumes over the years.[2] (Moorcock has also written a good deal of criticism and occasional journalism; two recent volumes assemble over a thousand pages of such writing, but Moorcock's editor John Davey admits that this represents only a fraction of what has been published.[3])

This vast fictive *œuvre*—at least 15,000 pages, I'd guess—falls into a bewildering variety of genres. While Moorcock is most often identified as a fantasist, more specifically as a practitioner of the much-reviled "sword-and-sorcery" subgenre (and he has indeed written quite a few books that fall into that category), he has also written "straight" science fiction (a rather small number of novels and stories); "sword-and-planet" romances that fall between the epic fantasy and SF genres; alternative histories; historical novels; and straight "literary" fiction. (He has as well scripted movies and graphic novels, provided lyrics for songs recorded by Hawkwind, Blue Öyster Cult, and his own band The Deep Fix, and written the scenario for a computer role playing game.) Moorcock has a keen awareness of generic traditions, but that doesn't mean he feels obliged to work within them. His novels have the habit, annoying for the pigeonholing critic, of constantly shifting among genres, of drawing elements from various traditions at once.

Moorcock has written a great number of books, in a great number of modes and categories. But his books are by no means uniformly successful. It goes without saying that genre fiction is fueled by different readerly pleasures than more conventional "literary" fiction: science fiction and fantasy offer the reader the splendors of unknown technologies, vividly imagined alien species, settings radically or subtly different from our own world, causality-challenging supernatural forces (magic, sorcery, gods and demons), and the opportunity to imaginatively engage in modes of physical and mental heroism rarely to be found in the reader's mundane existence. Readers of such genre fiction, it is often argued, place a lower premium than more snobbish literary types on depth of characterization, strength or subtlety of prose style, carefully observed social insight, and measured and balanced plotting. In such purely *literary* terms, some of Moorcock's novels are very badly written indeed, their flimsy characters and ramshackle, hasty plots all too patently betraying their hurried composition. And even in terms of genre fiction, a few of Moorcock's books simply fail to satisfy the reader's desire for vivid invention and colorful adventure. (But such utter failures are indeed few—even Moorcock's most frenetically tossed-off productions usually have some redeeming fictive element, some character, setting, or situation that embeds them in the reader's memory.)

I'm rather more interested in the distance Moorcock has consistently placed between himself and his more ill-written—from a specifically *literary* point of view—novels. While he has never outrightly disowned any of his writings, and has always undertaken whatever he writes with the intention of giving his readers full value for their time and money, he has also maintained a clear distinction between the fantasies he has written—often in rapid succession, with bewildering speed—and the more thoughtful works to which he has devoted much longer periods of time planning and drafting. Moorcock does not dismiss the former works, but their production is clearly subordinate to that of his more "weighty" works. What this distancing bespeaks is Moorcock's very real literary ambitions, his desire to write books of lasting merit, as well as mere entertainments. The tension between Moorcock the entertainer and Moorcock the "serious" novelist is perhaps most evident in his writing during the 1980s, when large, complex non-fantasy works like *Mother London* or the first two Pyat novels counterpointed such unabashedly generic fantasies as *The War Hound and the World's Pain* and *The Fortress of the Pearl*.

But it would be grotesquely oversimplifying to set a "serious," "literary" realist Moorcock too sharply in contrast to a fantasist diversion-maker, for over the past two decades Moorcock has brought his science fiction/fantasy works to a high pitch of literary weight and complexity, so that the books of the Second Ether series or the Moonbeam Roads novels (at least in part) bear comparison, in terms of stylistic polish and thematic complexity, with anything he has previously written. More important, however, is the fact that Moorcock's work, even in its most seemingly escapist modes, has always grappled with the sorts of larger moral issues that one associates with his true forebears, the major Victorian, Edwardian, and nineteenth-century Russian novelists. Moorcock is an intensely *moral* novelist, and from the very beginning his fiction has sought to explore the basic causes of human unhappiness and suffering: the perennial states of conflict, malaise, and dissatisfaction that he has named, in one title, the "world's pain."[4]

Fantasy literature has always been able to deal with serious moral and spiritual issues, but too often it's done so in the black-and-white terms of "good" and "evil." J. R. R. Tolkien's *The Lord of the Rings*, the vast presence hovering over English-language fantasy since the 1960s, is replete with nuanced, sometimes amusing examples of heroism and ordinary *goodness*; but in Moorcock's own reading, Tolkien's portrayal of *evil*—the unseen, malevolent Sauron, his grotesque minions, the various neutral characters he has "turned" to his side—is for the most part remarkably one-dimensional and unconvincing. Moorcock, as a child of the Blitz, and a child of Jewish ancestry, grew up in the wake of the Holocaust, under the shadow of regimes that could only be called "evil." But his fantasies, while they have their good guys and bad guys, strenuously resist the manichean dualism of evil and good.

Instead, the duality that most fascinates Moorcock lies between two opposed ways of individually and socially being-in-the-world: order and disorder. In the fantasy novels these states become personified as quasi-deities, Lords of Law or Lords of Chaos. (In his earliest works, Moorcock uses "chaos," "anarchy," and "entropy" largely interchangeably. Over time, he will favor "chaos": *entropy* is a process, rather than a state, and *anarchy*—the absence of external authority, rather than chaos—will come to be his chosen political inclination.) The Eternal Champion, reincarnated a thousand times, called to war in a thousand different realms, will fight for one principle or the other. But he (or occasionally she) fights for Chaos or Law not as an absolute *good*, but to establish an equilibrium between the two—a Balance. Such a Balance, refigured in various forms across the various novels, is the "cure" for the world's pain.

The moral principle advanced in more or less all of Moorcock's books, then, is that of an Aristotelian—or Horatian, or Confucian—ethical mean. It's presented in larger-than-life personification in the fantasy novels, sometimes as a giant set of scales in the sky, at other times as a jewel-studded shaft or a quasi-Arthurian Holy Grail. In other books, Moorcock explores the destructiveness of all manner of excess: sexual obsession (or "erotomania") in *The Brothel in Rosenstrasse*; hero worship in *Behold the Man*; racial and ethnic pride and bigotry in the Pyat novels. Throughout, his characters seek (and very occasionally achieve) states of equilibrium, islands of personal and social equity in which happiness can perhaps flourish.

As an ethical principle, the Horatian mean ("nothing in excess") is apt to sound a trifle banal—but no more so than any other universal. And boiling fictional worlds down to their thematic "messages" is a pretty reductive game (*Ulysses* = "Be happy with the love you've found, however imperfect"; *To the Lighthouse* = "make little islands of order in the chaotic rush of life"; *Moby-Dick* = "Avoid obsessing over large metaphysical mysteries"). We read fiction for the most part not to learn moral lessons, but to be immersed in worlds and consciousnesses other than our own. And Moorcock's work provides us not just with an alternate world, but a whole plethora of bewilderingly various yet cunningly interlinked universes—a "multiverse," populated by a multitude of characters. There is a didactic side to Moorcock, but he rarely lets it overshadow what he considers his primary calling as storyteller: to divert, to entertain, to enthrall with the variety of his invention. There have been many moments when Moorcock has grown uncomfortable with the label of "genre" writer, but he's always proudly aspired to be a *popular* writer. The Eternal Champion and his avatars may come and go, the Black Sword in its various manifestations may flicker in and out of the picture, but in all of the coruscating scenes of Moorcock's multiverse there is one implied constant: the reader.

* * *

The chapters that follow are an exploration of that multiverse. They approach Moorcock's work roughly chronologically, with occasional thematic and stylistic divagations. I want not merely to survey his work, but to convey a sense of how his writing has evolved, both stylistically and conceptually, over the past half-century.

Tempted as I was to begin with *The Silver Warriors*, my personal Moorcock ur-text, instead I start at a more logical point: the story "The Eternal Champion," which introduces the figure of whom so many Moorcock protagonists are avatars. From there, the first chapter examines the earliest formulations of Moorcock's multiverse, and takes a close look at the early appearances of his most iconic character, Elric of Melniboné. Elric is Moorcock's most famous, most immediately identifiable creation; for better or worse, he is to Moorcock as Conan is to Robert E. Howard, or Sherlock Holmes to Arthur Conan Doyle.

My second chapter turns its attention to Moorcock's activities, mostly over the second half of the 1960s and the first half of the 1970s, outside of the field of fantasy. As the outspoken and iconoclastic editor of *New Worlds*, he was at the forefront of what came to be known as the "New Wave" of British science fiction, though the boldness of his editorial rhetoric tended to outpace that of his fictive productions. One creation of that period retains its fascination: Jerry Cornelius, a mythic anti-hero for the new drug- and rock 'n' roll-centered counterculture of the atomic age— and a blatant recasting of Elric into contemporary form. Moorcock would write four Cornelius novels between 1965 and 1977; the latter two, *The English Assassin* (1972) and *The Condition of Muzak* (1977), are tours-deforce of modular, late modernist narrative, radical advances on the straightforward storytelling of his fantasy.

Even as he championed formal discontinuity in *New Worlds* and the Cornelius books, Moorcock was busily producing more conventional fantasy narratives, and my third chapter focuses on these books, along with his other works through the end of the 1970s. The seven books of Hawkmoon and the six Corum novels date from this period, and explore new avatars of the Eternal Champion. In the "Nomad of the Time Streams" trilogy, Moorcock experimented with alternative histories of the twentieth century and grappled with the implications of imperialism, revolution, racism, and postcolonialism. The "Dancers at the End of Time" novels, set in a post-mortality, post-morality far future, are ostensibly more light-hearted and comic, evincing Moorcock's debt to Ronald Firbank and other humorists, but at their heart is a moral question: in a world without death or want, how would human beings make meaning of their lives? The sprawling *Gloriana; or, The Unfulfill'd Queen* (1978) is Moorcock's (temporary) farewell to the fantasy genre, his homage to his mentor Mervyn Peake, and an index of his growing ambition towards "literary" status.

My fourth chapter examines precisely those fictions in which Moorcock most explicitly lays claim to "mainstream" literary status, beginning with the formally innovative *Breakfast in the Ruins* (1972). Less structurally fragmented—indeed, quite narratively straightforward—are the volumes of the vast "Between the Wars" tetralogy (1981–2006), which recount the picaresque adventures of Maxim Arturovitch Pyatnitski—engineer, inventor, visionary, anti–Semite, and crypto-Jew—from his 1900 birth in Ukraine to his presence at Dachau. The widely acclaimed *Mother London* (1988) is a love letter to the London of Moorcock's childhood and youth, to the myths of sociality and communality that sustained Londoners through the Blitz and after, in contrast to the poisonous racial and nationalistic myths upon which Colonel Pyat battens.

While *Mother London* and the Pyat novels brought Moorcock a good deal of mainstream literary attention, his hiatus from fantasy was actually quite short-lived, and my fifth chapter explores what amounts to a "second wave" of Eternal Champion novels written over the 1980s and early 1990s—two new Elric books and a sequence of novels featuring not a single character, but the von Bek family, over several generations. These books introduce a more complex and robust conception of the multiverse than had appeared in the earlier works, even as they downplay the figure of the Eternal Champion. Paradoxically perhaps, over the course of the 1990s Moorcock collected the bulk of his published works in uniform "omnibus" editions, precisely under the title of the "Eternal Champion." In the compiling of these omnibuses one can see his first concerted effort at unifying—through revision, through characters' name changes, through added bridge passages—his disparate and untidy *œuvre*.

The sixth and final chapter traces the concept of the multiverse as it evolves through even more intense modifications. In the "Second Ether" series (1995–1996), the multiverse itself, much inflected by Moorcock's reading in chaos theory, has become the primary focus of Moorcock's invention. The struggle between Law and Chaos continues, but the singular figure of the Eternal Champion has largely dispersed into a shifting cast of disparate characters. More recently, Moorcock has rebooted the Elric franchise in the three long "Moonbeam Roads" novels, which cast Elric himself as almost a secondary character to various contemporary von Beks, and which aim, by winding together the threads of dozens of earlier stories, to bring the Eternal Champion saga as a whole to a resounding and complex conclusion. And in his most recent novel, *The Whispering Swarm* (the first of a projected trilogy), Moorcock has mingled historical fantasy and straightforward autobiography, pressing his writing in a entirely new direction.

Moorcock's work is only slightly less multifaceted than his fictive multiverse. I certainly can't in the compass of a single book do justice to it, or even to all of the bits of which I'm fondest. The following, then, is less a detailed map of Elric's Bright Empire or a Baedeker to Jerry Cornelius's swinging and decaying London, than a Rough Guide to some salient landmarks of a rich and various continent. It was Frank Frazetta's glowering Urlik Skarsol who beckoned me into Moorcock's labyrinth, but every new reader finds his or her own entry point to Moorcock's library of whirling and intersecting worlds. This book, I hope, places some signposts in that initially bewildering multiplicity, and analyzes some of the sources of this writer's unique pleasures and powers.

A Note on Texts

In what follows I will be quoting as much as possible from the most recent, "definitive" texts of the Gollancz "Michael Moorcock Collection" (twenty-eight volumes, 2013–2015). Those who are still reading their Moorcock in ragged DAW or Mayflower paperbacks, however, can be comforted by the fact that most of the revisions he has made for various reprintings are minor, cosmetic. Most, but not *all*—and I will be paying some attention to the more significant changes he has made to his works over the years.

Moorcock has published over seventy separate novels or collections of linked stories and at least fifteen more miscellaneous collections of short stories. His books have been repeatedly reprinted and repackaged in various "omnibus" editions, often in volumes of differing content that share the same titles; a comprehensive bibliography of his works (a nightmarish prospect for the bibliographer!) would run to many hundreds of entries. In order to simplify references, I have tried as much as possible to avoid quoting from different editions bearing the same title: thus, for instance, when I quote Moorcock's important introduction to the White Wolf omnibus edition of *The Eternal Champion* (Stone Mountain, GA: White Wolf, 1994), I cite that introduction as reprinted in *Into the Media Web*, since I elsewhere quote material from the 2013 Gollancz *The Eternal Champion*. Sometimes, however, it has been impossible to avoid quoting volumes with the same or very similar titles. Readers should pay careful attention to the reference notes.

1

The Multiverse and the Champion

Michael John Moorcock was born in a London suburb on December 18, 1939, some fourteen weeks into the Second World War. "My earliest memories," he writes, "are of air-raid shelters, dog-fights, searchlights, barrage balloons, collecting shrapnel and bits of planes on the Common—which we swapped as peacetime kids trade bubblegum cards—of ruined buildings, of endless landscapes where bombs had cleared eccentric spaces amongst shops and houses."[1] He grew up in a single-parent household—his father decamped at the end of the war—and while he had no great success at a heterogeneous collection of private schools, he was an avid reader from early on. By the time he left school at fifteen, he had already produced a number of his own magazines (*Outlaws Own*, *Book Collector's News*), the most notable of which was *Burroughsania* [sic], dedicated to the work of the American novelist Edgar Rice Burroughs, creator of Tarzan of the Apes and John Carter of Mars.

Moorcock was a professional writer by the end of his teens, turning out an astonishing array of material: he wrote for *Tarzan Adventures* (for whom he produced stories of the John Carter-clone "Sojan the Swordsman"); he wrote for the Sexton Blake Library, "the longest running detective series in the world"; he scripted comic strips featuring "Dogfight Dixon, RFC; Dick Daring of the Mounties; Captain Condor of the Space Patrol; Karl the Viking; Robin Hood; Kit Carson; Buck Jones; Buffalo Bill; Strongbow the Mohawk; and Zip Nolan of the Highway Patrol."

In this popular fiction Grub Street, Moorcock learned "to write very economically, to plan scene, dialogue and narrative so that they had the maximum effect"; he developed "a tremendous facility for writing quickly about anything."[2] Revision was out of the question: "I wasn't writing for an editor, I was writing for a printer. The press was ready, waiting for my copy; and it would be ready for more copy tomorrow, and more this time next week."³ If he found a story not up to his standards, the solution was not to revise or rework that story, but to write another: to do better the next time around.

The beginning of the sixties found Moorcock, already several years into his career as writer, ready to begin seriously exploring the fields of science fiction and heroic fantasy in which he would make his name. In a concentrated burst of activity over the first third of the decade he laid out many of the fictive elements that would underpin his work over the next half-century. Three of them are conceptual:

- The figure of the **Eternal Champion**, a hero-function, as it were, assuming different identities in different settings, fighting on various sides in various struggles, but always, sometimes paradoxically, *the same person*.
- The **multiverse**, an infinite series of occasionally interacting but mostly separate parallel universes, which provides local settings and habitations for the various avatars of the Eternal Champion.
- The struggle between **Law and Chaos**, order and disorder, that takes place in every society and every individual, and which in the Eternal Champion's various universes more often than not becomes externalized as an actual struggle between opposing entities and forces.

And even as he was conceiving and writing through the first formulations of these ideas which would dominate much of his popular fiction over the decades to come, Moorcock at the outset of his career was creating his most popular and enduring single character: Elric the doomed albino, last ruler of the Bright Empire of Melniboné, wielder of the soul-sucking black runesword Stormbringer—an avatar of the Eternal Champion, traveller of the Multiverse, a sworn devotee of Chaos who fights on the side of Law, on behalf of the Cosmic Balance.

* * *

Best to begin with "The Eternal Champion," since this story is where the Eternal Champion begins. "*The Eternal Champion*," Moorcock says, "was the first book I ever planned to write." He wrote an early draft when he was seventeen; five years later a novella-length version of the tale appeared in *Science Fantasy* (1962). Moorcock expanded this into a novel in 1970, which he revised in 1978 and again in 1992.⁴

The twentieth-century earthman John Daker becomes aware of his identity as Erekosë, the Eternal Champion, through an irresistable summoning: "*They called for me, that is all I really know. They called for me and I went to them, for I could not do otherwise."*[5] We know next to nothing about Daker, save that he lives in our own familiar world; once he has been summoned to the nameless world in which King Rigenos rules, he is immediately recognized as Erekosë, the long-dead champion of humankind. His task, as Rigenos explains to him, is to lead humanity in its ongoing battle with the "Hounds of Evil," the Eldren.[6]

The motif of the sleeping hero is a very old one indeed. King Arthur, William of Monmouth tells us, sleeps in the Isle of Avalon to return to England at her hour of greatest need; Friedrich Barbarossa, some legends say, will awaken one day to restore Germany to its ancient greatness; Holger Danske (or Ogier Danois in the Roland cycle) is promised to rise again at Denmark's moment of extremity. The teenaged Moorcock was of course familiar with these medieval versions of the sleeping and returning hero, but a more immediate inspiration for "The Eternal Champion" was almost certainly the American Poul Anderson's splendid 1953 romance *Three Hearts and Three Lions*.[7] In that novel, the Americanized Dane Holger Carlsen, working for the Danish underground in 1943 and pinned down by Gestapo forces on a beach near Elsinore, is abruptly whisked away to a medieval Europe of dwarfs, elves, witches, trolls, Saracens, and so forth, where he has become Ogier Danois—Holger Danske—a hero who can stand against the forces of Faerie who would plunge the entire world into chaos.

The moment when the inhabitant of our mundane world steps through the portal into another reality is one of the paradigmatic moments of fantasy, from Alice's plunge down the rabbit-hole onward. And it takes a particular inflection in heroic fantasy, when the protagonist serves as a focus of identification for the mundane reader, who is able vicariously to pursue fantasies of physical prowess, sexual adventure, and general heroism in a world in which the constraints of Western bourgeois society do not exist.

Anderson exploits the comic potential of this situation with considerable wryness in *Three Hearts*, to some degree imitating the tone of Twain's *Connecticut Yankee in King Arthur's Court* or L. Sprague de Camp and Fletcher Pratt's "Harold Shea" tales. Anderson's somewhat later story, "A Logical Conclusion" (1960), goes even further: Carl Greenough of the publishing industry and the barbarian chieftan Kendrith of Narr have had their souls switched by "the Goddess." At the end of Kendrith/Greenough's exploits (a naval fight, a siege, a daring raid and conquest, etc.), it turns out neither man desires to return to his "home" world. Greenough is of course delighted with the physical and sexual adventures of Kendrith's sword and sorcery world, while Kendrith is perfectly happy in contemporary New York, "among towers as high as mountains, served by machines more powerful than magic, the most fabulous parts of the world no further away than a few days' flying."[8] So the two men stay "switched."

In contrast, we know relatively little about John Daker's earth life, nor does he seem particularly traumatized (or for that matter energized) by his transition to the world in which human and Eldren struggle. Erekosë has been summoned, it emerges, to fight in a false cause. Humanity's crusade against the Eldren—whom we learn are gentle, technologically advanced, culturally sensitive—is based on a kind of mindless genocidal speciesism, a xenophobic bloodlust that seems somehow hard-wired into the human psyche. When Erekosë begins to doubt the rightness of destroying the Eldren, his own kind turn on him as a traitor. By the conclusion of the story, he has changed sides, and using the Eldren's advanced weaponry (military technology they themselves have renounced) he has wiped out the whole of humanity. He marries the Eldren princess Ermizhad and has Eldren immortality conferred upon him. "The Eternal Champion"'s ending is profoundly unsettling. Erekosë/John Daker reflects on the genocide he has carried out, and justifies his act—"I feel no guilt about what I did. I feel more certain than ever that it was the decision of some Other"—only to immediately confess doubt: "Did I do right? It is too late for that question. I have sufficient control, nowadays, not to ask it, for I could not answer but in seeking to do so would destroy my own sanity."[9]

In the person of Erekosë, John Daker has found himself to be a champion—but a champion of *what*? Roland fights for Christendom; Anderson's Holger Danske fights the forces of Chaos, the "Wild Hunt," on behalf of "Christendie and mankind" and "such of Faerie as wish men well."[10] In Erekosë, Moorcock has created a heroic champion who fights not for a nation or a species or a religious creed, but for a general principle—a principle which leads him to genocide. It is to say the least an ambiguous beginning for a figure who will emerge as one of the central foci of Moorcock's writings: not merely an *ad hoc* hero, but an "Eternal" Champion.

The earliest version of "The Eternal Champion" is rather vague about this, but one motif of the story is that John Daker is not merely Erekosë the champion, but has been or will be a whole roll-call of champions: "*Was I John Daker or Erekosë?*" he asks himself as he lies in a hypnagogic state, hearing the voices of Rigenos and his daughter Iolinda; "*Was I either of them? Many other names, Shaleen, Artos, Brian, Umpata, Roland, Ilanth, Ulysses, Alric, fled away down the ghostly rivers of my memory.*"[11] These names seem chosen more for their sonorousness than their specific reference—of the nine, only Brian (the quasi-legendary Irish king Brian Boru?), Roland, and Ulysses (Odysseus' Latin name) are readily identifiable—but the point is clear: at given moments, one particular hero plays a pivotal role in the world-struggle. And while that hero might have many names and identities over time and space, he (for the hero is usually though not always male) is in some deep sense *the same person*. John Daker has not merely gone to bed John Daker and awoken Erekosë, but—as *The Eternal Champion*'s sequel *Phoenix in Obsidian* will demonstrate more explicitly—has awoken to his own destiny as the *self-conscious* embodiment of the Eternal Champion, the occupier of that subject-position who is able to recall his own previous incarnations, and to feel the weight of the endless battles he is constantly reborn to fight.

When Moorcock first published "The Eternal Champion" in 1962, he had created only a few memorable fictive protagonists, among them the slight figures of Sojan the Swordsman (a sort of portmanteau of Conan and John Carter of Mars, whose adventures were serialized in *Tarzan Adventures*) and Jephraim Tallow (the hapless yearner of Moorcock's early unpublished novel *The Golden Barge*), and the rather more robustly interesting sword-and-sorcery antihero Elric of Melniboné. But with the figure of the Eternal Champion, he set in place a conceptual framework within which he could assert the simultaneous difference yet identity of whichever heroic or anti-heroic protagonists he would come to create. And soon his novels would begin to proliferate incarnations of the Eternal Champion. That nine-name dream in the first version of "The Eternal Champion" ("*Shaleen, Artos,*" etc.) would be revised and expanded over the years, until in the most recent publication of (the novel-length) *The Eternal Champion* it reads as a roll-call of Moorcock's most significant protagonists, the central characters of some forty-five books: "*Corum Jhaelen Irsei, Aubec, Seaton Begg, Elric, Rackhir, Ilian, Oona, Simon, Bastable, Cornelius, the Rose, von Bek, Asquiol, Hawkmoon ...*"[12]

* * *

When King Rigenos and his daughter Iolinda summon John Daker—Erekosë—from our mundane world to their own, they have little idea of *whence* they are summoning this storied warrior, who to their culture is a Sleeping Hero of the order of King Arthur, Holger Danske, or Friedrich Barbarossa. But Rigenos fears Erekosë has been held prisoner on the "Ghost Worlds," a realm "beyond Time, beyond Space, linked to the Earth by tenuous bonds," a realm to which the hated Eldren have access, and from which they can occasionally summon "Ghost Armies."[13] Later, when he has come among the Eldren, Erekosë learns from their prince Arjahv that the Ghost Worlds are "solid enough, but exist in an alternate series of dimensions to our own."[14] The Ghost Armies are members of a race seemingly akin to the Eldren, ordinary in their own realm, but endowed with extraordinary powers of moving and disappearing in that of King Rigenos and the Eldren—they operate, that is, according to different laws of physics.

Moorcock doesn't deeply explore the Ghost Worlds in "The Eternal Champion," but the concept and the name reappear in his first science fiction novel, *The Sundered Worlds* (serialized 1962–3 in *Science Fiction Adventures*, published in book form 1965). *The Sundered Worlds* is not a strong piece of writing. John Clute has commented diplomatically that "in the 1960s SF was a difficult nut to demolish for Moorcock."[15] Moorcock himself dismisses the book as "an ignorant imitation of pulp science fiction.... It's scarcely a novel at all. It's a series of large images and spectacular events."[16] Nonetheless, this rather creaky and lurid work of space opera introduces one of Moorcock's crucial recurrent concepts: the multiverse.

In *The Sundered Worlds*, the "Ghost Worlds" are another name for the "Shifter," a mysterious planetary system which appears and disappears on the rim of the galaxy at unexpected intervals. Renark, former Warden of the Rim, and his companion, Asquiol of Pompeii, journey into the Shifter, hoping to find some solution to the crisis that Renark alone has knowledge of—that their own universe is rapidly contracting, which will mean the extinction of the human race. That universe, Renark hypothesizes, is only one of many, one of a "'multiverse,' the multi-dimensional universe containing dozens of different universes, separated from each other by unknown dimensions."[17] The Shifter, it turns out, is a system which rotates at right angles, as it were, to the other universes, and thereby passes *through* them. In the Shifter, Renark and Asquiol acquire the knowledge necessary to move the entire human race—bodily, in a vast flotilla of spaceships—from our contracting universe into another (where, needless to say, another novella's-worth of complications ensue). At the end of the book, Asquiol has become something of a multi-dimensional figure, existing at once in various universes, while Renark has been dispersed throughout the multiverse as a whole, though his spirit seems to share the optimism of the newly empowered humanity: "The multiverse shifted, swirled and leapt, forever changing and delighting them with its chaos, its colour, its variety. All possibilities existed there."[18]

The English word "universe"—"the whole of creation, the cosmos" (OED)—is based in metaphor: the Latin *universus* is formed from the prefix *uni-* and the past participle of *vertere*, "to turn," so the "universal" is the whole as regarded in a single turning: everything seen as one. This metaphor clings to the earliest appearances of the word "multiverse," which signifies the "universe considered as lacking order or a single ruling and guiding power." As William James writes in 1895, "Visible nature is all plasticity and indifference, a multiverse, one might call it, and not a universe."[19] Moorcock's use of the word in *The Sundered Worlds*—"Jewelled, the multiverse spread around him, awash with life, rich with pulsating energy"—is the OED's earliest citation of the word as "a hypothetical space or realm of being consisting of a large number of universes, of which our own universe is only one."[20]

Moorcock is more or less right when he writes that "consciously I invented only one thing in *The Sundered Worlds*, a neologism, viz: The Multiverse, to describe the idea of the near infinity of co-existing space-time continua each fractionally different, in which certain struggles and stories are played out through eternity, on a vast number of planes of existence."[21] Since 1962, the novelist's concept has migrated into theoretical physics, it would seem, where a growing number of physicists postulate the existence of multiple universes besides our own. And Moorcock himself has continued to expand, complicate, and refine his multiverse—but more of that in its own time. For now, it suffices to ask what purpose the overarching concept of the multiverse serves in this fantasist's project of world- and story-making.

The making of new worlds, after all, is one of the fantasy author's characteristic activities: one need only think of L. Frank Baum's Oz, Burroughs's Barsoom, C. S. Lewis's Narnia, or Ursula K. Le Guin's Earthsea. J. R. R. Tolkien, almost certainly the most popular and influential fantasist of the twentieth century, spent most of his adult life elaborating the history, languages, and anthropology of his Middle-earth, a project of which *The Lord of the Rings* now appears as only the visible tip of the iceberg. In his 1938 lecture "On Fairy-Stories," Tolkien describes what he is up to as a kind of "Sub-creation," the making of an internally consistent "Secondary World" different from our mundane—"Primary"—existence.[22] Moorcock's secondary worlds, from the world of Elric and the Young Kingdoms, to the Cornish and Irish worlds of Corum, to the far-future Europe of the Hawkmoon novels, don't really bear comparison to Tolkien's in terms of depth and detail of imagining. Indeed, Moorcock confesses, "I've scarcely any pleasure at all in making up worlds. What pleasure there is is very short-lived. Half an hour and I'm bored with it."[23]

Tolkien's painstakingly elaborated secondary world, like Robert E.

Howard's rather more slapdash Hyborian Age or Le Guin's Earthsea, is a self-contained universe. We enter it as readers in our imagination, and we follow the fortunes of characters for whom this is the *only* world. In contrast, we experience Barsoom, Oz, Narnia, and the medieval Britain of Anderson's *Three Hearts and Three Lions* through the consciousness of characters from our own world.[24] The transitional device taking the character from the mundane realm to the fantastic may range from well-calculated to silly—the wardrobe and the magic rings in Lewis's Narnia books, the tornado in *The Wonderful Wizard of Oz*, the astral projection of *A Princess of Mars*—or it may simply be finessed, as when Holger Carlsen passes out in World War II and wakes up in the Middle Ages.

In the first two decades of his multiversal writing, Moorcock isn't much interested in dwelling on his "portal devices": Asquiol takes his space fleet from one universe to the next by some unelaborated nifty space opera technology; John Daker is summoned from earth to become Erekosë on the world of the Eldren by an magical incantation; in *The Eternal Champion*'s sequel, *Phoenix in Obsidian*, Erekosë is again summoned away to become Urlik Skarsol in a different world. In *The Sailor on the Seas of Fate* Elric rides a mysterious ship into another realm, where he fights alongside Corum, Erekosë, and Hawkmoon; Oswald Bastable, in the "Nomad of Time" trilogy, is knocked from one alternate twentieth century to another by (among other things) a Nepalese wizard's curse and a nuclear explosion; and so forth. Only in the late 1980s and beyond will Moorcock become keenly interested in exploring the particular routes and technologies of multiversal travel.

What is important is not the portal, but the porosity of the worlds—the fact that one *can* travel from one to another—and those worlds' greater or lesser degree of similarity. What Moorcock in essence has done, in arguing that his works together present pictures of a single multiverse, is to provide a scientific (or science-fictional) rationalization for the thematic continuities of his created worlds. They are similar because they are related, a "near infinity of space-time continua each fractionally different"—and to a greater or lesser degree alike. In the decades after he introduced his multiverse in 1962, Moorcock would begin playing with the concept's potential, essentially staging his expanding array of fantasy novel-sequences as a series of variations upon one another's situations and characters (as we shall see in the chapters to come). The central figure of the Eternal Champion remains in place, in different avatars in different sequences, but Moorcock will repeatedly evoke a frisson of pleasant recognition in his readers by recycling antagonists and supporting characters, by playing variations upon previously presented narrative situations, and even by putting more than one Champion avatar on stage at the same time.

* * *

The subgenre popularly known as "sword and sorcery" (the term is Fritz Leiber's; Moorcock's own suggestion was that such stories should be known as "epic fantasy"[25]) rarely gets much critical respect; it is in the words of Samuel R. Delany, one of its most fascinating contemporary practitioners, the "most despised sub-genre of paraliterary production."[26] The popular imagination holds that sword and sorcery is the paradise of arrested male adolescence: broad-thewed and dim-witted barbarians stride across pseudo-medieval landscapes, fighting wizards and giant snakes, rescuing (and bedding) grateful but sketchily characterized young women—all for the entertainment and titilation of socially maladapted teenaged boys.[27]

The tales of Conan the Cimmerian, the barbarian hero invented in 1932 by the Texan Robert E. Howard (1906–1936), are of course the prototype for this image, and Conan is indeed the fountainhead of twentieth-century sword and sorcery.[28] Howard published seventeen Conan stories in the pulp journal *Weird Tales* between 1932 and 1936, and left several more unpublished or unfinished at his death. The Conan stories were collected in book form by the small Gnome Press in the first half of the 1950s, but the real efflorescence of Conan was to come in the following decade, when the editor-writers L. Sprague de Camp and Lin Carter augmented Howard's published Conan texts with a farrago of unpublished Conan stories by Howard, Conan fragments completed by other hands, non-Conan Howard stories revised to feature the barbarian (for many of Howard's protagonists are easily interchangeable), and outright pastiches by other authors, to form a twelve-volume, chronologically-ordered life-story of the Cimmerian. The books sold millions of copies.[29] There followed a whole horde of barbarian imitators—Lin Carter's "Thongor," John Jakes's "Brak the Barbarian," Gardner Fox's "Kothar"—an extremely successful Marvel Conan comic book series, and, in 1982, the big-budget Arnold Schwarzenegger film *Conan the Barbarian*. It's safe to say that from at least the beginning of the 1970s, Conan has been the public face of sword and sorcery.

But if Conan was at the roots of sword and sorcery, the subgenre had from early on been rather more varied and nuanced than the Barbarian stereotype. Howard's Conan stories had proved immensely popular with

Weird Tales readers, and other writers were quick to adopt his formula, which placed a sword-wielding protagonist in a pre-industrial setting of physical challenge, magic, and fantastic creatures. Clifford Ball wrote about "Duar the Accursed," while Henry Kuttner created Elak, a dispossessed Atlantean prince. The sword-and-sorcery hero did not need to be a barbarian—or even a man, as C. L. Moore demonstrated with her tales of the medieval French woman warrior Jirel of Joiry.[30] In 1939 Fritz Leiber published the first of his stories to feature the unlikely duo of Fafhrd and the Gray Mouser, the former a hulking, blond barbarian, the latter a diminutive but supple and crafty urban thief. Leiber's stories make quite sophisticated use of the situations and settings Howard had outlined, and often advance a gentle parody of the muscular ethos Howard's hero personified.

When E. J. ("Ted") Carnell, editor of the British magazine *Science Fantasy*, asked the twenty-year-old Moorcock for "some Conan-type stuff," Moorcock was rather relieved to find the editor didn't want actual Conan pastiche, but something in the sword-and-sorcery line.[31] Moorcock had passed through a phase of Howard fandom (right after his Burroughs period), but by 1960 he found more to admire in the subtleties of Leiber's Fafhrd and the Gray Mouser and in the ambiguous, sometimes tortured protagonists of Poul Anderson's two heroic fantasies, *Three Hearts and Three Lions* and *The Broken Sword* (1954). And Moorcock was reading the novels of the French existentialists Jean-Paul Sartre and Albert Camus, in which alienated protagonists try to discover meaning—often, as in Camus's *L'Étranger* (*The Stranger*, 1942), through violence—in an alien, indifferent universe.[32]

The character Moorcock introduced in the June 1961 issue of *Science Fantasy*, in a story entitled "The Dreaming City," was as far from the self-confident, unself-conscious barbarian muscle-man as could be imagined. Elric of Melniboné is the last monarch of a ten-thousand-year-old empire now in decline, that formerly drew its strength from pacts with demons, from dark sorcery, and from its squadrons—now nearly extinct—of mounted dragons. Elric himself is a "moody-eyed wanderer," a "reckless reaver and cynical slayer,"[33] and a sorcerer of great skills, performing multiple acts of summoning and conjuration in that first story. He is cynical and sophisticated, much unlike Conan, but what sets Elric apart even more clearly from Howard's hero—and from most other sword-and-sorcery protagonists—is his physical weakness. As Moorcock presents him in "The Dreaming City," Elric is "an albino, owning no natural reserves of vitality." Elric is a physical weakling, doomed in the natural course of things to a shortened and largely inactive life: "Normally, he would be slothful, his reactions sluggish, his mind hazed. His eyesight would grow steadily worse as he grew older and he would probably die prematurely."[34] Elric can be the physically active protagonist of sword and sorcery—he casts exhausting spells, he leads an assault on an armed city, he does a fair amount of hewing and skewering—only because of his symbiotic relationship with Stormbringer, "his runesword of black iron ... forged by ancient and alien sorcery when Melniboné was young."[35] "The Dreaming City" is in large part concerned with Elric's coming to realize just how much he depends upon his semi-sentient sword, how "he and the sword were interdependent ... 'bound by hell-forged chains and fate-haunted circumstances.'"[36]

Swords of numinous power are rather common in the romance tradition. King Arthur's Excalibur and Roland's Durandal are only the most famous examples. Sigurd slays the dragon Fafnir, in the Völsunga Saga, with the sword Gram (*Nothung* in Wagner's Ring Cycle), forged like Durandal by the master smith Wayland, who is also said in some sources to have made Cortana, Holger Danske's sword. Cortana figures only briefly at the end of *Three Hearts and Three Lions*, but the unnamed titular blade of Anderson's *The Broken Sword* is a malevolent force felt throughout the novel.[37]

Elric's black runesword Stormbringer is more than just another magic weapon, though when he wrote "The Dreaming City" Moorcock had only begun to imagine the sword's sinister implications. The sword, as he would develop it in the Elric stories he published over the next three years, is a sentient, malevolent entity. It supplies Elric with energy, but it does so by sucking the souls of those it kills and then transferring some of their vitality to its albino wielder. And it has the disturbing habit of taking the lives of those whom Elric would most prefer left unharmed—beginning, in "The Dreaming City," with Cymoril, Elric's betrothed. By the end of the four continuous novellas that make up *Stormbringer* (1963–1964, published in book form 1965), it is made explicit that Stormbringer is itself a demon, a supernatural entity to be ranked among the various gods and demons Elric has battled or summoned in the past.

Elric, to put it simply, is the anti–Conan, the dark underside to the healthy and hygienic barbarism the Cimmerian embodies. Elric is subtle, overcivilized. When he presents himself in the "tasteless and gaudy" costume "of a Southern barbarian,"[38] the reader knows that Elric is making an ironic fashion statement that would be pointless and incomprehensible to Conan. And while Conan is content to follow whatever path presents itself, hoping only for women, wine, treasure, or adventure, Elric is painfully introspective and self-conscious, questioning his own motives and place in the world. In his dependence on Stormbringer, he is an addict, a "junkie" in the drug culture argot that would become more and more familiar as the sixties wore on; and in his use of the stolen vitality of those whom Stormbringer slays, he is a vampire, if a reluctant and self-loathing one. Conan, Moorcock rightly observes in "Conan: American Phenomenon," is a rather thorough manifestation of American frontier individualism and self-reliance, like Cooper's Natty Bumppo, Hopalong Cassidy, or Burroughs's Tarzan and John Carter.[39] In contrast, Elric can be located in a long tradition of European anti-heroes, from the Wandering Jew, Melmoth the Wanderer, Don Giovanni, through Byron's sexually attractive but morally ambiguous protagonists, down to Sartre's Antoine Roquentin and Camus's Meursault. And Elric is a specifically *post-war* figure, his conception marked by the experiences of the Blitz and the Holocaust, by Moorcock's recognition of the destruction and genocidal potential at the heart of enlightenment logic and modern civilization.

"The Dreaming City" introduces us to Elric at a turning point of his life. He returns in Imrryr, the capital of Melniboné, as an exile at the head of a raiding party of seafarers from the upstart "Young Kingdoms," the largely non-sorcerous principalities that have displaced the ancient and decaying Melnibonéan empire. He confronts his cousin Yyrkoon, who has usurped Elric's throne, and kills him—in the process accidentally killing his beloved cousin Cymoril. Imrryr is destroyed, and Elric has become an exile without a home, reviled by the surviving Melnibonéans as a traitor and distrusted by the men of the Young Kingdoms as a "woman-slayer."

Elric proved quite popular with readers of *Science Fantasy*, and Carnell encouraged Moorcock to contribute further Elric stories. In four stories over the next sixteen months (one of them, "Kings in Darkness," in collaboration with his friend James Cawthorn, whose drawings of Elric helped shape Moorcock's evolving conception of the character), Moorcock has Elric fighting various human and supernatural threats; searching unsuccessfully for the meaning of life ("While the Gods Laugh"); attempting (again unsuccessfully) to end his dependency on the black runesword ("Kings in Darkness" and "The Flame Bringers"); and discovering a new love and a seeming peace with the princess Zarozinia in the kingdom of Ilmiora. And in the four novellas that make up *Stormbringer*, Moorcock kills Elric off, and destroys his entire created world in the process.

Over the course of these nine stories—what we might think of as "first-wave" Elric fictions—Moorcock rather rapidly develops and fleshes out the elements of Elric's character and cosmology. I've already noted how Stormbringer, just another brooding blade in "The Dreaming City," becomes more and more sentient as the stories progress, and its link with Elric becomes more clearly a channel of vampirism. The Melnibonéans who Elric once ruled, as well, become more clearly differentiated from the inhabitants of the Young Kingdoms as the stories unfold. Their civilization is older, crueller, more decadent, dependent on relationships with various supernatural entities; this much is clear from "The Dreaming City." But by early 1962 Moorcock was beginning to think of the Melnibonéans as a race—perhaps even a species—apart from ordinary humans, on the order of the Eldren in "The Eternal Champion."

The Eldren have "long pointed" faces, "slanting eyes that seem blind in their strange milkiness, slightly pointed ears, high slanting cheekbones."[40] They certainly resemble the Melnibonéans, as we can see from the description of Elric's cousin Dyvim Tvar: "he bore the stamp of Melnibonéan nobility.... His cheek-bones were high and delicate, his eyes slightly slanting while his skull was narrow, tapering at the jaw. Like Elric, his ears were thin, near lobeless and coming almost to a point."[41] In *The Knight of the Swords* (1971), the first of the Corum novels, Moorcock will introduce a third similar race, the Vadhagh, whose characteristic features include "narrow, long skulls; ears that were almost without lobes and tapered flat alongside the head; fine hair that a breeze would make rise like flimsy clouds around their faces; large almond eyes that had yellow centres and purple surrounds."[42] This is a physiognomy that we're inclined to consider "elfin,"[43] though Tolkien, who'd presented the most fully realized picture of elvish society and culture in *The Lord of the Rings*, and for that matter Lord Dunsany, with whose *The King of Elfland's Daughter* (1924) Moorcock was familiar, have rather little to say about how their elves actually *look*. A more proximate source is Anderson's *The Broken Sword*, where Imric the elf-earl looks "with the strange slant eyes of the elf-folk, all cloudy-blue without white or pupil.... He was ever youthful, with the broad forehead and high cheekbones, the narrow jaw and the straight thin-chiseled nose of the elf lords. His hair floated silvery-gold, finer than spider-silk."[44] "A cold haughtiness marked their features," Anderson writes of his elves (or "Pharisees") in *Three Hearts and Three Lions*, "which were of a strange cast, high tilted cheekbones, winged nostrils, narrow chins."[45]

In Anderson, Dunsany, and to some degree in Tolkien, the elves are representative of, indeed *embody*, a realm apart—Faerie, the magical, the fantastic. They may be largely benign or indifferent to humans (as in Tolkien) or they may be cruel and mischievous (Anderson), but they are utterly *other*. Moorcock's Melnibonéans/Eldren/Vadhagh are as well quite distinct from ordinary humanity, but the differences he stresses are largely cultural rather than ontological. In each case, the older, more sophisticated culture and intellect of the "elfin" race (sometimes decadent, as with the Melnibonéans, sometimes overly aestheticized, as with the Vadhagh) is set in contrast to a younger, simpler humanity: boundlessly energetic (Elric often admires this quality in the men of the Young Kingdoms), sometimes rapacious, sometimes—as we see with King Rigenos's "humanity" and the "Mabden" of Corum's world—mindlessly violent and destructive. In many ways, these books and sequences are parables of cultural change, of the passing of old orders under the pressure of the new.

If the Eldren are to humanity as Ariel to Caliban, there is no such benignity in the Melnibonéans. There is nothing malign about their pacts with the various elemental deities of water, wind, and so forth, upon whom Elric occasionally calls, nor is there anything threatening about their dealings with various animal deities; but Moorcock continually stresses the Melnibonéans' pursuit of dark sorcery, and their connection with supernatural powers less savory than a wind elemental or a cat god.[46] Elric's particular patron deity is Arioch, Duke of Chaos. When Elric first summons Arioch in "The Dreaming City," the "Lord of the Higher Hell" is little more than a Lovecraftian amorphous shadow, an "intolerably alien shape."[47] As the Elric stories progress, Arioch will be more and more clearly characterized—he is cruel, he is fickle, he often takes the shape of a beautiful youth—and his place within the pantheon of Elric's world made more evident. Elric's world, that is, is ruled—more accurately, overseen—by two contending groups of deities, the Lords of Law and the Lords of Chaos. "The upholders of Chaos," Elric explains to his newly-met sidekick Moonglum in "While the Gods Laugh," "state that in such a world as they rule, all things are possible. Opponents of Chaos—those who ally themselves with the forces of law—say that without Law *nothing* material is possible."

In that particular story, Elric is seeking the "Dead Gods' Book," a storied tome that may contain a higher truth about the government of the universe. As he tells Moonglum, "Law and Chaos rarely interfere directly in Men's lives—that is why only adepts are fully aware of their presence. Now perhaps, I will discover at last the answer to the one question which concerns me—does an ultimate force rule over the opposing factions of Law and Chaos?"[48] When Elric and his companions finally confront the entity which guards the Book, Orunlu the Keeper is unable to answer Elric's question: "*There is no Truth but that of Eternal struggle,*" he says. "*There is only the Balance.*"[49] The Book itself has crumbled to dust ages ago, and Elric is left in the dark: "I am the eternal skeptic—never *sure* that my actions are my own, never certain that an ultimate entity is not guiding me."[50] Orunlu has already given him an answer of sorts, of course: that Chaos and Law, disorder and order, struggle on this earth but are ultimately subject to a "balance," to a kind of principle of equilibrium.

In a long letter about Elric published in the fanzine *Niekas* in early 1964, Moorcock cites Zoroastrianism, the ancient Persian belief system in which Ahura Mazda, the supreme god and creator of order, is continually at war with Ahriman, deity of chaos and falsehood, as one of the two primary inspirations for Elric's cosmology.[51] (The other is Anderson's *Three Hearts and Three Lions*.) The world certainly becomes a battleground in the novel *Stormbringer*, where Elric finds he must renounce his ancestral fealty to Chaos in order to combat the sorcerer Jagreen Lern, who has opened a pathway for all the forces of Chaos to engulf the world. Eventually, Elric summons the Lords of Law, led by Donblas the Justice Maker, to a pitched battle with "Chardros the Reaper, Mabelode the Faceless, and Slortar the Old and the lesser Lords of Chaos."[52] Law proves triumphant, but the world as we have come to know it, now wracked and distorted by the forces of Chaos, is reformed into a new, more lawful configuration. It will be the home of new races, but only after Elric's own death—on the blade of (unsurprisingly) Stormbringer, who resumes its form as the "last manifestation of Chaos which would remain with this new world as it grew.... Its wild voice laughing mockery at the Cosmic Balance; filling the universe with its unholy joy."[53]

To some degree, Elric's final struggle in *Stormbringer* parallels that of Anderson's Holger Danske in *Three Hearts and Three Lions*—the hero fights the encroaching forces of chaos and disorder on behalf of law, order, normalcy. Erekosë as well fights on the side of Law, as will Moorcock's next two incarnations of the Eternal Champion, Dorian Hawkmoon and (most explicitly) Corum Jhaelen Irsei. In later works, however, Moorcock comes to present Law, when pursued as an absolute, as just as great a threat as Chaos. Law and Chaos, that is, cannot be simply equated with *good* and *evil*. Chaos is disorder, but it is also life-giving change, evolution; Law is boundary and regularity, but it is also enforced conformity, the suppression of vitality and creativity. The ideal state, both for the individual and for society as a whole, lies in a mean between the two extremes. The Law versus Chaos opposition can be expressed as Realism versus Romanticism, Reason versus Emotion—perhaps its ultimate Freudian resolution is Thanatos versus Eros. The Eternal Champion fights by turns for one or the other value, but his final goal is always to maintain the *bal-*

ance between the two. In scores of Moorcock's novels, we find the fictive playing-out of a very down-to-earth life-philosophy. As Moorcock reflects wearily in 1997, "Badly educated people are suspicious of ambiguity and rational compromise. Something seems to have divided us. The old ideal of the Happy Mean, the perfect balance of interests and impulses, hardly ever seems to be aired, these days."[54] But Moorcock has been airing that ideal, in a myriad of variations, for over half a century now.

* * *

In some quarters of the fantasy community, Moorcock is known less as the creator of Elric or the architect of the multiverse, or even as a vocal proponent of anarchistic, communitarian ethical moderation, than as "that guy who hates Tolkien."[55] Pausing for a moment to think a bit about Moorcock's relationship with Tolkien can I think cast some light on the overall genre of heroic fantasy, on Moorcock's place within that genre, and on some of the central social themes that inform his works, whether fantasy, science fiction, or otherwise.

The Lord of the Rings, on which Tolkien had labored from 1936 to 1949, was finally published in 1954 and 1955, but it's safe to say that the book's enormous impact on fantasy writing did not come until a decade later, when the three volumes were released in paperback in the United States, first in an unauthorized edition from Ace Books and shortly afterwards in a slightly revised, authorized edition from Ballantine. In hardcover, the book had enjoyed respectable reviews but only modest sales; in paperback, it struck a definite chord with young American readers, and their enthusiasm spread back across the Atlantic. By the end of 1968 some three million copies of *The Lord of the Rings* had been sold.[56]

In response to the book's astonishing popularity, Ballantine issued paperback reprints of other British fantasists—E. R. Eddison, Mervyn Peake—and then commissioned the American writer Lin Carter to edit a full-scale imprint, "Ballantine Adult Fantasy," which issued almost seventy titles, both reprints (William Morris, George Macdonald, Lord Dunsany, etc.) and new titles.[57] The following decades would see a virtual deluge of new fantasy books (and series), some of them in slavish imitation of *The Lord of the Rings*, but all of them appearing to some degree in the "wake" of Tolkien's work. For many readers and—more importantly—writers of fantasy, Tolkien was the "gateway" text to the genre, the first extended work of fantasy they read, and the literary and architectonic standard to which they would hold whatever further texts they read or wrote (or, for that matter, an exemplar against which they would react[58]). In the decades

1. The Multiverse and the Champion   31

since its paperback publication in 1965, *The Lord of the Rings* has occupied a hegemonic position, both critical and popular, in the fantasy genre, has been a kind of acknowledged or unacknowledged central text to which all else is referred. Brian Attebery, in his otherwise subtle and skillful characterization of the fantasy genre as a "fuzzy set" rather than a clearly-demarcated enclave, concludes by pronouncing that "Tolkien's form of fantasy, for readers in English, is our mental template, and will be until someone else achieves equal recognition with an alternative conception. One way to characterize the genre of fantasy is the set of texts that in some way or another resemble *The Lord of the Rings*."[59]

The first thing to be stressed, of course, is that while this may be an accurate description of the fantasy genre (in English) as it has grown up in the past half-century, and while it may be right to identify Tolkien as a central figure for even a majority of fantasy readers and writers, Tolkien's "centrality" is a matter of contingent literary history, rather than an ontological fact about fantasy in general, or even about "heroic" fantasy. And assuming Tolkien as a constant point of reference can be misleading in approaching writers for whom *The Lord of the Rings* is most definitely *not* a central text—Moorcock, for one. In a review of a reissue of Anderson's *The Broken Sword* (which was first published the same year as *The Fellowship of the Ring*), Moorcock recalls that

> when I first read it as a boy, Anderson's book impressed me so powerfully that I couldn't then enjoy Tolkien's.... I couldn't take Tolkien seriously. Aside from his nursery-room tone, I was unhappy with his infidelities of time, place and character, unconvinced by his female characters and quasi-juvenile protagonists.[60]

"Aspects of Fantasy," the series of critical essays Moorcock published in *Science Fantasy* in 1963 and 1964, contains only brief references to Tolkien—clearly, of contemporary writers Moorcock found Peake, Leiber, and Anderson far more interesting and suggestive. Indeed, I think it's fair to say that while Tolkien was very much "in the air" when Moorcock began writing fantasy, *The Lord of the Rings* had almost no influence on his work, early or late: instead, his fantasy is rooted in a separate, largely American tradition that has much in common with the various pulp genres in which he was reading and writing in his youth—a tradition that runs from Howard and Burroughs, in its rawest and pulpiest form, to a rather more refined and literarily respectable shape in the work of Anderson and Leiber. There is no tincture of the Inklings in Elric's snow-white visage.

It was not until 1978, however, when Frodo-mania was well into its second decade and publishers were assiduously promoting new trilogies that would be "the next Tolkien,"⁶¹ that Moorcock confronted *The Lord of the Rings*'s author head-on in a little pamphlet published by the British Fantasy Society: "Epic Pooh." "Epic Pooh" is a stinging attack on Tolkien, Tolkien's associates the "Inklings" (especially C. S. Lewis), and Tolkien's legacy for contemporary fantasy. In part, Moorcock criticizes Tolkien for the texture of his prose, "the prose of the nursery-room.... It is sentimental, slightly distanced, often wistful, a trifle retrospective; it contains little wit and much whimsy."⁶² But the prose, it turns out, is only symptomatic of a more seriously underlying ideological tendency in Tolkien's work.

The Lord of the Rings, says Moorcock, "is *Winnie-the-Pooh* posing as an epic." Through the medium of a kind of fake-nostalgic, suburban pastoralism—the Shire is "that Surrey of the mind"—Tolkien promotes the same "sentimental mythos," the "wretched ethic of passive 'decency' and self-sacrifice," that had made it possible for the average Englishman to survive, and to justify, the Great War. The ethical core of *The Lord of the Rings* is a "sort of consolatory Christianity" that breeds political and social quietism: in the end, for Moorcock, "a fundamentally misanthropic doctrine."⁶³ And the novel has clear class implications: Tolkien

> sees the petit bourgeoisie, the honest artisans and peasants, as the bulwark against Chaos. These characters are always sentimentalized in such fiction because, traditionally, they are always the last to complain about any deficiencies in the status quo.⁶⁴

"*The Lord of the Rings*," Moorcock writes, "is a pernicious confirmation of the values of a morally bankrupt middle-class." In contrast to the heroic characters of the novel—hereditary royalty and nobility (Aragorn, Theoden, Faramir), non-human warriors who risk all to preserve their immemorial ways of life (Legolas, Gimli), petit-bourgeois Hobbits who rise to heroism through their innate decency—"Sauron and his henchmen are that old bourgeois bugaboo, the Mob—mindless football supporters throwing their beer bottles over the fence—the worst aspects of modern urban society represented as the whole by a fearful, backward-yearning class."⁶⁵

It's not going out on a limb to remark the cultural conservatism that underpins Tolkien's work, his wholesale rejection of industrial modernity in favor of the dream of a vanished agrarian England—that dream, in the writings of John Ruskin and William Morris, was immensely influential when Tolkien was coming of age around the turn of the century.⁶⁶ Despite Tolkien's famous disavowal of allegory or contemporary political implication in the novel,⁶⁷ it's obvious that the malign forces in *The Lord of the Rings*—from Sauron's jackbooted, imperialist orc regiments, to Saruman's

Uruk-hai manufactory, to Ted Sandyman's steam mill—represent the forces of industrial modernity as much as they do a more metaphysical "evil." Of course, one does not have to be a political reactionary to be disturbed by the social tendencies of modernity: Marxism itself is a body of thought that arises in response to industrialization. It is the *character* of Tolkien's reaction to modernity that repels Moorcock, perhaps best exemplified in two of the functions of fantasy Tolkien describes in "On Fairy-Stories": *escape* and *consolation*. The two are bound up together, and inextricable from the religious faith that underpins Tolkien's thought.

The "consolation" of which Tolkien writes is embodied in fantasy's "*eucatastrophe*," its "sudden joyous 'turn' ... a sudden and miraculous grace" which is clearly proleptic of the "happy ending" of the Christian mythos: "The peculiar quality of the 'joy' in successful fantasy," Tolkien writes, "can thus be explained as a sudden glimpse of an underlying reality or truth ... a 'consolation' for the sorrow of this world."[68] This world—the nightmare of mechanized modernity, and more generally the brief period of our mundane lives—is a "prison," and it is only natural to seek "escape" in World-making: "Why should a man be scorned if, finding himself in prison, he tries to get out and go home? Or if, when he cannot do so, he thinks and talks about other topics than jailers and prison-walls?" Such "escape" is not escap*ism*: "In using Escape in this way the critics have chosen the wrong word," writes Tolkien, "and, what is more, they are confusing, not always by sincere error, the Escape of the Prisoner with the Flight of the Deserter."[69] Fantasy's function is to provide an escape from an at times painful earthly existence, and thus to give a foretaste of "the oldest and deepest desire, the Great Escape: the Escape from Death."[70] The Christian implications of this are unmistakable.

"Tolkien and his admirers (many of them leftists) gave his escapism an emancipatory gloss, claiming that jailers hate escapism," writes the Marxist fantasist China Miéville, an admirer of "Epic Pooh"; "As the great anarchist fantasist Michael Moorcock has pointed out, this is precisely untrue. Jailers love escapism. What they hate is escape."[71] For Tolkien, the staunch Roman Catholic believer, fantasy provides a momentary escape from a world which is brutalized and deformed precisely by human fallenness, an irremediable state that can only be fully redeemed and remade in a Christian afterlife. For Moorcock (and Miéville) this is to confuse middle-class political and social quietism—the longsuffering stiff upper lip, the obedience to hierarchical authority—with an ontological state. The roots of the world's pain do indeed lie in human failure, but human beings as well have the potential to alleviate that pain, to remake the world through acts of kindness, communal solidarity, class self-determination, toleration of difference, and ordinary generosity. For Moorcock—no theist, and certainly no Christian—the world in which we now live is the only world we'll know. If we find ourselves feeling like prisoners in the world, perhaps works of fantasy can not merely offer dreams of open skies and pastures, but can help us imagine ways of dismantling our prison walls.

Tolkien's epic fantasy rejects modernity in favor of a deeply conservative, nostalgic vision of an ordered, hierarchical, agrarian world. For him, as John Clute comments, "the twentieth century was a prison train bound for hell."[72] The moral vision of *The Lord of the Rings* sets Good (always characterized by self-abnegation, responsibility, duty, and rightful hierarchy) against a monolithically presented Evil which is potent and dangerous, but never attractive, always emphatically *other*. But for Moorcock the stakes are too high in fantasy romance, and the potentialities too great, to settle for a nostalgic vision of the "greenwood." (I suspect he would be much in sympathy with a maxim of Bertolt Brecht's which Walter Benjamin recorded in his diary in 1938: "Don't start with the good old things but the bad new ones."[73]) And what threatens human society and individual well-being is not a clearly demarcated, alien "evil," but the excess of principles which lie within even the best of us. Moorcock's moral vision, which is admittedly rough, cartoonish, even *pulpish* in his early writings, but which will be fleshed out, complicated, and subtilized over scores of later books, is concerned not with good and evil, but with order and disorder, Law and Chaos, the extremes between which the ethical subject or the ethical society must steer in order to achieve a harmony, or "Balance" in this world—or in any other realm of the multiverse. The difference is that this is a balance, a harmony, which *can* be achieved in any world, if only by hard labor. "Consolation" and "escape" amount, in the end, to quietism in the face of the world's pain.

2

A Messiah for the Age of Entropy

Elric of Melniboné had proved popular indeed with readers of fantasy, and by his mid-twenties Moorcock found himself among the most prominent writers of the genre—though it was clear his ambitions strained against the constraints of genre writing. In 1965, he could have been described (or dismissed) as a promising young fantastist, creator of at least one memorable character, given to lofty metaphysical and moral statement, and somewhat addicted to purple prose. A decade later, however, he was widely recognized as one of the most influential figures across both fantasy and science fiction, a major mover and shaker of the field as a whole, and as a person of letters who had significantly broken down the barriers between "genre" writing and the continuing traditions of "high" modernism. This shift came about in part through two momentous events in Moorcock's career: His groundbreaking and controversial editing of the magazine *New Worlds*, an editorship which proved the rallying point of a (much-debated) "new wave" in science fiction writing; and his creation and development of the character Jerry Cornelius, a perfect ironic distillation of his historical moment and at the same time a "technique" ductile enough to carry forward into new decades and even, indeed, into the new millennium.

* * *

E. J. Carnell, the editor who had solicited Moorcock's first Elric stories for *Science Fantasy*, had been a central figure in the British science fiction community since the 1930s. In 1946 he had founded the magazine *New Worlds*, which by the end of the fifties was the most prominent and respected British SF magazine, publishing established and new authors both from Great Britain and the U.S. *New Worlds* published several of Moorcock's short stories, some in collaboration with his friend Barrington J. Bayley.[1] Moorcock even contributed a guest editorial to the April 1963 issue of the magazine, lamenting the state of much contemporary science fiction, which despite its snazzy technologies and inventive plots lacked "passion, subtlety, irony, original characterisation, original and good style, a sense of involvement in human affairs, colour, depth and, on the whole, real feeling from the writer." All too much contemporary science fiction, Moorcock grouses, consists of "the boy-author writing boys' stories got up to look like grown-ups' stories."[2]

The following year, there was even more to lament, as Carnell was forced to announced the imminent demise of both *New Worlds* and *Science Fantasy*, victims of competition from American magazines and a steady fall-off of sales since 1959.[3] In the event, Carnell was able to save the two magazines by selling them to a new publisher, and while he was invited to continue as editor, he decided to pass *Science Fantasy* and *New Worlds* over to fresh editorial hands. Moorcock was offered his choice and, perhaps surprisingly—for more of his own work had appeared in *Science Fantasy*—went for *New Worlds*. "I chose *New Worlds*," he later recalled, "because the title was open to a number of potential interpretations and I felt that if the magazine was worth taking over (I had been reluctant to edit a purely SF magazine; I had little relish for most SF) then it should become the vehicle for various ideas I had had for some time."[4] Some of those ideas were on view in a "dummy" issue of the magazine Moorcock had prepared in consulation with his friend J. G. Ballard: a large-format glossy, featuring "experimental work" by figures like William Burroughs and the "pop" sculptor Eduardo Paolozzi, "it would attempt a cross-fertilization of popular SF, science and the work of the literary and artistic avant-garde."[5]

Moorcock did not get his large format, at least at first—*New Worlds* continued as a digest-sized paperback—but he began his editorship in spring 1964 with something of a bang, hailing Burroughs, an American author best known for his novel *Naked Lunch* (1959) and closely associated with the "beat" movement, as "the first SF writer to explore all the form's potentialities and develop a new mythology—a new literature for the Space Age."[6] Science fiction, from at least as far back as the genre had first been codified by the great editor Hugo Gernsback (of *Amazing Stories*) in the late 1920s, had prided itself on being a "literature of ideas," a kind of writing that did not merely explore the intricacies of human social and affective relationships (as did "mainstream" fiction), but that thought about the human race's place within a larger cosmos, that extrapolated upon the implications of emergent (or just barely possible) technologies and social trends.[7] But that "extrapolative," intellectual component of SF was always liable to be overshadowed by the "amazing" element, the thrill-inducing machinery of adventure narrative and dazzling gadgetry. As Brian Aldiss points out, "magazine SF largely grew out of men's adventure fiction,"[8] and the majority of its writers were perfectly comfortable with those generic conventions.

Even in the vastly more sophisticated science fiction of the so-called "Golden Age" (roughly 1938 through the 1940s, the era of John W. Campbell's influential editing of *Astounding Science Fiction*) and the decade following, Moorcock and his associates found a disconcerting emphasis on hard science at the expense of psychology and social analysis, and a reliance on narrative modes that would have been entirely familiar to a reader from the turn of the century—as if modernism, all the grand narrative experiments of Joyce, Proust, Woolf, and Wyndham Lewis, had never happened. In addition, many writers associated with *New Worlds* felt that traditional science fiction, in its obsession with the stars and with the future, was paying too little attention to the events and forces changing society before its eyes. "We were looking at the Vietnam War," Moorcock recalls, "Kennedy's assassination, the computer revolution, the armaments industry, the manipulations of the media, the profound hypocrisy of the liberal bourgeoisie, the appalling condition of the majority of human beings on the planet, the useless currency of outmoded or inappropriate political language."[9]

As editor of *New Worlds*, Moorcock published a range of both established writers and writers early in their careers, and a number of them became so closely associated with the magazine that one might speak of them as *New Worlds* "regulars." J. G. Ballard is by far the most important. Almost a decade older than Moorcock, Ballard had committed himself to full-time writing in the early 1960s with a string of "disaster" novels: *The Wind from Nowhere* (1962), *The Drowned World* (1962), *The Burning World* (1964), and so forth. Much of the direction of Moorcock's early *New Worlds* editing was arrived at in collaboration with Ballard, who was as impatient as Moorcock with most popular science fiction of the day: "What Ballard and I had in common was that our knowledge of SF was not profound," Moorcock recalls. "Neither of us had read most of the well-known writers or stories. We had no particular taste for them. Ballard enjoyed [Ray] Bradbury. I enjoyed [Alfred] Bester. We imposed our own imagination on the rest of SF, thinking most of it was better than it actually was; when we had to read it (say, for reviews) we were therefore disappointed."[10] One way of conceiving what became the stable of regular *New Worlds* contributors, then, is that they were writers whom Moorcock felt (or hoped) might live up to his and Ballard's imagination of what science fiction *might* be.

Brian Aldiss, a decade and a half older than Moorcock and an established figure by 1964, was at first skeptical of *New Worlds*'s new turn, but soon became one of the magazine's regular contributors. He was joined by a number of British writers of Moorcock's generation—Langdon Jones, M. John Harrison, Michael Butterworth, Hilary Bailey (whom Moorcock had married in 1962), Giles Gordon, and others—and a few expatriate Americans, most notable among them John Sladek, Thomas M. Disch, and Pamela Zoline. The very prolific British novelist John Brunner was a frequent contributor, as was the young Norman Spinrad, based in New York.

In the early years of Moorcock's editorship, *New Worlds* published a good deal of familiar, conventional science fiction. "Aware that too swift a transformation would alienate" habitual readers, Colin Greenland notes, "Moorcock changed the contents of the magazine much more slowly than he pretended to."[11] The editorial polemics, that is, were rather in advance of the magazine's actual contents. But it soon enough became clear that *New Worlds* would be regularly publishing work that violated the expectations of longtime SF readers, and in a number of different ways.[12]

Many of the fictions published in *New Worlds*—and this would go on to cause legal problems—dealt with sexuality and sexual relations in a more explicit manner than was conventional in mainstream SF. Science fiction in the early 1960s was not exactly a puritanical genre, but its strong roots in the tradition of adolescent adventure fiction were evident in the degree to which it largely ignored the sexual side of human relations, and entirely eschewed the explicit presentation of sex that had proved such a provocative element in such modernist writers as Joyce and Lawrence. When writers in *New Worlds* openly presented sex, then, they were doing no more than bringing the genre in line with what had already been brought into the open in "mainstream" fiction—but they definitely shocked readers who consciously or unconsciously expected their SF to stimulate the imagination but not the hormones.

Whereas much of "classic" science fiction had involved space exploration, had taken the stars as its setting, the fiction *New Worlds* published tended to withdraw back towards earth. "I think science fiction," Ballard wrote in the magazine in 1962, "should turn its back on space, on interstellar travel, extra-terrestrial life forms, galactic wars and the overlap of these ideas that spreads across the margins of nine-tenths of magazine s-f."[13] In part, this was a reaction to the Sputnik launch of 1957, when (as David G.

Hartwell writes) "in a single instant the fact of space travel turned most of the classic space travel stories of science fiction into fantasies."[14] In much of traditional SF, outer space had been little more than a transposed version of the Wild West or the still unexplored corners of "darkest Africa" and the Orient in turn-of-the-century adventure fiction. For the writers of *New Worlds*, outer space was less often a wondrous frontier than an environment of privation, isolation, psychological extremity. As Moorcock puts it in *The Black Corridor* (1969), "Space does not care. Space does not threaten. Space does not comfort.... Space is a remorseless, senseless, impersonal fact."[15] Indeed, as Greenland notes, Moorcock and others "came close to establishing a new fiction stock type of their own: the Mad Astronaut."[16]

Even as they renounced or redefined the traditional science fictional province of outer space, the *New Worlds* writers tended to focus on the equally strange realms of human psychology. "The biggest developments of the immediate future," Ballard writes, "will take place, not on the Moon or Mars, but on Earth, and it is *inner* space, not outer, that needs to be explored."[17] Conventional SF had made much of speculative mental "technologies" such as ESP, telepathy, and other so-called "psi" powers; but the writers of *New Worlds* were more interested in the far reaches of "normal" human psychologies as revealed in states of extremity (as in Ballard's landmark 1964 story "The Terminal Beach"), or in the altered states achieved through drug use (as in Moorcock's 1964 "The Deep Fix").

Perhaps the most striking theme articulated by *New Worlds*'s writers was entropy, the physical, social, and psychological implications of the Second Law of Thermodynamics.[18] Everything, in short, runs down, falls apart, sinks into a common level of disorganization. It is a theme of powerful human pessimism, and one can see it played out in the works of any number of *New Worlds* contributors, from Langdon Jones's "The Eye of the Lens" (1968), to M. John Harrison's "Running Down" (1975), Thomas Pynchon's early story "Entropy" (reprinted in *New Worlds* in 1969), and Pamela Zoline's brilliant "The Heat Death of the Universe" (1967), which juxtaposes meditations on the Second Law with the psychological breakdown of a suburban California housewife.[19]

Such thematic preoccupations convinced many aficionados of conventional science fiction that writers in the *New Worlds* orbit were somehow "morbid" or "decadent," but they were equally outraged by Moorcock's opening the magazine to a variety of "experimental" narrative modes. Science fiction may have prided itself on being a "literature of ideas," but however advanced those ideas might be they were more often than not delivered in straightforward, linear narrative forms essentially unchanged since the Edwardian era. Under Moorcock's editorship, *New Worlds* began running stories cast in fragmentary, discontinuous forms, stories narrated in the free-flowing "stream of consciousness" modes pioneered by Joyce, Woolf, Faulkner, and others, stories drawing on such radical collage techniques as Burroughs's "cut-ups," and stories taking on even more unfamiliar forms, like Ballard's "condensed novels," eventually collected in *The Atrocity Exhibition* (1970).

As editor of *New Worlds*, Moorcock was kept busy not merely with the inevitable public and fannish fallout from his innovative program, but the day-to-day challenges of keeping the magazine afloat in a highly competitive economic environment.[20] *New Worlds*'s publishers went bankrupt in late 1966, and the magazine would have gone under save for an Arts Council grant (engineered in large part by Brian Aldiss) secured in early 1967. That grant enabled Moorcock to finally make the leap to the large glossy format he had long envisioned. But in 1968 the magazine's serialization of Norman Spinrad's novel *Bug Jack Baron* got them in trouble, both with their distributors and even on the floor of the House of Commons, on the grounds of "obscenity and libel." By late 1968 Moorcock alone had full responsibility for the magazine, and by the end of 1970 *New Worlds* was winding down as a monthly (occasionally bi-monthly) periodical. The magazine continued for some years as a paperback series under the editorship of various hands, and there were a number of "best of" collections drawn from its files, but for all intents and purposes *New Worlds* ceased with the September 1979 issue (number 216). In the context of science fiction history, its most important period was that of Moorcock's direct editorship, from 1964 to 1975.

* * *

Moorcock talked a bold (if sometimes inconsistent) line in his editorials, and the stories he published in *New Worlds* were sometimes groundbreaking indeed, but his own fictional contributions (often published under the pseudonym "James Colvin") were nowhere near as formally inventive and provocative as the work he was presenting by Ballard, Aldiss, Thomas M. Disch, and others. For all of his admiration for William Burroughs, he was not ready to discard the linearities of traditional storytelling, yet he wanted to capture some of his own era's characteristic challenges and paradoxes. The fantasy-hero Elric of Melniboné had proved a compelling creation with which to juggle questions of fate and destiny, free will and determinism, Law and Chaos. But Moorcock felt that the very particular obsessions of the present moment—"stuff associated with scientific advance, social change, the mythology of the mid-twentieth century"[21]—could only be addressed by a contemporary myth. And thus he created the dandy, flâneur, scientist, and assassin Jerry Cornelius, at once the most ambiguous and most perdurable of his long series of "champions."

Moorcock wrote *The Final Programme*, the first of his Cornelius novels, in January 1965; as he would recount it, he produced the first draft "in nine days, working at night and feeding my baby daughters as I wrote."[22] The image and the name of his hero came to him serendipitously, as he sat eating at a Notting Hill café: "This beautiful young man, with his ascetic features, elegant clothes and floating long hair, had suddenly appeared as I looked up. And behind him was the name of one of our local greengrocer's shops, Cornelius of London."[23] The Jerry Cornelius of *The Final Programme* is a hero for his moment, the embodiment of everything that made London of the 1960s a capital of the popular imagination, that made it "swing": fashion, art, pop music, drugs, sexual liberation. He is an ex–Jesuit, a Nobel Prize–winning physicist who has repudiated his own books, whose titles read like indices of the *Zeitgeist* (*Time Search Through the Declining West, Toward the Ultimate Paradox, The Ethical Simulation*).[24] He is a sexual adventurer of comprehensive tastes: at the beginning of the book, he is enjoying a tryst with the (male) Professor Hira in Angkor Wat, but he will sleep with a number of women over the novel's course—and his true love remains his sister Catherine. He commands seemingly unlimited wealth, and moves amid an environment of lavish luxury goods and dazzling gadgets: his Duesenberg and Rolls Royce autos, his jewel-studded electric guitar, the voice-activated gates of his Holland Park Avenue (Kensington) mansion, his silent and deadly needle gun. He is something like a cross between Mick Jagger, James Bond, and Jay Gatsby.

He is also more immediately a refashioning of the albino emperor Elric. In Jerry Cornelius, Moorcock transposes Elric to mid-sixties London, where the Melnibonéan's sorcery—the "secret knowledge" of the world's working proper to a fantasy setting—becomes Jerry's visionary physics and Professor Hira's Hindu cosmology. The better part of *The Final Programme*, in fact, is a rewriting of "The Dreaming City" and "While the Gods Laugh," the two 1961 stories that introduced Moorcock's sword-and-sorcery anti-hero; these stories provide the direct narrative scaffolding for about three-fifths of the novel. In "Phase 1" of *The Final Programme* the assault on Jerry's father's Normandy villa is adapted from the assault on Imrryr in "The Dreaming City"; every detail of the Elric story seems mirrored in this stretch of the novel, from Elric's servant Tanglebones—

who becomes, anagrammatically, John Gnatbeelson—to the sea-maze the reavers must navigate to reach Imrryr's harbor, which becomes the maze-passage from the Normandy cliffs to the elder Cornelius's mansion. Elric's usurping cousin Yyrkoon threatens him with a black runesword the twin of the his own Stormbringer, just as Jerry and his brother Frank duel with identical needle guns; and just as Elric's beloved cousin Cymoril dies on the point of Stormbringer, Jerry's sister Catherine is felled by his own needle.

The Final Programme's "Phase 2" more roughly parallels "While the Gods Laugh," in which Elric and Moonglum travel to the Silent Land, where they fight various elementals and descend into a magical cavern in search of the "Dead Gods' Book," which contains various weighty secrets. Similarly, in "Phase 2" Jerry and the enigmatic Miss Brunner travel to an abandoned underground Nazi complex in Lapland, where they corner and kill Frank, who has both the microfilm that was the object of their raid on the Normandy villa in "Phase 1" and a manuscript written by the American astronaut Newman, whom Jerry suspects had obtained some deep insight into the entropic processes of earth during his time in orbit. The Dead Gods' Book, Elric discovers, has decayed into dust; Newman's manuscript consists of "203 neatly numbered pages" of "ha ha ha ha ha" (etc.).[25]

More interesting than Moorcock's sometimes mechanical adaptation of his own plotlines—the Newman manuscript is little more than an outrageous MacGuffin—is his reworking of Elric's symbiotic relationship with his sentient runesword Stormbringer. In *The Final Programme*, the position of Stormbringer is filled not by an object but by a *character*: Miss Brunner, the vulpine computer programmer who has the unsettling habit of *absorbing* her lovers, bones and all. (She is echoed in this vampirism by Jerry himself, who "found that he didn't need to eat much, because he could live off other people's energy just as well."[26]) At the end of "The Dreaming City" Elric realizes that he and Stormbringer are irrevocably tied one to another, "Bound by hell-forged chains and fate-haunted circumstances."[27] *The Final Programme* presses this symbiosis a step further: at novel's end, Jerry Cornelius and Miss Brunner emerge from the womb of the massive computer DUEL (Decimal Unit Electronic Linkage) fused into a single pansexually irresistible figure, "Cornelius Brunner"—"a tall, naked, graceful being," "hermaphrodite and beautiful"[28]—who saves European humanity from increasing entropy by leading them in a lemming-like migration into the sea. Elric's tragedy has been recast as chillingly amoral comedy.

Jerry Cornelius, as his very initials might indicate, would seem to fulfill Professor Hira's speculations about the imminence of "a new messiah—

a messiah of the Age of Science."[29] But Moorcock himself has always been suspicious of leaders, much less messiahs. Among the pressing problems of this world of "196-" is precisely the loss of individuality, the amalgamation of previously distinguishable persons in "a crowd," "a single unit, a composite creature, many-limbed and many headed." We see this in a harrowing episode in the Chicken Fry restaurant in London, where Jerry, in order to escape an amoeba-like crowd, is forced to shoot his old acquaintance Shades, identified now only as "The Part."[30] In order to bring some salvation to this disintegrating and homogenizing body politic, to become the new age's "messiah," Jerry must surrender part of his own individuality to become Cornelius Brunner; and Cornelius Brunner's solution to the decline of the West is precisely to wipe out Western man. Erekosë, we recall, solves the problem of human aggression by exterminating humanity. Cornelius Brunner can pronounce ours "a tasty world," but only after its people have been removed.[31]

The Final Programme, which finally appeared in book form in 1968 (in a somewhat bowdlerized version[32]), is shot through with irony and comic asides, but on the whole is a straightforwardly constructed short novel, its most compelling theme the struggle of its hipster protagonist to maintain his equilibrium, even his identity, in a world sliding into disorder. Moorcock complicates matters in the second Cornelius book, *A Cure for Cancer* (1971), which is a fast-paced, comic affair, its action cartoonish, exaggerated, its science-fictional technologies deployed with all the subtlety of a low-budget comic book. Here Jerry has become a photographic negative of himself, his skin coal-black and his hair as white as Elric's. Miss Brunner is nowhere to be found (though there is a sympathetic male character, Captain Brunner); the principal antagonists are Bishop Beesley, a grotesquely fat, sweets-addicted cleric, and his daughter Mitzi. The landscape is a nightmarish vision of civilization sliding into chaos: Europe, occupied by millions of American military "advisors," is the new Vietnam. America itself, apart from stretches of the West in which Native American tribes are staging full-scale revolutions, is under authoritarian rule, dotted with concentration camps.

The plot is a hectic chase back and forth between continents, all against a backdrop of increasing entropy. Jerry, who runs an organization specializing in "transmogrifying" people, fitting them to survive in this new reality, is in search of his missing "black box," which is "a sort of randomiser. It can produce all the alternatives at once.... It breaks down the barriers. It lets the multiverse—well—'in.'" His goal, as with so many of Moorcock's protagonists, is "moderation in all things."[33] The Bishop, in contrast, wants to entirely arrest the process of entropy. Through his great steam-driven orrery, he claims, "I order the world. I bring realism—the virtues of the past."[34] Beesley may be something of a Lord of Law, but for all Jerry's dimension-shifting and cross-dressing—he seems to spend half the book in drag—Jerry is by no means a power of Chaos. At the book's conclusion, he brings his dead sister out of her cold-storage drawer and revives her with the black box. They make love in the snow of Holland Park, and then Catherine dies again. "He looked down at her with affection but without sorrow.... Then he walked away from there, leaving her lying surrounded by the snow. It had all been worthwhile."[35] Entropy, in the end, is irreversible. The most one can strive for, even one as flamboyant as this vibragun-wielding scientist-messiah, is a momentary equilibrium, a momentary stay against confusion.[36] But that is, after all, the human condition.

* * *

The notion that Jerry Cornelius is a "messiah of the Age of Science" must be taken ironically from the very start, it is clear, and Moorcock's critical examinations of the messianic are part and parcel of his more or less constant questioning of the concept of leadership and heroism itself. All of the avatars of the Eternal Champion, as we shall see, are to one degree or another anti-heroes, anti–Champions as it were. In "Behold the Man," a novella published in *New Worlds* in 1966, the year after he drafted *The Final Programme,* Moorcock advances his most searching critique of society's desire for messiah-figures.

The story, Moorcock recalls, "was conceived at the kitchen table of a Ladbroke Grove basement in Easter 1966, when some of us were discussing the nature of demagogues and how much their careers were driven by their own ambition, how much by the yearnings of the crowds who gave them their power."[37] The story's protagonist, Karl Glogauer, is a contemporary English Jew, a deeply conflicted and neurotic young man obsessed with Jung, Christianity, and the history of religion. By means of a fortuitously-available time machine, Glogauer travels to Palestine in 28 AD, where he hopes to discover the truth about the historical Jesus. Mary, wife of the carpenter Joseph of Nazareth, does indeed have a son named Jesus, but the young man is "misshapen," hunch-backed, can pronounce no words other than his own name: Glogauer has "seen a man he recognized without any doubt as a congenital imbecile."[38] Before coming to Nazareth, Glogauer has lived among the Essenes, has associated with John the Baptist, has seen firsthand the profound messianic desire of the Jewish people under Roman rule. If there is no Jesus—at least as later ages will come to know him through tradition and through the records of the gospels—then someone must supply that absence: and Glogauer himself steps into the pre-scripted role of the messiah. He *becomes* Christ, "healing" psychosomatic illnesses, relating as many of the parables as he can remember from the gospels, collecting about him a mass of followers desperate for leadership and salvation. "He was bringing a myth to life—a generation before that myth would be born. He was completing a certain kind of psychic circuit. He was not changing history, but he was giving history more substance." Glogauer is fulfilling his own need: "It was in his power to make Jesus a physical reality rather than the creation of a process of mythogenesis."[39]

Glogauer goes to his crucifixion with no hope of resurrection—he is, after all, entirely agnostic—and his last words on the cross are "It's a lie. It's a lie. It's a lie" (which the author of the Gospel According to Mark will interpret as *Eloi, Eloi, lama sabacthani?*—"My God, my God, why has thou forsaken me?").[40] It has indeed been a "lie": that is, the christological traditions that have been the basis of the whole edifice of Christianity, according to the novella's neat but paradoxical logic, have accreted around the very *absence* of a historical Jesus. But "Behold the Man" is a "true" parable of messianism. The messiah, the chosen and anointed one, appears not at the behest of the divine, but through the synergistic combination of the messiah's own psychological drives—Karl's desperate need to find meaning—and the people's needs: his followers "thought he led them, they in fact, drove him before them."[41]

The Science Fiction Writers of America gave "Behold the Man" the Nebula Award for Best Novella in 1967. Moorcock expanded the story to make a short novel, which was published in the UK in 1969 and the U.S. in 1970, at which point his religious parable garnered him, at least from the more staunchly evangelical parts of America, a number of angry letters and even some death threats. Moorcock cheerily replied to such letters by enclosing refunds for the purchase price of their writers' copies: "It has always seemed the fairest way to treat dissatisfied customers."[42]

"Behold the Man" is clearly an SF narrative, but the technological aspects of the story—the time machine itself, which is dwelt upon only to emphasize its womb-like nature—are of far less concern to Moorcock than the psycho-sociological messianic theme upon which it dwells. Similarly, *The Black Corridor*, the other science fiction novel Moorcock published in 1969 (written to some degree in collaboration with his wife Hilary Bailey), is less interested in the details of the future world it imagines or the technicalities of the space voyage which is its setting than in the psychological state of its protagonist, Ryan, left alone to tend the spaceship while the other members of his party lie in suspended animation. *The Black Corridor*, a harrowing little book, is a fine exercise in the exploration of "inner space" conducted in the traditional SF context of outer space. The spaceship *Hope Dempsey*, travelling at nearly the speed of light, is some four years into its journey to a nearby star, where sensors have located a habitable planet. For much of that time, Ryan has been awake by himself, while his wife and sons, other members of his family, and friends have slept. They have left behind—or rather, they have barely escaped—an earth sliding rapidly into chaos, nation-states fragmenting into local principalities, rampant xenophobia and regionalism, a general sense of anomie and paranoia gripping the populace.

Alone on the ship, Ryan begins to succumb to hallucinations, begins to lose the self-control upon which he has always prided himself. And as he loses his grip on his immediate surroundings (he sees ghostly figures dancing outside the ship, he imagines that he has awoken his brother to keep him company), the memories of his last months on earth come flooding back, and the reader learns that Ryan, in order to realize his dream of taking his family off of the earth, has carried out a whole series of acts of brutal and cold-blooded violence. He is, and has been all along, as paranoid in his own way as any of the members of the mobs he has sought to escape. The novel ends on a note of stasis, Ryan awake and seemingly clear-headed, all of the sleepers secure in their caskets. But it is evident that the old dream of science fiction, to travel to another world to start anew, has played itself out: wherever the human being goes in the universe, he carries with him the seeds of the same suspicions, paranoias, and disunities that threaten to make our own world uninhabitable.

* * *

Soon after *The Final Programme* was published in 1968, it became clear that with Jerry Cornelius Moorcock had created a full-fledged culture hero for his generation. This wasn't necessarily a positive thing, for Moorcock had intended Jerry in large part as an *ironic* commentary on the cultural optimism of mid-sixties London. As he later reflects, *The Final Programme*—"or at least its hero, Jerry Cornelius—was taken as a model by those same young men whose euphoria and ambition it satirized. They detected no irony. They saw Jerry as just what they wanted to be: a kind of hipper James Bond."[43] But for a number of the writers in the *New Worlds* orbit, Jerry Cornelius proved an irresistable figure to write about—not as a hero, but as a *myth*, a character by which they could explore their own

2. A Messiah for the Age of Entropy

impressions of the age. Moorcock had written a Cornelius short story, "The Peking Junction," for his friend Langdon Jones's anthology *The New SF*, and drafted another, "The Delhi Division." Having seen these stories (the latter in draft form), the American writer James Sallis asked Moorcock if he'd mind Sallis himself trying his hand at a Cornelius short, "since, in his opinion, the JC stories were a form in themselves."[44]

Sallis's story "Jeremiad" appeared in the February 1969 *New Worlds*, and soon a number of other *New Worlds* writers joined in the fun. Over the next two years the magazine published Jerry Cornelius stories (and one poem) by M. John Harrison, Brian Aldiss, Langdon Jones, Norman Spinrad, and Maxim Jakubowski.[45] Jerry Cornelius was, as Harrison put it, less a "character" than a "technique": he had become an open-source myth. As Spinrad put it, these writers were engaged in an act of collective mythopoesis: "If enough diverse writers successfully use the Jerry Cornelius myth in stories of their own, it will take on all the attributes of a genuine popular myth," a myth "around which they can blow experimental variations useful in the exploration of their own directions."[46]

This proliferation of Cornelius texts, I think it safe to argue, had a clear influence on Moorcock's own Cornelius writings. Harrison's "The Ash Circus" (in the April 1969 *New Worlds*) presents Jerry as the "English assassin," a title Moorcock would adopt for his third Cornelius novel, and Harrison's "The Nash Circuit" (August 1969) introduces Shakey Mo Collier, who would become a regular character in Moorcock's own Cornelius stories and novels. More significantly, the short-form Cornelius fictions, both Moorcock's and those by other hands, tend to be far less plot-driven, far more oblique and fragmented, far more reliant on setting and atmosphere than *The Final Programme* and *A Cure for Cancer* had been. If *A Cure for Cancer* sometimes approached the condition of the Chuck Jones cartoon, the Jerry Cornelius *story*, whether in Moorcock's or in another's hands, tended towards the condition of the vignette or the fragment, a moment snipped from an already-in-progress narrative, in which relationships, precedents, and motives are rarely made clear, in which characters move in an atmosphere of brooding, obdurate, but never quite clarified significance. It is but a brief step from such short stories to the radical discontinuities of *The English Assassin*, the next Cornelius novel, and the third of what Moorcock had realized some time earlier would be a tetralogy.[47]

Both *The Final Programme* and *A Cure for Cancer* are instantly recognizable products of the same cultural milieu as Pynchon's *The Crying of Lot 49* (1966) and Vonnegut's *Slaughterhouse-Five* (1969), and they are both in some ways meditations on entropy, what might be seen as the master trope of the whole *New Worlds* enterprise. In their narrative structures, however, despite the high-spirited tabloid-style chapter titles and the quoted advertisements and newspaper clippings scattered throughout *A Cure for Cancer*, they are relatively conventional: aside from a few dimension-shifting speedbumps in *Cure*, the two novels follow straightforward temporal and causal sequences; they proceed from beginning to end. In terms of structure, *The English Assassin* (1972) is something else altogether.

The English Assassin is a formally stylized novel, divided into four major sections, called "shots." Each "shot" contains ten brief (two- to five-page) chapters, in two five-chapter sections. Between the sections, at the center of each "shot," are two short unrelated chapters, titled "The Alternative Apocalypse," themselves sandwiched between collections of newspaper clippings ("Latest News") and brief autobiographical paragraphs ("Reminiscences") by "Maurice Lescoq" (a pun on Moorcock's own name). At the center of the novel as a whole, between the second and third "shots," is "The Peace Talks: The Ball," a longish chapter set at William Randolph Hearst's San Simeon castle (which had previously figured in *The Final Programme*), now transported to Ladbroke Grove and the site of an international gala ball in which all of the characters of the previous Cornelius novels, an array of figures from Moorcock's other books, and various real-life characters—royalty, members of government, divers pop stars, the members of the rock band Hawkwind, the novelists Jack Trevor Story and Kingsley Amis, C. S. Lewis and J. R. R. Tolkien ("dons who wrote children's novels at Oxford"[48])—and a host of others are gathered, only to be dispersed in an explosion of violence when Jerry Cornelius, the absent master of the household, reappears.

"The Peace Talks: The Ball" bears no direct relationship to the chapters that lead up to it, nor to the ones which follow, and this discontinuity is characteristic of the novel as a whole. The forty chapters that make up the bulk of *The English Assassin* are emphatically *modular*. Some of them, especially in the early part of the novel, follow upon one another in a straightforward (if attenuated) chronological and causal order; but many of them, like Lego bricks that can be removed and replaced with a piece of another color, seem to have little overt relationship to the chapters they stand between. The overall readerly texture of the novel resembles a photo album in which each new snapshot depicts an entirely new setting, may contain a different set of faces from the previous one. Some of the chapters are directly linked to one another, directly follow one another, although at a distance of thirty or forty pages; others seem to have no connection to the general current of the novel. As Greenland notes, "Each section is self-contained, as if we are visiting a story at several intermediate stages. The scenes are separate, brief but clearly lit; what happens between is shadowed and obscure."[49]

The same cast of characters is cycled in and out of the chapters of *The English Assassin*, but in different roles and guises: is Catherine Cornelius a prostitute in Miss Brunner's London brothel, as she appears in "The Lovers," or guard to the POW Captain Nye, as she appears four chapters later?[50] Is Frank Cornelius a seedy antiques dealer or the (seedy) commander of a destroyer? And while almost all the chapters' settings evoke a profoundly unsettled Europe, their temporal location—indeed, their location among various *alternative* temporalities—is continually shifting. "The Observers" takes place in a steampunk Guatemala City in the early twentieth century, while the next chapters return us to London in some undefined postwar moment, and "The Explorers" essentially recapitulates the first chapter of *The Final Programme*.[51]

Matters are complicated even more by the eight "Alternative Apocalypse" episodes sandwiched within the four "shots." In these vignettes, Jerry Cornelius appears alone or in company—walking through the ruins of London, watching a horde of fleeing hippies cross a collapsing Tower Bridge, ransacking Wordsworth's Dove Cottage, being crucified to the mast of a yacht off the coast of Kent—always in the context of an apocalyptic final breakdown of western society. These "apocalypses" have no discernable narrative connection to the rest of the novel, though they pick up themes and motifs from other parts of the book and from the previous Cornelius novels. Throughout *The English Assassin*, in addition to the bundles of clippings designated "Latest News," the text is littered with fragments of newspaper stories, advertisements, and publicity sheets—"found" texts, like the newspapers Picasso and Braque would paste into their cubist collages.

The novel's form is unconventional to say the least, reminding the reader of the experiments in narrative of such modernists and late modernists as James Joyce, Italo Calvino, Burroughs, and the writers of the French *nouveau roman*. Moorcock however does not see his discontinuous form as being in the lineage of an aesthetic avant-garde, but as part and parcel of the themes he is striving to pursue. "Books—any art—must have shape, but the shape can be very different," he writes in a 1976 notebook; "It's an attempt to describe and dramatize my own view of the world—i.e., one which is non-linear. I can see so many possibilities all at once I can't choose one—and I would not wish to choose one. I'm not confused by multiplicity—I'm delighted by it."[52] The radically unconventional forms of such novels as *The English Assassin*, *The Condition of Muzak*, *Breakfast in the Ruins*, and *Mother London* are not exercises in aesthetic experimentation, nor are they meant as challenges to the reader (one recalls Joyce's comment on *Ulysses* that "I've put in so many enigmas and puzzles that it will keep the professors busy for centuries arguing over what I meant, and that's the only way of insuring one's immortality").[53] "It was never my intention," says Moorcock, "to write 'difficult' books."[54] It's not that Moorcock does not admire the achievements of high modernism; *Ulysses* "is a tremendous, brilliant book; but it's not the same kind of book that I write.... I'm still a popular novelist."[55] "The faceted form, the musical form, the non-linear form," he argues, "is to prevent the reader from making conventional links and deductions."[56] But it is *not* to make the novel an exercise in puzzle-solving, "not to make the reader work, because I don't believe in that; [rather] to give the reader a good time, but an *unfamiliar* good time."[57]

There are many pleasures, both familiar and unfamiliar, in *The English Assassin*. There are a number of new characters joining Frank, Catherine, Miss Brunner, Professor Hira, and the Beesleys: Shakey Mo Collier (whom Moorcock adopted from M. John Harrison), Major and Captain Nye, blue-eyed exemplars of the virtues of old-style British imperialism; Prinz Lobkowitz, scion of middle-European aristocracy; Sebastian Auchinek, Jewish partisan and theatrical manager; the old Slav Colonel Pyat. Una Persson, one of Moorcock's most memorable female characters, comes into her own in *The English Assassin*.[58] (She had appeared briefly the previous year in *The Warlord of the Air*.) She is intelligent, beautiful, self-assured, handy with a firearm, lover to Jerry, Catherine, Auchinek, and no doubt others, but entirely her own woman. She is perhaps the only character in the novel who seems continually on top of whatever situation she finds herself in; in books to come, Moorcock will further develop her as a "temporal adventuress."

Most important and memorable of the characters Moorcock introduces in *The English Assassin* is Mrs. Cornelius, Jerry, Catherine, and Frank's mother. "Mrs. C." (Honoria) is perhaps Moorcock's single greatest creation; he has said on several occasions that she is his favorite. She is proudly Cockney, intensely rooted in working-class London; she is vast, vulgar, and possessed of formidable appetites for food, liquor, and sex; she is something of an embarrassment to her children. Above all, she is shrewd, as sure to survive the apocalypse as a cockroach, and she is kind-hearted.

Missing from most of *The English Assassin*, however, is Jerry Cornelius himself—at least as an active, conscious presence. A number of the novel's modules follow the progress of his body, in a kind of hibernation, as it moves across Europe: the carton carrying him washes up in a cave in Cornwall, is carried to Berlin, then transported back to London by train, passing through a number of hands along the way. In other, thematically related episodes, he is dying on a raft far out at sea; he is imprisoned in a box on the deck of a warship in the Mediterranean; he is a dead and decaying apelike creature lying in a castle on an island in Grasmere Lake; and in two episodes, we are encouraged to identify him with the carefully packaged skeleton of a child in the hold of an airship en route to the Indian Ocean.

The English Assassin ends on a comic note. Mrs. Cornelius, with Catherine and the repulsive Frank, is visiting the seaside, England in ruins behind them. As the matriarch dozes in her beach chair, Catherine and a group of children digging in the sand uncover Jerry's casket. He emerges from his state of hibernation in a scene that is a cross between Sleeping Beauty and *Dracula*—he is lovingly reunited with Catherine, and simultaneously drains Frank of his vital energy—then, dressed in a Pierrot's costume and strumming a ukulele, he bears his sister and lover away on the yacht *Teddy Bear*.

* * *

Moorcock had drafted *The Final Programme* in a little over a week. The last novel of his Cornelius tetralogy, *The Condition of Muzak*, which was not published until five years after *The English Assassin*, clearly took far longer to write; and it is correspondingly more complex and realized than that first book, incorporating all of the themes and characters of the three earlier Cornelius novels, replaying them and turning them inside out, making them into something far richer and more strange than they had been on their first appearances. The technique is self-consciously musical, and the titles of the sections of *The Condition of Muzak*—"Prelude," "Introduction," "Development," "Recapitulation," and "Coda," interspersed with brief episodes of "Tuning Up"—echo classical sonata form: or, in Moorcock's own account, symphonic form. "*The Condition of Muzak*," he says, "was the first book I wrote that really moved as a symphony in my head."[59]

The Cornelius Quartet as a whole is preceded by a "Note to the Reader": "Although the books may be read in any order, the reader might wish to know that the structure of the last volume reflects the structure of the overall tetralogy."[60] *The Condition of Muzak*, then, repeats and builds upon what has come before it in the three earlier books, but in a significantly changed key, a shifted tonality. The themes and the narratives of *The Final Programme*, *A Cure for Cancer*, and *The English Assassin* reappear in *Muzak*, but to a large degree stripped of their exuberance and ebullience, toned down, weighed down by a grimy realism wholly absent from the first two books of the tetralogy, at least: restated as it were in a minor key, or in the muted tones of "Muzak," which a final note informs us is "a trade name for piped music used in restaurants, supermarkets, bars and other public places."[61] "The condition of music" is Walter Pater's phrase, from the 1877 edition of his manifesto of aestheticism, *The Renaissance: Studies in Art and Poetry*. "All art," Pater writes, "*constantly aspires towards the condition of music.*" By "the condition of music," Pater means the ultimate subsumption of "form" and "content," the "perfect identification of form and matter" that one experiences in instrumental music, where the affective impact of the artwork is experienced directly, without the distraction of narrative, of representation, of mimesis.[62] But if the "condition of music" is a state of aesthetic sublimity, the condition of *Muzak* reflects the power of entropy to grind down all sublimity, to reduce all the beauties and ideals in its scope to its own commercialized, background level.

We see this Muzak-principle at work as *The Condition of Muzak* restages the first three Jerry Cornelius novels, each of them stripped of the glamour and excitement of its original appearance. The first five chapters of the "Introduction" section give us what amounts to a prequel to *The Final Programme*; the second half presents a kind of "bridge" between that novel and *A Cure for Cancer*. Jerry and Miss Brunner are no longer merged ("I thought we were going to be together always," Jerry sulks), but discarding the other half of "Cornelius Brunner" seems no more complicated than "clamber[ing] out of his stockings and suspenders."[63] Where, in *A Cure for Cancer*, the photographic-negative Jerry had been coal-black to his very teeth, even his pubic hair snow white, here we see him blackening his face and bleaching his hair like an actor assuming a minstrel-show role.[64]

These sections, with their air of scene-setting, their heavy-handed building of backstory, work intentionally to deflate the sparkling and strange science fantasy of the first two novels, to reveal the needle-gun toting Jerry Cornelius of *The Final Programme* or the vibra-gun wielding satyr of *A Cure for Cancer* as temporarily assumed *roles*: Jerry was never *quite* Jerry Cornelius; he was only playing him. The novel is concerned largely with roles and play-acting, as was presaged in Jerry's donning of the Pierrot costume at the end of *The English Assassin*. And indeed *The*

2. A Messiah for the Age of Entropy   53

Condition of Muzak is shot through with references to the old Continental tradition of the *Commedia dell'Arte*, in which the actors play variations on a set of fixed roles—Harlequin, Pierrot, Columbine, and so forth.

The central sections of *The Condition of Muzak* are reminiscent, both thematically and stylistically, of *The English Assassin*. Stripped of his hipster roles, of his technological gadgets and far-flung support systems, Jerry is in retreat, constantly regressing towards the condition of stasis in which he spent most of that previous novel. Finally he does entirely withdraw into hibernation, burrowing into his lair in the overgrown Derry and Tom's roof garden—the setting of the opening scene of *A Cure for Cancer*, itself a repeat of the Cambodian jungle of the beginning of *The Final Programme* and more generally reminiscent of the womb-enclosures into which Moorcock's protagonists retreat or penetrate. From there he is extracted by Major Nye and Professor Hira and ushered back into a revitalized London. As he convalesces, Miss Brunner and Major Nye pronounce a final obituary on his mythological status. "And he used to be tipped as the Messiah to the Age of Science," Miss Brunner says scornfully. Major Nye is kinder: "You tried to use [technology] to maintain the old order. Your friend Beesley wanted to turn it against itself, to destroy it altogether. But Cornelius enjoyed it for its own sake. Aesthetically ... he wasn't the world's Messiah," Nye concludes; "He wasn't the Golden Trickster. He was his world's Fool."[65]

In the ten years Jerry has been sleeping, he has become a legendary figure, a "sleeping king" like Friedrich Barbarossa, Holger Danske, or Erekosë. Now, when he awakens, he is crowned King of a new, utopian Britain, split into seventy-two tiny principalities, each ruled by its own rajah, maharajah, mandarin, chief executive, or Celtic or Caribbean leader. And following a bravura, Dickensian description of the Christmas celebrations following his coronation, there is a reprise of the awakening scene from the first section of *The Final Programme*; only this time it is Frank who dies, rather than Jerry's sister. Catherine is Columbine, the beloved from the *Commedia dell'Arte*. But Jerry is not the crafty trickster Harlequin, as he had implicitly assumed throughout the first two books of the tetralogy, but Pierrot, the weeping clown. "Harlequin somehow metamorphosed into Pierrot," he muses; "I used to believe I was Captain of my own Fate. Instead I'm just a character in a bloody pantomime." It is Una Persson who is the true Harlequin, who can awaken Catherine/Columbine from her drugged sleep: "Pierrot couldn't wake her, you see," she tells Jerry. "Only Harlequin has the power to do that. Pierrot has no power—only charm."[66]

Much of *The Condition of Muzak*, then, stages an elaborate deconstruction of the "myth" of Jerry Cornelius. But even the happy equilibrium reached at the end of this episode, when Catherine and the newly-crowned Jerry relax into each others' arms, is undercut by the novel's "Prelude" and "Coda," which present us with a grimly realistic Jerry Cornelius, a spotty young man living in a grubby apartment with his mother and sister, dreaming of rock 'n' roll stardom, practicing guitar and getting stoned in his room, staring from his balcony (a sordid echo of the Derry and Tom's roof garden) and fantasizing about the nuns in the convent across the street.

The "Coda" narrates a rags-to-somewhat-tawdry-finery story. Frustrated in his aspirations to be a pop star—at his first public gig with his band The Deep Fix, a drug-fuddled Jerry falls through a hole in the stage and smashes his guitar—Jerry begins taking roles in local theater, and eventually achieves prosperity making television commercials as a sort of Noël Coward-Leslie Howard lounge lizard. He may drive a real Rolls Royce Phantom, but he's gotten it by making Rolls Royce advertisements. The Jerry Cornelius of *The Final Programme*, trend setter of fashion, design, and lifestyle, is no more than a media-filtered image, a role impersonated by this "real" Jerry Cornelius, indifferent musician and (one imagines) indifferent actor. The tetralogy as a whole is rounded off by its first real death—a death after which one expects no resurrection: that of Mrs. Cornelius. Moorcock has encased the fantasy of *The Condition of Muzak*, fantasy which is at once a continuation, an elaboration, and a critique of the fantasy of the tetralogy's first three books, within a frame of irreducible realism: realism which shows how rock 'n' roll is watered down into Muzak, how the glittering flourishes of the harlequinade are a series of rote movements gone through by tired actors, how all the hectic activity of human life eventually ends in the entropic dead level of mortality.[67]

* * *

The principal Jerry Cornelius tetralogy is perhaps Moorcock's single most achieved work. (I confess that it is my favorite among his writings.) *The Final Programme* and *A Cure for Cancer* are consistently amusing and exciting narratives, and the more modular, discontinuous collages of *The English Assassin* and *The Condition of Muzak* are rich and surprising reading experiences. The tetralogy as a whole is neatly and poignantly summed up and bound together in its final volume, a novel which has something of the same culminatory power as Proust's *Time Regained* or the closing chapters of Joyce's *Ulysses*.

As self-contained and complete as the tetralogy may be, Moorcock would go on to write a good deal of Cornelius fiction outside of these four books. This goes well beyond the short stories—something of a genre in themselves, and which Moorcock has continued to write occasionally into the new century—and includes several more novel- and novella-length fictions. The attraction is obvious: given the narrative ductility of the Cornelius "form," coupled with a familiar set of characters, Moorcock can transpose his Cornelius ensemble to whichever present he wishes to address. Among the short stories, for instance, "The Romanian Question" (1991) confronts the fall of the Soviet bloc, while "The Spencer Inheritance" (1998) thinks about the death of Princess Diana, the place and future of the British monarchy, and the phenomena of publicity and stardom.

The longer extra-tetralogical Cornelius writings are rather a mixed bag.[68] Moorcock wrote *The Great Rock 'n' Roll Swindle* (1980, also titled *Gold Diggers of 1977*) as something of an authorized tie-in to the Sex Pistols film of the same name, while *The Entropy Tango* (1981) reads like an extended, slowed-down—entropic, really—coda to *The Condition of Muzak*. *Firing the Cathedral* (2002) and *Modem Times 2.0* (2011) situate Jerry and company in the uncertain new world of post–September 11 paranoia and neo-imperialism, surveying the domestic devastation of neo-liberal economic and social policies. (In these latter Cornelius stories, Miss Brunner, in grotesquely aged form, more often than not appears as "the Baroness," a pointed association with Margaret Thatcher.)

Two of the "long-form" works stand out. *The Adventures of Una Persson and Catherine Cornelius in the Twentieth Century* appeared in 1976, between *The English Assassin* and *The Condition of Muzak*. It is Moorcock's attempt, he noted a bit later, "to write a kind of women's adventure novel"[69]—in contrast, one assumes, to the "boys' own" adventure stories that had constituted much of his own formative reading. The novel is a series of vignettes, slices of the two women's individual adventures at various points in the twentieth century (or rather, various possible twentieth centuries), for Una and Catherine are experienced time travellers. Una's adventures tend to involve war and violence; Catherine's, sexual and romantic entanglements. Una is confirmed in her role as a "temporal adventuress," a member of the League of Temporal Adventurers, as she has already appeared in the *Dancers at the End of Time* novels.[70] Jerry too will in various short stories and novellas be increasingly figured as a time traveller. In one sense, this is Moorcock's way of rationalizing the time- and space-shifts central to his fictive technique in *The English Assassin*.

"If there was any remotely coherent message in *The Adventures*," Moorcock reflects, "it was that women's first loyalty must be to their own sex if permanent change in the status quo is to be achieved."[71] This is part and parcel of the strong feminist position at which Moorcock had arrived by the early eighties (encouraged in large part by his close friendship with the American thinker Andrea Dworkin), evident as well in his 1983 anarcho-feminist pamphlet *The Retreat from Liberty*, in which he argues that such limited-focus political causes such as the Campaign for Nuclear Disarmament are to some degree distractions from the central issue of the age: women's rights and women's equality.[72] "Through the principles of feminism," Moorcock writes, we might save society "from the existing jingoistic chauvinists of all kinds whose self-deceiving lies threaten to lead us along the road to an even more tarrying kind of destruction: both personal and political."[73]

The Alchemist's Question, which was published in 1984 with the subtitle "Being the Final Episode in the Career of the English Assassin,"[74] comes perilously close to being fictive propaganda on behalf of such principles. At the very least, it is an odd and ungainly production, set firmly in the Cornelius universe(s), but with a narrative pace and overall plot structure more reminiscent of Moorcock's more pulpish fantasies. Una Persson, Catherine Cornelius, and a small band of refugees from the now-obliterated Time Centre (a kind of operations center for the League of Temporal Adventurers) seek to thwart Miss Brunner's Thatcherian plan to plunge the world into nuclear winter and return to the regimented society of a previous era. "We must break up the walls Miss Brunner's erected.... We need a good base; a new beginning. After that, things will spread in all directions again. The alternatives will be there to choose from." This time around, however, Una stresses, "the centre ... will be run on female principles."[75] The problem with his failed merger with Miss Brunner in *The Final Programme*, Jerry recognizes, is that "Miss Brunner dismissed my mother's importance.... She listens to men because she thinks they've got the secret. She dismisses women."[76] Miss Brunner is, in short, a Thatcherite woman, a woman who seizes the power that men wield by taking on a man's mindset. At novel's end, there has been another merger, this time between Jerry and Catherine, who have come together in an alchemical crucible and been transformed into a glowing golden egg, the "philosopher's stone."[77] The egg is an emblem of new life, new hope, new possibilities; and when the egg speaks, six months later, it repeats "Cornelius Brunner's" words in a distinctly feminine voice: "'It's a tasty world,' *she* said."[78]

It's premature to speak of Jerry Cornelius's "afterlife," for Moorcock himself is still writing the occasional Cornelius story and incorporating the character into such projects as the graphic novel *Michael Moorcock's Multiverse* (1999), but it's safe to say that Jerry is—after Elric of Melniboné—Moorcock's most recognizable and popular character. He has appeared in a number of media, and had a wide influence. In 1973, the director Robert Fuest directed a stylish but rather one-dimensional film of *The Final Programme*, with Jon Finch as Jerry and Miss Brunner played by Jenny Runacre; Moorcock had written a script for the project, which Fuest had rejected in favor of his own treatment. The French comic artist Moebius (Jean Giraud) incorporated some glancing references to Moorcock's work in his series *Le Garage Hermétique* (originally *Le Garage Hermétique de Jerry Cornelius*) which ran from 1976 to 1979 in the magazine *Métal Hurlant*. More full-throated in its borrowings both from the Cornelius mythos and from Moorcock's notion of the multiverse in general— though with full acknowledgment—was Bryan Talbot's complex, dense, and magnificent *The Adventures of Luther Arkwright* (1978–1989), which is among the most important and influential British graphic novels. Cornelius stories continue to be written and published. Like Conan the Barbarian, John Carter of Mars, or Sherlock Holmes, there is every indication that the creation might well outlive its creator.[79]

* * *

During the years in which he edited *New Worlds*, Moorcock worked hard to promote writing that he felt would give new life to the science fiction field, but this doesn't mean that he was promoting only a single *kind* of writing. Rather, as Samuel Delany argues, "it was only a narrow range of writing that Moorcock excluded [from *New Worlds*]—but a range whose oceanic acceptance elsewhere Moorcock felt had swamped, if not drowned, the field."[80] In other words, Moorcock's editorial agenda at *New Worlds* (a "clear, vital, and consistent" program, in Delany's words) involved opening science fiction to a broad range of elements, both stylistic and thematic, that had been in play for some time in the broader fields of popular and literary writing, and simultaneously downplaying many of the *differentiae* of science fiction that had over the past decades ossified into conventions.

It was natural that such a program would arouse some resistance among the writers, editors, and fans of established forms of SF, and spirited arguments raged across the pages of periodicals and fanzines even more strongly when *New Worlds* came to be hailed as the spearhead of a "New Wave" in SF writing.[81] The term "New Wave," in obvious emulation of the so-called "nouvelle vague" French filmmakers of a few years before (Jean-Luc Godard, François Truffaut, Éric Rohmer, and others), was by some accounts coined by the American writer Judith Merril, editor since 1956 of a highly-regarded "year's best" SF anthology. In 1968 Merril released *England Swings SF*, an anthology presenting work by almost all of the core members of the *New Worlds* group. *England Swings SF*'s contributors' notes (composed by Merril, and interlaced among more conventional statements by the contributors themselves) constitute a kind of running manifesto on behalf of the New Wave.

While there were a number of Americans—Zoline, Disch, Sladek, Sallis—in Moorcock's London orbit, *New Worlds* and whatever literary "movement" it represented were primarily a British affair. In the United States, a largely unrelated but similarly "oppositional" group of younger SF writers were shortly to become identified as the American New Wave, an association to some extent crystallized by Harlan Ellison's anthology *Dangerous Visions* (1967). Christopher Priest has argued that the American New Wave editors, in attempting to emulate *New Worlds*, had to a large degree "missed the point" of Moorcock's editorial program:

> The purpose of the New Wave, if indeed it can be said to have a purpose, was to release writers and readers from the preconceptions of the pulp magazine idiom. The American argument was about a *product*: a "type" of story with an invented label. The *process*, which Moorcock and others had been encouraging writers to explore, was to find an individual approach to writing speculative fiction.[82]

While this seems a fair enough assessment of what Moorcock as editor was up to, I have no doubt that it considerably oversimplifies a series of very complex dynamics, both in individual writing careers and in the field as a whole.

In general I distrust the nominalization of literary-historical processes. Such abstract nouns as "Romanticism," "Modernism," "Confessional Poetry," or the "New Wave" may serve a couple of purposes: convenient categorizations for literary and cultural historians; or more or less temporary banners under which (mostly younger) writers can march during the precarious stages of their careers in which individual agendas can best be advanced within a "group" formation. The New Wave served the latter purpose for maybe a bit longer than half a decade, from the mid-sixties to the early seventies; now it is serving the former for too many historians of science fiction.[83] I find very persuasive Delany's argument that the generational and oppositional model (a New Wave opposing an "Old Wave," eventually multiplying and propagating itself to become a new mainstream of SF production), a model accepted by too many historians and critics of science fiction, is oversimplifying, and that it would be more useful to think of *New Worlds* and the writers associated with it not as a "wave" but as an "island" of literary production. Of the "American New Wave," Delany writes, "Harlan Ellison's 1967 anthology *Dangerous Visions*, for example, though an island of an entirely different density and structure and with an entirely different fallout, has been hopelessly confused with the New Wave because the two were roughly contemporaneous."[84]

Even from a distance of half a century, it is difficult precisely to assess Moorcock's *New Worlds* tenure. At times, one is astonished by the boldness of his editing and the clear-sightedness of his critiques of contemporary culture, SF and otherwise; at other times, one finds oneself lending a little assent to Lester Del Rey's grousing: "Moorcock claimed that what he wanted was fiction with ideas; but he never seemed to define what he meant by that."[85] If nothing else, Moorcock's editing of *New Worlds* catapulted him into the forefront of the science fiction community. (And the financial exigencies of the magazine, as we shall see in the next chapter, led to an explosive increase in his production of fantasy writing.)

What is most striking about Moorcock's editorial program and writing during this period is not so much his desire to introduce modernist narrative techniques and up-to-date thematic material into SF—though that is indeed important—as his more general desire to break down the walls of genre, to modify, refunction, or discard altogether the conventions dividing science fiction from "literary" writing. And vice-versa, for SF has as much to offer "literary" fiction as "literary" fiction does SF. This impulse to explore and then move beyond genre, along with his never-forgotten obligation to the reader—the obligation above all to *entertain*—is one of the constants of Moorcock's career.

3

New Avatars, New Time Streams and a Farewell to Fantasy

Between 1965 and 1974, the years when he was most closely associated with *New Worlds*, Moorcock published an enormous number of books, both under his own name and under a variety of pseudonyms. But while he was advocating a program of psychological and literary experimentation from his editor's desk, there was precious little of the experimental in most of the forty-odd books he wrote over that decade. Instead, he was turning out—by the yard, as it were—generic fantasies, along with a few science fiction pot-boilers. "I wrote fantasy works to commission for US publishers, primarily Lancer Books," Moorcock later explained:

> I think I received $1000 a book. It was a fortune. I would produce a full-length book in three days. Each manuscript was exactly 180 pages long. In what little spare time there was between issues of the magazine, I wrote these books to support my family and, by then, the magazine itself, since our budget did not meet our needs.[1]

Of course, to turn out novels so rapidly, even for a writer hardened in the school of pulp popular fiction, a wordsmith who thought little of turning out fifteen to twenty thousand words a day, required Moorcock to rely on narrative and generic formulas, and most of his fantasy novels of this period are very formulaic indeed.[2] But while their narratives may follow familiar rhythms and their characters take familiar shapes, these further novels of Elric and Erekosë, and the new series featuring Corum and Dorian Hawkmoon, are never less than entertaining, and are sometimes positively gripping. They show Moorcock developing and refining his figure of the Eternal Champion and further elaborating the conflict between Law and Chaos that forms the underpinning of his epic fantasy.

By 1975, with *The Quest for Tanelorn*, the concluding volume of a second Hawkmoon series, it was clear that Moorcock was ready to wrap up and wind down the whole Eternal Champion mythos. His writing was moving in a number of fruitful new directions. *The Warlord of the Air* (1971) was an alternate history novel hearkening back to H. G. Wells, while the "End of Time" trilogy (1972–1976) unwound and reconfigured the moral themes and motifs of his epic fantasies in a playful, Voltairean register. By the end of the decade, Moorcock was laying plans for a large, non-generic work, the "Between the Wars" tetralogy, and he bade farewell to fantasy (temporarily, as it would turn out) with *Gloriana; or, The Unfulfill'd Queen*, a vast and baroque work that was in large part an homage to one of his great original influences, Mervyn Peake.

* * *

Moorcock between 1965 and the end of the seventies presents something of a paradoxical figure: even as in his editorial statements for *New Worlds* he continually railed against the constrictions of genre writing and against the expectations of SF and fantasy fandoms who wanted not something *new*, but more of what they already knew they enjoyed, his own writing more often than not fell firmly within genre expectations. This is nowhere clearer than in the trio of "Michael Kane" novels he published with Compact Books in 1965, which were outright pastiches of Edgar Rice Burroughs's Mars novels. *Warriors of Mars*, *Blades of Mars*, and *Barbarians of Mars*—all titles reminiscent of Burroughs's *A Princess of Mars*, *The Gods of Mars*, and so forth—were published under the pseudonym "Edward Powys Bradbury." As Moorcock explains, "it seemed to me just then it wasn't a good idea to be talking about the breaking down of genre conventions whilst producing a trilogy of romances which exemplified, even exalted, those conventions."[3] (The books were reprinted under Moorcock's own name a few years later, and with his preferred titles *City of the Beast*, *Lord of the Spiders*, and *Masters of the Pit*.)

Moorcock wrote these three books "in just over a week,"[4] and had a grand time paying homage to Burroughs, an idol of his youth, and poking some gentle fun at the sometimes insufferable do-gooder John Carter. The novels themselves are little more than lively imitations of the Barsoom model, reproducing precisely Burroughs's scenario of a contemporary earthman transported to a Mars of strange animals, swordplay, and more or less constant action. Where Burroughs has green Martian giants, Moorcock has *blue*; on Barsoom one rides an eight-legged animal called a thoat, while on Moorcock's Vashu one rides an apelike *dahara*; John Carter's barbarian sidekick is Tars Tarkas, while Michael Kane's is Hool Haji; and so forth. Moorcock has given a bit of thought to the matter of Mars's mixed technology, what one might think of as the central contradiction of the "sword and planet" sub-genre. That is, it is a trifle hard to conceive why Burroughs's Barsoomians, having access to anti-gravity-equipped flying machines and radium firearms with a range of hundreds of miles, would bother riding thoats and fighting with swords. On Moorcock's Vashu, such anomalously advanced bits of technology are few and far between, the leavings of the Sheev, a vanished technologically advanced race.[5]

As the name *Sheev*, reminiscent of the Hindu god Shiva, indicates, Moorcock draws much of the cultural paraphernalia and nomenclature for his Martians from South Asian culture. Michael Kane repeatedly remarks how the script and ornamental motifs on Vashu remind him of Sanscrit; and since the Mars to which Kane travels is the Mars of the distant past, when earth was still ruled by dinosaurs, he can imply at the onset of the trilogy that our own human civilization may be descended from migrating Vashuvians.[6] In the passages in which Kane improvises a balloon airship, and later oversees the manufacture of a fleet of such ships, we see an early manifestation of Moorcock's obsession with lighter-than-air flying machines. They are the primary transportation in his teenage "Sojan" stories, and will reappear to greater effect in *The Warlord of the Air* (1971), *The English Assassin* (1972), *The City in the Autumn Stars* (1986), and numerous other books.

In the mid–sixties Moorcock also published several pseudonymous thrillers and a handful of leaden science fiction novels.[7] One of their few memorable moments is the flamboyant figure of Emmanuel Bloom, the titular character of *The Fireclown* (1965, reissued in 1969 as *The Winds of Limbo*), who would reappear to much greater effect in *The Transformation of Miss Mavis Ming* (1977). But his bread-and-butter writings between 1967 and 1974, and the works which established him as one of the most popular fantasists alive, were extensions of the Eternal Champion template: the expansion of "The Eternal Champion" into a full-length novel, followed by a sequel; new Elric books; and most importantly, two new, very different avatars of the Champion, whose tales would play out over thirteen volumes—Duke Dorian Hawkmoon of Köln and Corum Jhaelen Irsei, the Prince in the Scarlet Robe.

Moorcock imagines a very striking world indeed for Hawkmoon, who is at the center of *The History of the Runestaff*, a tetralogy published between 1967 and 1969 (*The Jewel in the Skull*, *The Mad God's Amulet*, *The Sword of the Dawn*, and *The Runestaff*).[8] The novels play out in a far-future Europe, several thousand years after the "Tragic Millennium"—a nuclear war, presumably—has largely destroyed our own civilization. The land masses are more or less familiar, but the names of the cities and regions have changed (Paris is *Parye*, Spain is *Espanyia*, Wales is *Yel*) and political boundaries have reverted to quasi-medieval regions rather than contemporary nation-states. Europe is a mass of small, squabbling principalities who are gradually falling under the dominion of the evil empire of Granbretan (Great Britain). Duke Dorian Hawkmoon is the fallen ruler of Köln (Cologne): "In a spirit consciously at odds with the jingoism of the day," Moorcock comments, "I chose a German for a hero and the British for villains."[9]

There was much nostalgia for empire in the United Kingdom in the postwar period, but Moorcock would have none of it. The anti-imperialist sentiment that runs through most of his books is perhaps strongest and most explicit in the Runestaff tetralogy. The war-hardened Count Brass, ruler of the idyllic Kamarg delta in the south of France (the Camargue to us), may admire the "consistency" and "order" that Granbretan's conquests are imposing upon Europe—"What will you have? The princedoms of Europe dividing into smaller and smaller segments, war a constant factor in the life of the common man?"—but the poet-philosopher Bowgentle sees more clearly what Granbretanian dominion means: "The order they bring is superficial, the chaos they bring destroys men's souls."[10]

The Dark Empire of Granbretan, ruled by the two-thousand-year-old King-Emperor Huon, a wizened, fetus-like figure who drifts in the "milk-white fluid" of his Throne Globe (echoing Karl Glogauer's womblike time machine in *Behold the Man*), is a vividly realized evil. Londra, the capital, is an enclosed city of vast, baroque, perverse architecture, bisected by the River Tayme, stained blood-red by some chemical effluent. The Granbretanians themselves manifest a weird comingling of regimentation and individual perversity. It is the fashion for everyone of any social standing to conceal his or her face behind a mask, usually representing some animal. The Empire's various operatives are organized into various animal "orders": the Hounds, the Vultures, the Pigs, etc., each member wearing the mask of that species. Aviators who pilot Granbretan's ornithopters are Crows, military engineers are Badgers, the King-Emperor's personal guard are Mantises. It is a breach of etiquette to allow one's naked face to be seen, and only the lowest, most despised castes go bare-faced. By concealing their visages under the simulacra of beasts, the Granbretanians are denying their own and others' humanity, are refusing the true sociality always involved in meeting another's gaze. And the concealment of the face allows the underlying bestial nature—cruel, rapacious, sadistic—to openly emerge.

"In Köln," Bowgentle tells Count Brass, "their sport was to crucify every girlchild in the city, make eunuchs of the boys, and have all adults who would save their lives perform lewd displays in the street.... Their entertainment is to debase all humanity."[11]

Any number of terms could characterize the Granbretanian culture of cruelty—"unnatural," "perverted," "sick"—but at its root, as we see in the case of Baron Meliadus of Kroiden (that's the London suburb Croydon), Hawkmoon's principal antagonist in the tetralogy, is a kind of twisted *aestheticism*. Meliadus proposes to Flana Mikosevaar, the King-Emperor's sole living relative, that she join him in a conspiracy to unseat Huon and restore the vitality of Granbretan, perhaps even extending its empire to the stars. "Granbretan's adventures could last a million years!" he exclaims, and when Flana wonders whether "adventure and sensation" are all that is worth pursuing, Meliadus replies, "All is chaos, there is no meaning to existence, there is only one advantage to living one's life and that is to discover all the sensations the human mind and body is capable of feeling." Flana can only agree: "That is our creed, true."[12]

This Granbretanian "creed" clearly rests on existentialist foundations—"there is no meaning to existence"—but the practical application it draws from life's meaninglessness hearkens back to the infamous 1873 conclusion to Walter Pater's *The Renaissance*: "A counted number of pulses only is given to us of a variegated, dramatic life," writes Pater. "How may we see in them all that is to be seen in them by the finest senses?... To burn always with this hard, gemlike flame, to maintain this ecstasy, is success in life."[13] Many of the lords of Granbretan are sensationalists of a lower order, pursuing the pleasures proper to greed, sadism, and so forth; but a striking number—Meliadus, the erotomane Flana, the knowledge-seeking sorcerer-scientists Kalan and Taragorm—pursue their ends out of self-consciously *aestheticized* motives.

In the Elric stories, the Melnibonéans are decadent, and the lassitude of decadence has caused them to lose their Bright Empire to the insurgent vitality of the Young Kingdoms. In contrast, the spiritual decadence of Granbretan is yoked to a ferocious energy, a furious drive to subordinate all of Europe and beyond to the order of servitude. Hawkmoon, deposed leader of the conquered city of Köln, is a numbed and traumatized prisoner of the Dark Empire at the beginning of the tetralogy. He is sent by the lords of Granbretan, principally Meliadus, to subvert Count Brass's Kamarg, one of the few enclaves holding out against them. Instead, Hawkmoon ends up allying with Count Brass, marrying his daughter Yisselda, and by the conclusion of *The Runestaff*, leading an army to Londra to top-

3. New Avatars, New Timer Streams, and a Farewell to Fantasy   65

ple the entire Granbretanian empire—and of course slaying Meliadus in single combat.

How all this comes about is far too complex (and at times, frankly hurried) to recount, but it's fair to say with Moorcock's finest critic John Clute that the tetralogy relies altogether too much of the gathering of "plot coupons," items "all of which the characters must collect before ... they can send off to the author for the ending."[14] In *The Jewel in the Skull*, Hawkmoon must travel to Turkia where the wizard Malagigi can nullify the brain-eating black gem Baron Kalan has implanted in his forehead; in *The Mad God's Amulet*, he travels to Ukrania, where he takes possession of an amulet that gives him measureless strength in battle, and then to the plane-shifting city of Soryandum in Syria for a crystal machine that will shift the whole of the Karmarg into an alternate Europe, thereby rescuing it from the Dark Empire's siege. Much of the second half of the tetralogy takes place in "fabled Amarehk" (America), where Hawkmoon obtains the Sword of the Dawn, which can summon the Legion of the Dawn (endlessly replenishing ranks of phantom Amerindian warriors), and the Runestaff itself, an object of profound but mystical power.

While the sometimes slipshod texture of the writing in *The History of the Runestaff* reflects the books' hasty composition, Moorcock is more or less right (if a trifle self-congratulatory) to remember the books as cunningly constructed: "I think the books themselves are probably little gems, structurally speaking—not that I've actually read them," he tells Colin Greenland.[15] The tetralogy exhibits a nicely balanced mirroring of movements and events. *The Jewel in the Skull* and *The Mad God's Amulet* begin and end with idylls in the Karmarg, in between following the out-and-back course of Hawkmoon's journey to Ukrania and the Middle East. The latter two volumes reverse this movement, with Hawkmoon's westward journey to Amarehk and his return. The black jewel, whose malignant threat dominates the first novel, is revived in the fourth. And unlike in his previous fantasy novels, where the narrative focus is always firmly upon a single character, Moorcock skillfully maintains tension by shifting viewpoints from character to character between chapters and sections.

"Balance," in many ways, is the central theme of the tetralogy, symbolized and embodied in the Runestaff itself. This numinous object would seem to be the prime mover behind the events of the novels: Meliadus, we are told, sets the action of the whole series in motion when he swears an oath on the Runestaff; Hawkmoon is repeatedly told by the mysterious Warrior in Jet and Gold (who pops up in best *deus ex machina* fashion when he's most needed) that both of them are servants of the Runestaff, though Hawkmoon has no idea what that means. Each of the "books" into which the novels of the tetralogy are divided is prefaced with an excerpt from "*The High History of the Runestaff*," passages which take an eagle's-eye view of the ongoing action, and emphasize the behind-the-scenes working of the Runestaff. Hawkmoon himself, continually receiving new directives from the Warrior in Jet and Gold, the Runestaff's messenger, begins to feel bereft of free will: "I resent the feeling of being the puppet of some supernatural agency," he tells his friend Huillam D'Averc—and this is only one of many such complaints.[16] (Elric, as well, frequently grouses about being manipulated by Law and Chaos.)

In Dnark (New York) Hawkmoon encounters the Runestaff itself and its embodied spirit, the boy Jehamia Cohnalias, who tells him that "here in Dnark we seek only equilibrium. That, after all, is the goal and reason for existence of the Runestaff."[17] Later, Orland Fank, the guardian of the Runestaff, will explain: "The world does not change, Dorian Hawkmoon. There is merely the occasional shift in equilibrium and if that shift goes too far in one direction, then the Runestaff attempts to right it."[18] The Runestaff, then, is the Balance, the same scales seen in the sky in the last scenes of *Stormbringer*, demonstrating the restored equilibrium of Chaos and Law.

At the end of the tetralogy, defeating the Beast Lords of Granbretan while holding the staff high, Hawkmoon has emerged as the champion of the Runestaff. He has fought on behalf of a cosmic force, true enough, but Orland Fank reminds him that what the Runestaff symbolizes and embodies can only be achieved through the freely-willed actions of individuals: justice "can be manufactured in small quantities.... But we have to work hard, fight well and use great wisdom to produce just a tiny amount.... Justice is not the Law, it is not Order, as human beings normally speak of it; it is Equilibrium, the Correction of the Balance."[19] Here Moorcock explicitly corrects readers' perhaps mistaken impression that his Champion fights only for Law (as Elric supports Law against his ancestral patrons of Chaos, and Corum will fight to banish the Lords of Chaos from his planes). For Hawkmoon, despite the relative absence of the rhetoric of Law and Chaos in the Runestaff tetralogy, is clearly a manifestation of the Eternal Champion—something Moorcock makes plain in his revision between the first edition of *The Secret of the Runestaff*, where Orland Fank bids him farewell—"Remember that, Hawkmoon. Remember it"—and later editions of *The Runestaff*: "Remember that, Sir Champion Eternal."[20]

* * *

In 1970, Moorcock expanded his novella "The Eternal Champion" into a full-length novel. Such reworkings of previously-published material—the revising of a shorter work to novel length, the presentation of tenuously connected short stories as a single book-length work (the "fix-up")—are common in the science fiction and fantasy fields; the year before, against his own better judgment, Moorcock had expanded "Behold the Man" to novel length.[21] Later in 1970 Moorcock published *Phoenix in Obsidian*, a sequel to *The Eternal Champion*. *Phoenix* is notable for the extent to which it shows Moorcock beginning to think of his epic fantasies as together comprising a single grand narrative, a series of variations upon one another. Though the story of Urlik Skarsol, the Black Sword, the Lady of the Chalice, and the mysterious Silver Warriors has a good deal of grim power on its own, it is even more resonant placed as it is conceptually at the intersection of *The Eternal Champion*, the already published Elric stories, and the Runestaff tetralogy.

Erekosë, summoned away from his Eldren bride Ermizhad to become Urlik in *Phoenix in Obsidian*, is beset with vivid memories of his other existences: "*I was Elric of Melniboné and I defied the Lords of Chaos.... I was Dorian Hawkmoon and I fought against the Beast Lords of the Dark Empire.... I was Jeremiah Cornelius.... I was all of these and more than these.*"[22] He dreams of the Warrior in Jet and Gold; he encounters the dwarf Jermays the Crooked, who had aided Elric in the last section of *Stormbringer*.[23] And most strikingly, he finds himself destined (if reluctantly) to wield a Stormbringer-like Black Sword, similarly rune-marked, humming, and sentient, and similarly given to cutting down standers-by and occasional allies—if not possessed of Stormbringer's soul-sucking and -transferring qualities.

From the beginning of *Phoenix in Obsidian*, Urlik-Erekosë is haunted by the possibility that he has been *condemned* to be the Eternal Champion, "that I had been responsible, in some incarnation, of a cosmic crime, so terrible that it was my fate to be swept back and forth across eternity."[24] Somewhat later, he begins to suspect that his punishment is not that he *is* the Eternal Champion, but "that I be *aware* of my incarnations and thus know my true tragedy."[25] The crime, he comes to realize, was that "in some previous incarnation—whether in the past or the future, for Time in my own context was a meaningless word," he had rid himself of the Black Sword, had refused the Champion's symbiotic relationship with his blade. When Urlik Skarsol finally takes up the Black Sword (in *Phoenix*, it is also the "Cold Sword"), he is well-nigh invincible. He frees the Lady of the Chalice from her captivity by the unpleasant Bishop Belphig, thereby showing that the moon-born Silver Warriors (another version of the Eldren) are in reality no threat to the humans of the Scarlet Fjord, and finally, by slaying the Lady on the ice in what amounts to an alchemical-Arthurian grail ritual, he restores life to the dying sun, and saves the whole planet from its wintry senescence.

The Sword itself, however, is like Stormbringer purely *evil*. As Champion Urlik has refused or tried to cast away the black blade many times before; but the sword is the Champion's inevitable companion, even a part of himself. It is Elric's Stormbringer, Hawkmoon's Sword of the Dawn, Roland's Durandal, Erekosë's poisoned, perhaps radioactive blade, Jerry Cornelius's needle gun: "*sometimes my weapon was a sword, at others it was a spear, at others a gun.... But always, I bore a weapon that was the Black Sword or a part of that strange blade.*"[26] The Cold Sword is the real thing; when Urlik takes it up, he realizes that "it was rare for me to hold the actual blade. Usually I had a weapon which drew its power from the Black Sword, which was a manifestation of the Black Sword." "This is the Whole Sword!" he exclaims, hefting it.[27] He has taken up, in its full presence, what his other avatars—save Elric—have handled only in a partial manifestation.

Just as in *Phoenix in Obsidian* we see Moorcock developing and generalizing the relationship of the Champion and his symbiotic, evil sword across his growing range of Champion-avatars, so he is also beginning to develop the concept of Tanelorn, the place of refuge and rest to which the Champion aspires. The city of Tanelorn was first introduced in the Dunsany-esque story "To Rescue Tanelorn...," published in *Science Fantasy* in December 1962, after the first five Elric stories (which would be collected in 1963 as *The Stealer of Souls*) and before the four long stories that make up *Stormbringer*. "To Rescue Tanelorn..." is set in Elric's world of the Young Kingdoms, and involves the decision of the Lords of Chaos, represented by Narjhan, to destroy Tanelorn, "a lonely, long-ago city, loved by those it sheltered." They resent the city because "most of these troubled travelers who dwelt in peaceful Tanelorn had thrown off earlier allegiances to the Lords of Chaos"—without, however, swearing fealty to the Lords of Law.[28] When Tanelorn is menaced by a vast beggar army led by Narjhan, Rackhir the Red Archer (formerly a warrior priest sworn to Chaos, but now a Tanelornian) cannot appeal to the Lords of Law, but must go in search of the mysterious "Grey Lords," who will offer supernatural aid that saves the city. In the course of his multi-dimensional quest for the Grey Lords (a quasi-allegorical quest, with strong echoes of James Branch Cabell, for Rackhir journeys through the realms of Chaos and Law,

3. New Avatars, New Timer Streams, and a Farewell to Fantasy 69

encountering a good deal of philosophizing about the meaning of life), Rackhir encounters the immortal Guardians, Eldren-like figures who reveal that they had created Tanelorn, "the last of our cities," as a place of rest.[29] Along with the hermit Lamsar's final pronouncement, "Tanelorn will always exist while men exist…. It was not a city you defended today. It was an ideal," this is the only hint in "To Rescue Tanelorn…" of a larger symbolic or metaphysical resonance for the city.[30] But Tanelorn will shortly come to assume a more important role in Moorcock's cosmology of Law, Chaos, and the Eternal Champion.

In *Phoenix in Obsidian*, Urlik Skarsol is most immediately tormented by the fact that he has been parted from his Eldren love Ermizhad, and his thoughts and dreams are full of his longing to be reunited with her. In one of the most vivid of his dream-visions he first hears of the city Tanelorn. A figure resembling Ermizhad tells him that Tanelorn "*has existed through eternity.*" "*Tanelorn,*" she says, "*exists in many Realms, on many Planes, in many worlds, for Tanelorn is eternal. Sometimes hidden, sometimes there for all to visit—though most do not realize the nature of the city—Tanelorn shelters many Heroes.*"[31] Later, in expounding the nature of the Multiverse to Ulrik, the Lady of the Chalice explains that while Earth is mirrored in a myriad of other worlds, "Tanelorn is mirrored elsewhere—but with one difference, it does not change. It does not decay as the other worlds decay. Tanelorn, like you, Sir Hero, is eternal."[32] By the novel's end, Urlik has resolved to seek this mysterious, timeless Tanelorn, which holds the hope of reunion with Ermizhad, and perhaps even respite from his continual struggles and reincarnations as the Eternal Champion.

* * *

In *The King of the Swords* (1971), the last novel of Moorcock's first trilogy featuring Corum Jhaelen Irsei, the Prince in the Scarlet Robe, Corum and his companion Jhary-a-Conel actually visit Tanelorn. In this particular manifestation—for there are as many different Tanelorns, it would seem, as there are manifestations of the Eternal Champion, but all of them in some deep sense *the same*—Tanelorn is a place of metallic, azure beauty:

> It was a blue city and it gave off a strong blue aura which merged with the expanse of the blue sky which framed it, but its buildings were of such a variety of shades of blue as to make them seem many-coloured. These tall spires and domes clustered together and intersected and adjoined each other and rose in wild spirals and curves, seeming to fling themselves joyfully at the heavens as if silently delighting in their own blue beauty, in all their colours from near-black to pale violet, in all their shapes of shining metal.[33]

This particular Tanelorn is not a place of rest for Corum, but it does hold, in the person of the imprisoned god Kwll, the key to final victory in the struggle against the Sword Rulers—the Lords of Chaos—which has occupied the whole of the trilogy.

The first three Corum books (*The Knight of the Swords*, *The Queen of the Swords*, and *The King of the Swords*, all 1971) were among the many fantasies Moorcock turned out in rapid succession during this period, and were clearly conceived as a trilogy from the outset. In Corum, Moorcock creates yet another traumatized protagonist, yet another antithesis to the healthy, muscular virility of Conan (or Thongor, or Brak) the Barbarian. Elric is a physical weakling, dependent for life itself on his symbiotic relationship with his sword; Erekosë-Urlik-John Daker is perennially seized by doubts and misgivings, and tormented by admittedly partial self-knowledge; Hawkmoon begins the Runestaff tetralogy as a shell-shocked prisoner of war, and lives with the ever-present menace of the black jewel embedded in his forehead. But Corum out-traumatizes them all. He is the last survivor of the Eldren-like Vadhagh; his family and the rest of his race have been brutally exterminated by the barbarian Mabden, and Corum himself has been bereft of a hand and an eye by the repulsive Mabden Earl Glandyth-a-Krae.

In the downfall of the Vadhagh before the bestial Mabden, Moorcock recasts a number of his earlier scenarios: the war King Rigenos pursues against the Eldren in *The Eternal Champion*; Bishop Belphig's manipulation of the Silver Warriors in *Phoenix in Obsidian*; and the fall of Melniboné to the Young Kingdom reavers in "The Dreaming City." In writing of the Mabden, Moorcock speculates that he had in mind the various first-millennium invasions of Cornwall: the trilogy draws closely upon Cornish names, history, and folklore—the result of "an exceptionally wet Cornish August when the most interesting book I had available was a Cornish-English dictionary with no corresponding English-Cornish section."[34] More significant, however is the degree to which Moorcock portrays the Vadhagh as an ancient and *decadent* race: not cruel in their decadence like the Melnibonéans, but detached from the evolving world, too involved with abstract philosophy and the creation of music, artworks, and poems to recognize the threat the younger races, which they regard as little more than animals, pose them.

Corum survives his dismemberment through supernatural aid, he is rehabilitated by and eventually falls in love with Rhalina, a Mabden woman of a rather more civilized tribe than Glandyth-a-Krae's (compare the cross-species romances of Erekosë-Ermizhad and Elric-Zarozinia), and he

3. New Avatars, New Timer Streams, and a Farewell to Fantasy 71

acquires supernatural replacements for his missing members: the Eye of Rhynn, which can see into the netherworld, and the six-fingered Hand of Kwll, which can summon thence a variety of fighting forces.[35] He will need these uncanny prostheses, for it becomes evident that the Mabden destruction of the Vadhagh and their threat to Rhalina's folk is not merely the result of population pressures, geopolitical shifts, or outright imperialism, but a manifestation of a world out of balance: the Sword Rulers, or the Lords of Chaos, have come to dominate the realm in which Corum moves, and his task over the course of the trilogy—aided in the latter two books by Jhary-a-Conel, professional "companion to Champions"—is to progressively expel each of them to limbo, installing in their place the Lords of Law.

There is a twist at the end of *The King of the Swords*, however. When Corum has returned his borrowed hand to the god Kwll, freeing him from the timeless Tanelorn, Kwll and his brother Rhynn proceed to slay the Chaos lords—and for good measure they kill the Lords of Law as well: "Now you mortals are free of gods on these planes," Kwll tells Corum. "Now you can make your own destiny."[36] The gesture is one that Moorcock makes repeatedly. The Lords of Law and Chaos both, in the long run, are no more or less than manifestations of conflicting tendencies within the human temperament. The sooner the world is rid of such deities, such supernatural displacements of human responsibility, the sooner human beings can go about crafting their own destinies in a self-conscious, creative manner. Corum as Champion must welcome this change, for all of the avatars of the Champion are to some degree burdened with the sense that they are merely puppets in the hands of larger forces. Jhary-a-Conel, in contrast, leaves Corum's world for more familiar spaces: "I go to seek worlds where gods still rule, for I am not suited to any other…. Gods—a sense of omniscience not far away—demons—destinies which cannot be denied—absolute evil—absolute good—I need it all."[37] Jhary, the Companion to Champions, is only at home in the worlds of heroic fantasy. One suspects that his leave-taking reflects Moorcock's own impatience with the supernatural dualisms of his created worlds, and the limitations of sword and sorcery as genre.

* * *

The King of the Swords is also notable for an episode towards the end, right before Corum and Jhary-a-Conel reach Tanelorn, in which Corum meets and teams up with two (to him) unfamiliar figures—Elric of Melniboné and Erekosë—to fight the dwarfish sorcerer Voilodion Ghagnasdiak. This highly unusual event, three avatars of the Eternal Champion on the same plane of existence, is only made possible by the "Conjunction of the Million Spheres," a moment in which the various separate universes of the Multiverse come into alignment, when "old laws are broken and new ones established—the very nature of space and time and reality are altered."[38] Thriftily, Moorcock tells the story of the three heroes' fight in Ghagnasdiak's plane-shifting tower twice: once from Corum's perspective in *The Knight of the Swords*, and again from Elric's in "Three Heroes with a Single Aim," the third section of the Elric novel *The Sleeping Sorceress* (1971).

Though he had killed off Elric in "Doomed Lord's Passing," the final section of *Stormbringer*, Moorcock had returned to writing of his albino anti-hero, still his most popular and immediately recognizable protagonist. Again there is a precedent in Conan. "The Phoenix on the Sword" (1932), the first published Conan story, presented a middle-aged Conan already king of Aquilonia. The sixteen more stories Robert E. Howard published before his death ranged across Conan's lifespan from early manhood on, in no chronological order. Later L. Sprague de Camp, Lin Carter, and others would take up the task of sorting Howard's stories by internal chronology, constructing a linear biography for Conan, and filling in the blanks in the barbarian's career. Similarly, while Elric had certainly died at the end of *Stormbringer*, that was no impediment to Moorcock's going back and inventing adventures from earlier in his life—which he proceeded to do.

The new Elric material reflected Moorcock's more recent discipline in writing Hawkmoon and Corum novels. Unlike the earliest Elric works, which were entirely stand-alone short stories, *The Sleeping Sorceress* and *Elric of Melniboné* (1972)[39] were conceived of as novel-length works from the start (though their plots admittedly retain some of the modularity of the "fix-up"). *Elric of Melniboné* is a prequel to the events of "The Dreaming City," setting up the relationship among Elric, Cymoril, and Yyrkoon, and narrating Elric's discovery of the black sword Stormbringer. The events of *The Sleeping Sorceress* take place between those of the early stories "The Singing Citadel" and "The Stealer of Souls."

All in all, one has a clear sense that by the end of the first half of the 1970s Moorcock was anxious to wind up the entire Eternal Champion mythos, to turn his full attention to some of the other fictive modes he was exploring. There would be two last concentrated bursts of Championwriting, however: a second Corum trilogy and three more books of Hawkmoon, "The Chronicles of Castle Brass." Where the first Corum trilogy had drawn on Cornish language and folklore, Corum's second outing— *The Bull and the Spear* (1973), *The Oak and the Ram* (1973), and *The*

Sword and the Stallion (1974)—has a strongly Irish flavor, and an altogether chillier atmosphere. As with the Runestaff tetralogy, the novels rely a trifle too much on obvious "plot coupons" (the "bull," "spear," "oak," etc., of their titles), but on the whole this trilogy is one of Moorcock's most tightly plotted, cunningly constructed, and emotionally engaging fantasy sequences. Corum is never quite at home in this icy world to which he has been summoned to fight the Fhoi Myore, mindless and grotesque Chaos gods—his own world, but hundreds of years in the future—and his own death at the end of *The Sword and the Stallion* has an air of the inevitable. If the end of *The King of the Swords* marked the end of the era of gods, then *The Sword and the Stallion*'s conclusion, with Corum's death, signals the final banishment of the supernatural from the world. As the Dagdagh tells the dying protagonist, "Now this world is free of all sorcery and all demigods."[40]

Moorcock wrote his second Hawkmoon series under considerable financial duress. "The first editions of these books," he comments in one omnibus, "were dedicated to Harrods of Knightsbridge and to Bill Butler of Unicorn Books. Harrods were threatening to sue me for a small fortune and Bill owed me one. I amiably suggested that they get together and cut out the middle man, but legal departments are, like policemen, professionally humourless."[41] The "Count Brass" novels—*Count Brass* (1973), *The Champion of Garathorm* (1973), and *The Quest for Tanelorn* (1975)—are among the weakest of Moorcock's fantasy novels, so far as nuance of style and sturdiness of narrative construction go; much of the time, one has the unmistakable feel that the author is simply going through the motions. They follow Hawkmoon's career after the Battle of Londra with which *The Runestaff* concluded, and find him battling an improbably surviving Baron Kalan, who has found the means to manipulate time and aims to restore the Dark Empire. Moorcock's time-travel speculations here are far less coherent than in "Behold the Man" (1966) or *The Warlord of the Air* (1971), and the trilogy refuses to hang together as a unit; Moorcock seems a bit tired of the whole business. Things come alive a trifle in *The Champion of Garathorm*, however, when Corum's companion Jhary-a-Conel turns up in Hawkmoon's world and, through a series of subterfuges too involved to go into, gets Hawkmoon to infuse his soul—the soul, we learn for the first time in the Hawkmoon corpus, of the Eternal Champion—into the body of Ilian, Princess of Garathorm, the first *female* avatar of the Champion.

The Quest for Tanelorn serves as a grand final gathering of all of the strands of Moorcock's Eternal Champion mythos. Here not three but *four* manifestations of the Champion come together: Hawkmoon, Elric, Erekosë, and Corum, brought together by the blind captain of a mysterious ship to fight the incursion into the Multiverse of the monstrous alien siblings Agak and Gagak, who are capable of sucking the energy from entire universes, and who thereby threaten the Multiverse's very existence. In the episode of Voilodion Ghagnasdiak's tower, Elric, Erekosë, and Corum found their strengths multiplied when they linked arms; in *Quest*, the four Champions literally fuse into a single giant fourfold warrior. These two episodes of heroes "crossing over" from one created world to another (or to an intermediate, neutral world) are meant to provoke the pleasure of recognition in the reader; they are Moorcock's knowing winks to his fandom. He even plays the neat trick of cross-cutting internal chronologies: the episode of Agak and Gagak, which will be narrated from Elric's point of view in *The Sailor on the Seas of Fate* (1976), is Corum's second meeting with the albino; he recognizes Elric from their adventures against Voilodion Ghagnasdiak—which has yet to take place in Elric's life. Conversely, in the Voilodion episode ("Three Heroes with a Single Aim"/*The King of the Swords*) Elric feels a strong sense of recognition when he encounters Corum, who has yet to meet the Melnibonéan in his own time-continuum.

There is an overwhelming sense of "winding-down" as *The Quest for Tanelorn* draws to its close. Hawkmoon and Erekosë come indeed to Tanelorn, "the still, unalterable centre of the multiverse,"[42] where they are confronted by a black demon—the spirit that is Stormbringer, the Cold Sword, and Hawkmoon's Black Jewel, and whom the boy Jehamia Cohnahlias, the spirit of the Runestaff, names as "Fear. Mankind's greatest enemy."[43] Erekosë is reunited with Ermizhad, but only for a few moments, for in a final struggle the two Champions destroy the Black Sword/Black Jewel, the Runestaff, and the Cosmic Balance itself, at the cost of Erekosë's life. Hawkmoon will return to a world emphatically freed of the struggles of the Lords of Law and Chaos. "[H]ow can mortals hope in a sphere dominated by bickering gods, by the warring of those they desire so much to respect?" asks Erekosë; Orland Fank provides an answer somewhat later: "Gods are but metaphors.... As metaphors they might be very acceptable—but they should never be allowed to become beings in their own right."[44] Tanelorn, that place of stability and peace, was created, the blind captain reveals, by himself and his brother the steersman: "'We have only one name,' said the Captain. And the steersman said: 'We are called Man.'"[45] Tanelorn is a human creation, a man-made equilibrium that we can each obtain by overcoming "gods and the worship of fallacy, fear of our own humanity."[46] A world without gods, Huillam D'Averc ventures, may mark

3. New Avatars, New Timer Streams, and a Farewell to Fantasy 75

"the beginning, perhaps, of comedy."⁴⁷ *The Quest for Tanelorn* stages a profoundly didactic—if perhaps a trifle over-schematized—ending to the run of almost twenty books that have preceded it: "This ends the long story of the Eternal Champion,"⁴⁸ Moorcock signs off on its last page. He has brought to a close the epic tales of Erekosë, Elric, Hawkmoon, and Corum, and will turn his attention to worlds where neither swords nor sorcery—and least of all *gods*, whether of Law or Chaos—hold sway.

* * *

The "world-making" aspect of fantasy, so prized by the myriad admirers of Tolkien's richly-textured *Lord of the Rings*, has never deeply engaged Moorcock. "I think the notion of worldbuilding is a failure of literary sophistication," he says; "I only invent what's necessary to explain the mood of a character. I haven't thought about an imaginary world's social security system; I don't know the gross national product of Melniboné."⁴⁹ The point of fiction is to create interesting characters and set them in conflict, either with one another or within themselves: the world in which they are placed is no more than an adjunct to, a setting for that conflict. The invented worlds of Moorcock's fantasy, unsurprisingly, are sometimes rather sketchily imagined. But his lack of interest in the details of social and economic structure, of patterns of forestation and geographical shifts, of how characters manage to find or carry provender for their riding animals, and so forth, is usually compensated for by the vividness with which he presents his characters' moral and emotional situations.

One alternative to building worlds from scratch, however, is to reimagine one's own world, and this is the course Moorcock pursues in *The Warlord of the Air* (1971), an affectionate homage to the Edwardian fiction Moorcock read as a child, especially that of E. Nesbit and H. G. Wells. *The Warlord* combines two separate pleasures, as Colin Greenland notes, "two paradigm shifts: the future through the eyes of the past, with the alternative history."⁵⁰ It's worth teasing these two apart for a moment. *Warlord* presents "the future through the eyes of the past" because it is, in short, a pastiche Edwardian "scientific romance," a version of the futuristic novels Wells was publishing around the turn of the century; indeed, its most immediate model is clearly Wells's *The War in the Air* (1908), which narrates how an early twentieth-century world war fought with technologically-advanced air power brings an end to civilization as Wells's generation knew it. *The Warlord of the Air* is presented as an actual document, the 1903 testament of Oswald Bastable, an English soldier who has been catapulted seventy years into the future. But the 1973 in which Bastable arrives, and where he becomes an officer aboard various lighter-than-air airships, is not *our* present day—hence the "alternative history." To complicate matters further, when Bastable is returned to 1903 to relate his story, it is not his own 1903, but the *reader's* (i. e., ours), a 1903 subtly different from the one he left.

Bastable's story is mediated through an elaborate frame narrative in which Moorcock himself discovers, among his late grandfather's effects, the transcript of Bastable's first-person account. This elaborate paratext, including a ten-page narrative of how Michael Moorcock (the grandfather) came to meet and befriend Bastable on a remote Indian Ocean island, strongly evokes Victorian and Edwardian narrative techniques, as does Bastable's own narrative voice. The "original" Oswald Bastable was the narrator of E. Nesbit's novels for children, *The Story of the Treasure Seekers* (1899), *The Wouldbegoods* (1901), and *New Treasure Seekers* (1904). He is the eldest among his siblings, plucky and resourceful, at times a trifle mischievous and sometimes a bit self-satisfied. In Moorcock's novel, he has grown up to be a fairly colorless, faintly priggish, and deeply patriotic late-Victorian liberal, wholly convinced of the goodness of empire.

In the 1973 in which Bastable finds himself, there has been no Great War, and the European powers (along with the USA) have divided the entire world among them. When he first visits a London made new and shining, its worldwide empire maintained by its fleets of airships, Bastable feels he is in a true Utopia, the final goal of Victorian progressivism: "Poverty had been banished! Disease had been exiled! Misery must surely be unknown!"[51] As the novel unfolds, Bastable comes to realize that the paradise of the metropole is founded upon the misery of the colonies, that England's prosperity is a result of the immiseration of its subject peoples around the world, and that a world-wide conflagration of anti-colonialist revolution is at hand. In a plot movement familiar from *The Eternal Champion* and *Phoenix in Obsidian*—the hero is transported into an unfamiliar world where he casts his lot with one side in a conflict, then realizes that the opposing party has justice on its side and promptly switches allegiances—Bastable changes sides. His patriotic loyalty to England cannot obscure his innate sense of "fair play," and his recognition that the anti-colonial revolutionary O. T. Shaw is ultimately right in seeking to free the masses dominated by empire. "When I had first been hauled into the world of the 1970s," Bastable reflects, "I had thought I found Utopia. And now I was discovering that it was only a Utopia for some. Shaw wanted a Utopia which would exist for all."[52]

The Warlord of the Air mounts a critique, then, of Victorian imperi-

3. New Avatars, New Timer Streams, and a Farewell to Fantasy 77

alism, but it relates just as immediately to the postcolonial moment during which it was written, the emancipatory conflicts in Kenya, in Algeria, and especially in Vietnam.[53] (As Moorcock comments, "We're always writing about our world, whether we're conscious of it or not."[54]) *The Warlord of the Air*'s alternative twentieth century presents a thought experiment: What if two world wars had not largely broken up the European powers'—especially Great Britain's—colonial empires? What if the world-system had continued in its imperialist stage, the vast inequities suffered by the colonized entirely invisible, by reason of distance and ideology, to the citizens of the metropoles? The result which Bastable witnesses is a revolutionary conflagration vast as a world war, culminating in his own act of dropping an atomic bomb on the allied shipyards at Hiroshima.

This "echo," as it were, in an alternative 1973 of the historical 1945 Hiroshima bombing, is only one of many connections Moorcock draws between his alternate history and our own. In the world Bastable visits, Rolling Stones frontman Mick Jagger is a lieutenant on a British airship, while Ronald Reagan is a half-crazed, racist scoutmaster. The Conservative parliamentarian Enoch Powell (best known for his 1968 anti-immigration "Rivers of Blood" speech) is a major in the air force and an amateur archaeologist. In China, at O. T. Shaw's "City of the Dawn," Bastable meets "Comrade Spender" (presumably the English poet Stephen Spender) and the very aged Russian revolutionary theorist Vladimir Ilyitch Ulianov—whom our own history knows as Lenin. Bastable's deepest affection, however, is for the Polish expatriate airship captain Korzeniowski (a temporally displaced Joseph Conrad, who would have been 116 in 1973).

Moorcock thoroughly indulges his own fascination with lighter-than-air flight in *The Warlord of the Air*, and with its vividly-depicted vision of an Edwardian future—the British Empire still intact, steam engines as the primary transportation technology, dirigibles criss-crossing the skies—the novel has a fair claim to be the most important precursor of the "steampunk" movement in imaginative literature (and in fashion), as well as an important inspiration for such exercises in Edwardian retrofitting as Alan Moore's graphic novel series *The League of Extraordinary Gentlemen*. Moorcock's two further Bastable novels, *The Land Leviathan* (1974) and *The Steel Tsar* (1981), attempt to repeat the alternate history formula, but with far less success.

* * *

Moorcock sought to address certain large socio-historical matters in the Bastable books, and he did so with enthusiasm though perhaps little subtlety: British colonialism and imperialism in *The Warlord of the Air*, American racism in *The Land Leviathan*, and the failed promise of Russian "communism" in *The Steel Tsar*. Beside this heavy fare, the far-future comedy of the *Dancers at the End of Time* trilogy—*An Alien Heat* (1972), *The Hollow Lands* (1974), and *The End of All Songs* (1976)—might seem positively frothy. The Bastable books hearken back to the earnestness of the Victorian novel and the moral pedagogy of the Edwardian "boys' own": the End of Time novels evoke far more lurid precursors in the glittering decadence of the late Victorian *fin de siècle*, and in the fiction of that late-born admirer of the *fin de siècle*, Ronald Firbank (1886–1926). The last years of Victoria's reign saw a remarkable blossoming of the "aestheticism" forecast in the conclusion to Pater's *The Renaissance*: artists like James McNeill Whistler and Aubrey Beardsley, and such writers as Oscar Wilde, Max Beerbohm, Ernest Dowson, and Lionel Johnson emphatically turned their backs on the social and moral responsibility demanded by mid–Victorian culture, and sought to explore the extremes of emotional, sensual, and aesthetic experience. By some, this development in culture was called "decadent"—and not always as a term of opprobrium. Arthur Symons, himself among the aesthetes, describes his own cultural cohort in 1893 in "The Decadent Movement in Literature": "it is no doubt a decadence; it has all the qualities that we find in the Greek, the Latin, decadence: an intense self-consciousness, a restless curiosity in research, an over-subtilizing refinement upon refinement, a spiritual and moral perversity."[55]

This would seem a fair description of the mindset of the inhabitants of Moorcock's End of Time, perhaps his purest and most extended examination of decadence. They live many thousands of years in the future, on an earth whose sun is almost exhausted: but they are the inheritors of millennia of the most advanced technology, now embodied in self-sufficient and sentient "cities." By means of "power rings" which command the energies of the cities (which in turn draw energy from far-flung sources across the universe), the inhabitants of this end-time utopia can alter their environments, their very bodies, at will; they can create and destroy whole continents at a whim; and they are for all intents and purposes immortal, since anyone why dies by some mischance can be immediately resurrected by her or his fellows. There is no disease, no poverty; there is space enough for each inhabitant to build the environment of her or his fancying; the world has become a playground, a canvas upon which these eccentric demigods can paint their most extravagant fantasies.

The denizens of the End of Time are among Moorcock's most endearing creations, as colorful as their names: the master chef Argonheart Po,

3. New Avatars, New Timer Streams, and a Farewell to Fantasy 79

whose elaborate environments are always edible; Mistress Christia, the Everlasting Concubine, continually exploring new variations on the act of sexual congress; the moody romantic Werther de Goethe; Sweet Orb Mace, who shifts gender from scene to scene; O'Kala Incarnadine, the Iron Orchid, the Duke of Queens, Bishop Castle, and a host of others. They spend their lives in a never-ending succession of parties, outings, and entertainments, vying with one another to create "effects" from the vast (and often hilariously misunderstood) cultural repository of the past. As Lord Jagged of Canaria puts it, "We are the sum of all previous ages, are we not? And as a result there is nothing that marks this age of ours, save that one thing. We are the sum." To which Jherek Carnelian replies, "There is nothing left to invent, my lilac lord. The long history of mankind, if it has a purpose at all, has found complete fulfillment in us."[56]

Jherek, as his name implies, is something of a variation on Jerry Cornelius, a kind of Candide-like, happy instantiation of the Eternal Champion. Among his fellows at the End of Time Jherek is reckoned the most knowledgeable antiquarian of "dawn age" culture (our own): each corner of his "typical" nineteenth-century ranch house ("done in fiba-fome and thatch") is "supported by a wooden Indian, some forty feet high," with "a magnificent pearl, twelve inches in diameter, in his turban, and a beard of real hair."[57] For all of his piecemeal knowledge of dawn age culture, Jherek is utterly ignorant of, but desperate to learn about and experience, what Raymond Williams would call the "structures of feeling" of the nineteenth and twentieth centuries: what they meant by "love," "morality," "virtue," and a whole lexicon of words that have become obsolete in his own ahistorical utopia. And herein lies the moral paradox which Moorcock addresses in the End of Time trilogy: human beings have always sought to abolish want, to level out inequity, to achieve a society in which people could find fulfillment, not in productive drudgery, but in aesthetic pursuits—even, indeed, to transcend death. But if such a society were to be achieved, what would distinguish true art from dilletantism? And is there any basis for morality in a life that is not bounded by mortality?

Jherek comes to confront such questions in his pursuit of the inadvertent time-traveller Mrs. Amelia Underwood, who has arrived at the End of Time from Bromley, Kent, 1896, bringing with her all the cultural and moral baggage of a middle-class Evangelical identity. Jherek's passion for Mrs. Underwood is initially an experiment in antiquarian emotion, but blossoms into real affection, unfolding over the three novels in a by turns hilarious and affecting pursuit back and forth across time between Victorian England, the End of Time, and the early Devonian Period. For her part, Amelia Underwood learns to lay aside some of her strait-laced prejudices, and even to love Jherek in return: she comes to realize that what she had originally dismissed as "decadence" in the society of the End of Time is actually a kind of *innocence*. "To be sinful," she tells her lover, "one must have a sense of sin. That is my burden, Jherek, and not yours."[58]

When it becomes evident that it really *is* the end of time, that the heat death of the universe (hastened by the cities' profligate use of the universe's energy) is actually at hand, Lord Jagged of Canaria devises a means by which the world's denizens can carry on as they always have, by recycling the same seven-day period of time over and over; only now, there can be no further time travel into or out of the End of Time. Amelia is dismayed by the prospect "that things will remain as they are throughout eternity, that the same dance will be danced over and over again and that only the partners will differ." When Jherek assures her of his undying love, she responds, "What is love without time, without death?"[59] In the end, Jherek and Amelia opt to leave the End of Time and settle in the Palaeozoic—some alternate Palaeozoic to ours, evidently—and become the parents of a new human race, accepting mortality as a natural part of humanness. It is a reprise, of course, of *Paradise Lost*, and the Genesis legend upon which Milton based his poem, but wholly secularized. Jherek willingly takes on mortality for the sake of love and for the prospect of actual *creation* (of a new race, that is); it is unclear to the very end, however, if he will ever take on a burden of unearned guilt, the "original sin" of Christian theology. When Amelia asks him, "What is it I must explain to you, my dear?" and Jherek replies, "Guilt," her only answer—and the end of the trilogy—is a kiss.[60]

Moorcock's End of Time fictions themselves are something of a parable of the narrative implications of the Second Law of Thermodynamics: the denizens—"dancers"—at the End of Time form a closed system, and the author must continually introduce outside elements (time travellers, space explorers) to sustain the narrative energy. In the *Dancers at the End of Time* trilogy Mrs. Amelia Underwood is clearly the principal "outside element," but there are also various space-travelling alien arrivals, including the doom-prophesying Yashurisp and the dwarfish, perpetually horny Lat. Moorcock repeats the procedure in the several shorter End of Time stories he published in *New Worlds* as the novels were appearing. "White Stars" introduces a misplaced squad of twenty-fourth-century space marines (a clear parody of Robert A. Heinlein's 1959 *Starship Troopers*[61]); "Ancient Shadows" gives us Dafnish and Snuffles Armatuce, time travellers from a period even more morally strict and physically abstemious than

Amelia Underwood's; and most spectacularly, Emmanuel Bloom, the messianic "Fireclown," fresh from his disappearance into the sun in *The Winds of Limbo* (1965), blazes onto the scene in "Constant Fire."[62]

At some point Moorcock's friend the novelist M. John Harrison suggested "that the denizens of the End of Time could be seen as the Gods of Chaos by the likes of Elric and his kind."[63] The remark inspired Moorcock to write the delightful squib "Elric at the End of Time," which sends up the whole genre of heroic fantasy by transporting Elric directly to the End of Time, which he assumes is indeed a realm of Chaos, and whose bemused but accommodating inhabitants—who stage a rousing battle and creature-chase for his benefit—he takes for Chaos Lords. Many of Moorcock's more serious fans, deeply invested in the figure of the doom-laden, self-pitying albino prince, were not amused. But Huillam D'Averc's words at the end of *The Quest for Tanelorn*—"the beginning, perhaps, of comedy"—seemed to coming true: Moorcock had made a space for high (and low) comedy within his own corner of fantastika, and it would prove to be a mode with deep popular appeal, as Douglas Adams's *Hitchhiker's Guide to the Galaxy* (1978) and Terry Pratchett's "Discworld" novels (from 1983 on) would demonstrate.

* * *

As he neared the end of his fourth decade, and as the seventies drew to a close, Moorcock anticipated a major shift in his writing career. With *The Quest for Tanelorn* he had wrapped up the multi-series epic of the Eternal Champion. For DAW Books, his U.S. paperback publisher, he had assembled all of his Elric stories into a six-volume sequence, ordered by internal chronology. The four Jerry Cornelius novels had been issued in handy single-volume form, emphasizing the linkages and continuities of that work. His popularity as a fantasist was perhaps at its height, but his reputation as a writer of "serious" ambitions, despite the very weighty issues dealt with in *Behold the Man*, the Bastable novels, and elsewhere, and the fact that his Cornelius novels had been published as non-genre works, was to some degree—and especially in the U.S.—overshadowed by his abundance of rapidly-produced sword-and-sorcery potboilers. Moorcock had in mind work in a more realistic vein, novels which would deal directly with the history of his own century. *Gloriana; or, The Unfulfill'd Queen* (1978), then, was intended as "my last fantasy ... something of a swan song, an affectionate farewell to the gorgeous and exotic, to Fancy of Coleridge's classic definition, if not imagination."[64]

Gloriana is an ambitious book indeed, and the two literary models with which Moorcock identifies the novel indicate the scope of his ambitions: *Gloriana* is dedicated "to the memory of Mervyn Peake," the author of the *Gormenghast* trilogy, one of the great achievements of British fantasy and indeed of twentieth-century English fiction; and in an author's note, Moorcock comments that while *Gloriana* "is neither an Elizabethan Fantasia nor an historical novel, this romance does have some relation to *The Faerie Queene*," Edmund Spenser's vast Elizabethan epic poem, one of the cornerstones of the literary canon.[65] Moorcock had first met Peake in the 1950s, before he began showing the symptoms of the ill-understood Parkinson's Disease that would bring his death in 1968. A youthful enthusiast, Moorcock assiduously promoted Peake's work, then temporarily out of fashion, through the 1960s and beyond; "After Bunyan," he writes, "Peake had been my chief inspiration to write adult fantasy."[66] Moorcock's first surviving novel-length work, *The Golden Barge*, is a very close—if not very successful—pastiche of Peake.[67]

Born in 1911, Peake was already well-known as a painter and an illustrator when *Titus Groan* appeared in 1946, to be followed by *Gormenghast* (1950) and *Titus Alone* (1959). There is nothing else in English literature quite like the trilogy. It is in some sense a fantasy—though it has no trace of the supernatural or paranormal—since the whole world of Gormenghast Castle and its environs is invented. The *Gormenghast* books draw largely on the Gothic tradition, not least for the haunted and claustrophobic atmosphere of Gormenghast Castle, with its mazes of superimposed passages and apartments and its age-old encrustations of ritual and repetition, all taut with the tension of a dozen complex and deeply-laid plots. If Peake's setting is Gothic, however, his proliferation of characters is positively Dickensian—they are menacing, pitiable, hilarious, grotesque, pathetic, and emphatically *alive*.

Titus Groan and *Gormenghast* follow the first seventeen years of Titus, the seventy-seventh Earl of Gormenghast, from his birth to his coming of age and his renunciation of his home and birthright. His principal antagonist is the renegade former kitchen boy Steerpike, who rises through the force of his insane, malevolent intellect from the sculleries to the heights of power. In *Gloriana*, Moorcock echoes the character of Steerpike in the schemer, traitor, and social climber Captain Arturus Quire, assassin, spy, and all-round rogue, who sows dissension in the court of Albion and eventually becomes the lover of Queen Gloriana herself. As Colin Greenland points out, "Quire is a rational Steerpike. Steerpike is mad. Quire is in some ways the most sensible character in the book."[68] Quire may be rational, but he is an aesthete, an artist, and the "art" of his manipulations and treacheries has no relation to morality: he is Moorcock's portrait of the artist as an amoral constructor of spectacle, one horrific outcome of the *fin de siècle* aesthetes' notion of the autonomy of the artwork, of the act of art-making, and its utter divorce from social and moral considerations.

For Moorcock, "the *Gormenghast* trilogy is the apotheosis of that romantic form which had its crude beginnings with [Horace Walpole's] *Castle of Otranto*, in which the vast, rambling, semi-ruined castle is a symbol of the mind itself."[69] Gormenghast Castle itself "could represent a human skull and the warrens and catacombs within stand for the inner working of the psyche."[70] The same is true of Gloriana's palace in London. As in the Freudian model of the mind, where the ego and the superego are erected over still-living but repressed memories and the drives of the unconscious id, the public face of Gloriana's court—its celebrations, masques, progresses, its everyday privy council meetings and receptions—coexists with another world exiled into the labyrinths of blocked-up passages and abandoned chambers beneath or within the walls of the palace, where dwell whole races of people cast out of court society, and where the memory and living evidence of Gloriana's dead father, the demonic tyrant Hern, is still vibrant.

This sense of the court as a *layered* environment, where death and corruption lurk just below the surface of blooming health and vitality, is one of Moorcock's principal themes in *Gloriana*, and one that has strong resonances with *Gormenghast*. His other perhaps more conscious concern is social and political, and is also tied in with the notion of doubleness. And here we might pause to consider *Gloriana*'s other cited source, Edmund Spenser's *The Faerie Queene*. Spenser's long poem is of course one of the ur-texts of heroic fantasy: over its vast length—some 36,000 lines—heroic knights ride forth to battle giants, dragons, evil wizards, shape-shifting temptresses, and all manner of supernatural and natural foes. But *The Faerie Queene* is also, as Spenser explains to Sir Walter Raleigh in a letter appended to the first (1590) installment of the poem, "a continued Allegory, or darke conceit," in which Spenser aims "to fashion a gentleman or noble person in virtuous and gentle discipline" by personifying each of the important virtues in given characters: the Redcross Knight of Book I is holiness, Sir Guyon of Book II is temperance, and so forth.[71] In "Gloriana," the fairy queen herself, Spenser signifies "glory in my general intention, but in my particular I conceive the most excellent and glorious person of our soueraine the Queene"—Elizabeth I.

The elaborate chivalric and fantastic trappings of *The Faerie Queene* are the machinery of a moral allegory. But they are also the decoration and justification of a very real political structure. As a colonial administrator in Elizabethan Ireland, Spenser was (as one critic calls him) "a pen-pusher in the service of imperialism."[72] He was deeply involved in the politics of his own historical moment, and while *The Faerie Queene* grapples with those politics in specific sophisticated ways, one general intention of the poem—as Moorcock well recognizes—is to swathe the messy, bloody, and fundamentally unjust "birth of the British Empire as we came to know it" in a high-minded, moral cloud of chivalric virtue.[73] In Moorcock's *Gloriana; or, The Unfulfill'd Queen*, Gloriana, Queen of Albion, both represents and embodies a "golden age" of wealth, world domination, and equipoise, but is herself too taken in by the chivalric myth to recognize the seamy machinations and ruthless *Realpolitik* that have sustained her reign.

The outward symptom of this disjuncture, the logic of the narrative suggests, is Gloriana's inability to reach orgasm, to be "fulfilled." She can only reach that life-changing climax after the entire machinery of chivalry has been broken down in a final torrent of violence. The ending of the novel is deeply disquieting: Gloriana experiences her first orgasm when she is raped by the treacherous Captain Quire, whose plots and subterfuges have brought her once-harmonious court to the brink of civil war. The rape is intended to "demystify her," Moorcock commented in 1991—but he also confessed that the scene "was a clear mistake, morally and socially, and probably the wrong way of resolving" the narrative.[74] When he had the opportunity to issue a revised edition of the book in 1993, Moorcock rewrote the scene so that Gloriana achieves orgasm not by being raped by Quire, but by fighting him off and overcoming him with a newly discovered sense of power, of personal selfhood apart from her identity as Queen.[75]

While the conclusion of the novel is disappointing, both in its burst of bloody action and melodramatic revelation, and in its thematic (not to mention ideological and moral) confusion, *Gloriana; or, The Unfulfill'd Queen* is one of Moorcock's most striking achievements. It is a more than fair attempt to pay homage to his early influence Peake, where *The Golden Barge* was such a signal failure. And as an intended capstone to Moorcock's career in fantasy, it is a remarkably self-contained work, in contrast to the manner in which so many of his earlier works draw upon one another for characters, themes, and narrative motifs. There are a few winks and nudges—Jephraim Tallow reappears from *The Golden Barge*, but in a considerably transmogrified form, "Prince Hira of Bom Bai" and "the warlike

Prince Pyat of Ukrainia" are mentioned, names familiar from the Cornelius books[76]—but aside from Una, Countess of Scaith, the Queen's companion (who has a distinct resemblance to Una Persson but gives no hint that she is the temporal adventuress of the Cornelius and Bastable novels), there are no significant "repeats" from the loose weave of Moorcock's other fiction.

Gloriana's Albion is a kind of alternative early modern England, in which Albion's empire has spread far further than England's had in Elizabeth's day (most of North America, it seems, is the colony of "Virginia"), where the greatest external threats to the east—Tartary, Muscovia, Arabia—are either under Albion's dominion or divided one against another by the cunning foreign policy of Gloriana's chief advisor Montfallcon. But the book is, as Moorcock notes, "neither an Elizabethan Fantasia nor an historical novel"; while it draws upon the iconography of Elizabeth's reign, its language is not at all pseudo-Elizabethan. The poet Ernest Wheldrake's civic verses have more in common with the Carolean masque than with Spenser, Sidney, or Raleigh.[77] But the imagined world of *Gloriana*, both like and unlike early modern England, is a strikingly detailed and colorfully, vividly imagined one; and Moorcock presents a gripping picture of the moral corruption that underpins the myth of Gloriana, Albion's personified golden age.

For that matter, *Gloriana* is by far the best-written and most carefully constructed of Moorcock's novels to date. The prose shows a new flexibility, ranging from the rapid-fire evocation of action to sprawling periods of lyrical description, and the shifts in narrative focus, the cumulative withholding and revelation of plot information, and the masterful use of setting—the shifting seasons, the contrast between exterior and interior scenes—all bespeak an author finally making the time to master his craft. Most of Moorcock's fantasy novels thus far had taken him a matter of days to write; *Gloriana*, in contrast, took him "six weeks of sheer hell ... agony, dreadful, vivid, neurological pain."[78] The book was intended as a farewell to fantasy, a swan song; in the event, it would mark only a hiatus in his fantasy-writing, but it stands *sui generis* among his works. Wisely enough, Moorcock has never attempted its sequel.

4

Reality and Its Bitter Myths

Moorcock had begun his career writing adventure stories, westerns, detective stories, fantasies—all exercises in popular entertainment, exercises in "genre" writing. By the 1970s he had attained an impressive prominence, but to a large degree that prominence was still confined within genre: the fantasy narratives of Elric and other Eternal Champion avatars, the science fiction of *New Worlds* and Jerry Cornelius. Despite his impatience with the minutiae of "world-building," he had created an impressive variety of vivid (if at times sketchy) universes for his stories: Melniboné and the Young Kingdoms; the two separate worlds in which Corum moves, each of them embedded within a multiplicity of additional "planes"; Hawkmoon's far-future earth, scarred by nuclear war and traversed by both technology and magic; the alternate twentieth centuries of Oswald Bastable; the rich decadence of the End of Time; the Cornelius books' sexed-up and tilted versions of the late twentieth century; Gloriana's Albion; and so forth. And all of them, implicitly or explicitly, are to be related as aspects of a single multiverse. The one world Moorcock had barely explored, however, was his own twentieth century, unaltered either by the impossibilities of fantasy or the speculations of science fiction.

Samuel Delany distinguishes among science fiction, fantasy, and what he calls "naturalistic fiction" on the basis of their "subjunctivity." Reportage—historical writing or journalism, for instance—takes place at the subjunctive level of *"this happened."* Naturalistic fiction's subjunctivity "is defined by: *could have happened,"* fantasy's is *"could not have happened,"* and science fiction's is *"have not happened."*[1] Delany's distinction is a subtle and provocative one, and very useful, though I'm not very happy with the term "naturalistic" fiction, which carries too much weight of literary history—Naturalism as a literary movement and so forth. "Mundane" fiction, a term favored by some critics, seems unintentionally pejorative. I will settle, despite the term's own historical baggage, with the I hope self-explanatory phrase "realistic fiction."[2]

These three modes of fiction are each situated in a clear relation to the world in which we live, the "real" world. While realistic fiction deals with the "real" world in a straightforwardly mimetic fashion, fantasy imbues it with elements generally considered impossible (supernatural forces, mythical species, etc.), or creates its own worlds incorporating such elements; science fiction alters the real world by means of *novums*—technologies, social structures, historical developments, scientific knowledges, and so forth—which are *at present* impossible, but which the progress of science could plausibly render reality.[3] But whether she works in a fantastic, science-fictional, or realistic mode, the writer is always confronting human experience, commenting upon a range of affective and social relations shared with her audience.

Moorcock had demonstrated by his mid-thirties that he was anxious to deal with "big questions" whether he was writing fantasy or science fiction—bearing in mind always, however, that he considered it his first responsibility to provide his readers satisfying entertainment. "Behold the Man" was a fine SF story, but it also posed fascinating questions about the phenomena of religious faith and mass movements. The Cornelius novels are parables of role-playing in an entropic society, while *The Dancers at the End of Time* questions the social and experiential roots of human morality. The sword-and-sorcery antics of the various Eternal Champion avatars take place against the largest socio-moral backdrop of them all: the eternal oscillation within the human psyche, and across human society as a whole, between Law and Chaos. But there were certain aspects of the human adventure, in particular the very specific catastrophes of his own twentieth century, that could be better approached, not by analogizing them or allegorizing them in science fiction or fantasy, but by simply writing *about* them, using them as the scaffolding for fiction which would be neither fantastic nor science-fictional: which would be if not precisely "realistic," then in some deep sense "historical."

And to be frank, for Moorcock the persistent role of "genre" writer had begun to rankle. Whatever large ideas he might develop, whatever formal innovations he might hone, his work was still largely relegated to the disreputable suburbs of the literary field marked "fantasy" or "SF," and not given the same serious consideration it would obtain had it been published simply as "fiction."[4] One way for Moorcock to write beyond the constraints of genre fiction, then, would be to take on the subjunctivity of "naturalistic," "mundane" fiction—for a while to set aside the *"have not happened"* and "*could not have happened*" in favor of the "*could have happened.*" The resulting books, the four large volumes of the Pyat sequence and *Mother London*, are Moorcock's bid for literary respectability on "mainstream" literature's own turf: but since Moorcock is Moorcock, his books demand attention very much on their own terms. These books are sprawling, claustrophic, chaotic, over-ordered, replete with vivid detail, dull, riveting, ultimately indigestible—but indigestible in the same way the great works of Dickens, Tolstoy, George Eliot, Dostoevsky, and Joyce are: they refuse to conform to our market-fostered notions of what a well-formed novel should resemble, and remain in our consciousness, unprocessed and undismissable, reminding us of the human enormities and occasional human triumphs of the century that gave us Auschwitz, Hiroshima, and the end of the British Empire.

* * *

One precursor to this "realistic" turn in his writing is *Breakfast in the Ruins*, a curious, haunting, and intense little book Moorcock published in 1972, the same year as *The English Assassin*. Like *The English Assassin*, *Breakfast in the Ruins* is an extremely modular book; it consists of nineteen chapters, the first and last of them constituting a "frame narrative" within which the others are presented. The frame itself in quite unsettling. In the first chapter, Karl Glogauer, a shy commercial artist who bears a good deal of resemblance to the neurotic protagonist of "Behold the Man" (with whom he shares a name), is enjoying a quiet afternoon in Derry and Tom's Roof Garden when he is approached by a Nigerian tourist who invites him back to his hotel room. From there, the frame narrative extends itself through the rest of the book as a series of italicized passages at the beginning and end of each chapter. Karl and the black man have sex; they engage in various sadomasochistic games; they talk a great deal. Karl immerses himself in a bath which dyes his skin black, and by morning the Nigerian has turned white, his eyes "pale, blue." Once masterful and handsome, he has become nervous and lifeless: "He looked thin and his silk suit hardly seemed to fit any longer."[5] Karl, in contrast, has a new-found energy and freedom, gained it seems by his very transgressions of his middle-class sexual and racial norms. He has become, in some sense, the grinning, self-assured black Jerry Cornelius of *A Cure for Cancer*—though that self-assurance has come at the price of being subject to his society's racism: he tells the fat tourist who bumps into him, "Don't worry, boss," and salutes when a punter tells him, "I'll say that for you fellows, you know how to keep cheerful."[6]

4. Reality and Its Bitter Myths   89

The heart of the novel, however, is not this strange transformation but the seventeen vignettes it encloses. In them we meet a progression of Karl Glogauers, aging from seven to twenty-two, in historical moments ranging from the Paris Commune of 1871 to wartime Vietnam in 1968. The seven-year-old Karl watches his mother, mistaken for a *pétroleuse*, shot by government soldiers in 1871; in 1892, nine-year-old Karl, a mixed-race houseboy in Capetown, has his prized butterfly collection destroyed by a blundering house-guest; in Calcutta in 1911, the twelve-year-old (half-Indian) Karl arranges for an "accident" to befall an English sailor who has tried to cheat him in a drug deal; the fifteen-year-old Karl, dining with his girlfriend at a speakeasy in 1929 New York, embarrasses his father, out on the town with a woman not his mother; the eighteen-year-old Karl plays violin in a prisoners' orchestra in Auschwitz, 1944; in Kenya in 1959, the twenty-one-year-old Karl, an Army sergeant, tortures a Mau Mau prisoner; and in Vietnam, Karl, a twenty-two-year-old American soldier, participates in the massacre of a village suspected of Viet Cong sympathies. The vignettes range from the socially awkward to the horrific, with an emphasis on the latter.

The only element of fantasy or science fiction that enters these vignettes is in the final one, "London Life: 2020: City of Shadows," which is written in the future tense and depicts an eighty-one-year-old Karl Glogauer, holed up in his Ladbroke Grove home in the ruins of London, burning books in the fireplace and waiting to die. Otherwise, these vignettes are starkly realistic, a series of snapshots of the inequities, injustices, and brutalities of the past century, from the violent suppression of the Commune, through a whole parade of insurgencies, counter-insurgencies, and wars down to Vietnam. "Karl Glogauer" is a constant through these shifting settings: brutal and officious in 1959 Kenya, business-like in 1911 Calcutta, scared and nauseated in 1968 Vietnam. The frame narrative makes no attempt to rationalize or naturalize these appearances, to explain them as repeated "incarnations" or the effects of time-travel. They are the formal constituents of the novel, the fragments of lives that have been juxtaposed to make a collage-like whole.

Likewise, there is no explanation for the "What Would You Do?" passages that end each chapter. Moorcock adopted these from a feature he and Barrington Bayley collaborated on in the magazine *Boys' World* in the early 1960s,[7] but whereas *Boys' World* presented practical quandaries (*Your California neighborhood is being rocked by an earthquake—where do you go to make yourself safe?*), *Breakfast in the Ruins*'s "What Would You Do?" segments present moral dilemmas more often than not characteristic of the twentieth century: An enemy soldier is raping a young girl in the church; should you, as priest, kill him, risking reprisals from the occupying forces? As a liberal white in a predominantly black town gripped by race riots, how do you preserve your own safety in the face of a destructive black mob?[8]

Breakfast in the Ruins is a novel much concerned with the heritage of racism and colonialism in contemporary society. It offers no answers, but raises many troubling questions. As a kind of dark joke, with mortality much on his mind, Moorcock appended an "Introduction," signed by "James Colvin" (one of his pseudonyms): "Michael Moorcock died of lung cancer, aged 31, in Birmingham last year. The whereabouts of Karl Glogauer are presently unknown."[9] A joke in extremely doubtful taste, it would rebound on Moorcock from time to time: "That fucking biography. Shortly after it came out I was at a Hawkwind gig, stoned out of my brain, and these people kept coming up to me, and I thought I was dead. They kept saying 'You're dead, you're dead.' Later I realized that they were saying, 'But we thought you were dead.'"[10]

* * *

Breakfast in the Ruins was a momentary turn towards realism in the hectic welter of Moorcock's early-seventies productivity. (Between 1971 and 1973 he published fourteen novels, including ten Eternal Champion fantasies, two Cornelius books, and *An Alien Heat*, the first Dancers at the End of Time novel.) It was only later in the decade, when he had completed the Cornelius tetralogy and bidden (a temporary) farewell to fantasy with *Gloriana; or, The Unfulfill'd Queen*, that Moorcock turned his full attention to a fictive treatment of the twentieth century in *Byzantium Endures* (1981), the first volume of a vast tetralogy that would be known as "Between the Wars" or, more simply, The Colonel Pyat Quartet.[11]

Moorcock had been contemplating a sequence of novels that would in some ways come to grips with the Holocaust since the mid-seventies, and the vehicle upon which he eventually settled was a minor character in the Cornelius tetralogy, Colonel Pyat. Pyat first appears in *The English Assassin* as a military man and one of the sets of hands through which Jerry's hibernating body passes on its journey across Europe.[12] Later in that novel he appears newly married to Mrs. Cornelius, only to be shot by a vengeful Prinz Lobkowitz. At the end of *The Condition of Muzak*, a sequence which brings all the characters back to a level of gritty realism, Pyat runs a shop in North Kensington selling second-hand "fur coats, evening capes, cloaks, hats and gloves."[13] He is still courting Mrs. Cornelius, in his morose way, and it is Colonel Pyat who phones Jerry to tell him his mother is taken ill at tetralogy's end. This Pyat, a "spear-carrier" in the Cornelius books (John Clute's phrase), and based to some degree "on an old Polish man I had known around Ladbroke Grove,"[14] would become Maxim Arturovitch Pyatnitski, the endlessly voluble narrator and central character of the Pyat Quartet: *Byzantium Endures* (1981), *The Laughter of Carthage* (1984), *Jerusalem Commands* (1992), and *The Vengeance of Rome* (2006).

Byzantium Endures begins with a framing paratext, a form familiar enough from eighteenth- and nineteenth-century novels, that seeks to buttress the narrative's verisimilitude and disclaim authorial responsibility for what will follow: Moorcock is not the *author* of the book in hand, but merely the selector and editor of Pyat's memoirs, " a terrifying collection of manuscript, hand-written in six languages on almost every possible size and colour of paper, collected in eleven shoe-boxes." (Moorcock explains that he has supplemented this morass of written materials with many Sunday afternoons' worth of Pyat's tape-recorded "monologues."[15]) Pyat, who died in 1977, is convinced that the world will be anxious to read "his reminiscences of Mrs. Cornelius, who had died in 1975. He knew that I [Moorcock] had already, in his terms, 'exploited' her in my books." Pyat believes that Mrs. C. is "probably as famous as Queen Elizabeth,"[16] and while Moorcock is unable to disabuse him of this notion, the writer gradually becomes fascinated with the course of the old man's life, with the historical and moral weight of his massive and self-centered narrative. For Pyat, it will turn out, encapsulates in his own experience much of the unique promise and horror of European history over the first half of the twentieth century.

Maxim Arturovitch Pyatnitski—for that's the name by which he will identify himself most firmly—is "a child of my century, and as old as the century. I was born in 1900, on 1 January, in South Russia: the ancient true Russia from which the whole of our great Slavic culture sprang."[17] Of course, every detail of his birth and childhood has been altered or rendered other by history. His birthday is reckoned to be New Year's Day by the Julian Calendar, which the Soviets would abandon in 1918, thereby making him born on January 14, New Style. Kiev, the city of his upbringing, will be part not of Russia, but of the Ukrainian Soviet Socialist Republic (now simply Ukraine); and the very city of his birth, Tsaritsyn, will be renamed first Stalingrad and then Volgograd, marking the tides of history in its name-changes. Pyat's own names are even more chameleon-like: in the first two novels of the tetralogy alone, he is Maxim Arturovitch Pyatnitski (by turns "Doctor," "Major," and "Colonel"), Dimitri Mitrofanovitch Kryscheff, Mr. Papadakis (only briefly), Max Peterson, and Matt Pallenburg (not to mention a slew of Russian diminutives—"Simka," "Mishka," etc.).

Pyat's *real* name, we learn on the last pages of *The Vengeance of Rome*, is Moishe Aaronovitch Peskonechnya. He is Jewish, son of a kosher butcher, grandson of a rabbi.[18] This is the contradiction at the heart of the tetralogy, for Pyat has spent a repulsive number of the almost two thousand pages up to this point in fierce anti–Semitic invective, and in denying that he has any Jewish ancestry whatsoever. "I am not, as is frequently suggested by the illiterates amongst whom I am forced to live, Jewish," he proclaims on the first page of *Byzantium Endures*; "The great Cossack hawk's beak is frequently mistaken in the West for the carrion bill of the vulture."[19] On the basis of his racial views alone, Pyat is one of the most repugnant characters in English literature. He hates and despises the Jews above all, but also has well-developed prejudices against Turks, Greeks, Arabs, blacks, Muslims, Roman Catholics, West Indians, Asians, and other racial, ethnic, and religious groups. And he vents these prejudices in periodic tirades that sometimes go on for pages at a time. Reading Pyat's memoirs, one realizes very quickly indeed, means spending a good deal of time in the company of a very unpleasant person.

Pyat's prejudices are more deep-seated and systematic than a casual dislike of the other, an unconsidered xenophobia. Instead, they are part and parcel of a fully-formulated worldview, the essence of which is to some degree laid out in the Quartet's titles, which together pronounce a sentence: "Byzantium endures the laughter of Carthage; Jerusalem commands the vengeance of Rome." "Byzantium" or "Rome" is the representative or seat of Western civilization, the exemplar of all the elements—technological progress, equitable justice, moral uprightness, literature and the arts—that distinguish civilized humanity from barbarism. The Semitic settlements of "Carthage" or "Jerusalem" represent the forces that would undermine or destroy this civilization, the impulses of rampant greed, pitiless commercialism, sexual and social decadence, and moral turpitude. "Carthage" is the Jews, of course, but it is also Islam, the Bolsheviks, the American Democratic and British Labour Parties, the ever-present threat of mindlessly proliferating Asia.

Pyat's conception of "Western Civilization" as locked in a death struggle with an inimical other is of course a depressingly familiar one. Its most extreme expressions in the first part of the century are perhaps *The Protocols of the Elders of Zion*, a "blueprint" for Jewish world domination forged by Russian anti–Semites in the first years of the century, and Adolf

4. Reality and Its Bitter Myths   93

Hitler's autobiographical manifesto *Mein Kampf* (1925–6). Any number of public figures less extreme than Hitler believed that a Jewish conspiracy was undermining the foundations of civilized order: Henry Ford underwrote the American distribution of the *Protocols*; the American poet Ezra Pound came to believe that the First World War had been instigated by the unholy collusion of armaments merchants and Jewish banking interests, and said so in his long poem *The Cantos*. The central catastrophic event of the century, the Nazi Holocaust, was neither the doing of a single dictator nor a single nation. In the introduction to *Byzantium Endures*, Moorcock quotes his "old friend and sometime collaborator M. G. Lobkowitz" (himself a fictional character from the Cornelius mythos): "'The great tragedies of history,' he said, 'are the sum of all our individual tragedies. It takes several million Pyats at least to conspire in the fate of the twelve million who died in the camps.'"[20]

The fact that Pyat is an anti–Semitic *Jew* is key to the strange affect of the Quartet as a whole, for at no point are we given any indication that he believes himself to be concealing anything about his own identity: so far as he is concerned, his missing father was a Don Cossack. Pyat presents himself throughout as a paragon of openness, a veritable Montaigne of self-revelation. But he is also a monster of egotism (*The Laughter of Carthage* begins, "I am one of the great inventors of my age"[21]), sublimely convinced of his own intellectual and moral superiority over pretty much everyone else. Hand in hand with Pyat's egotism is his appalling impercipience, his almost ludicrous inability to understand the minds and motives of the people around him and the implications of the situations into which he is thrown. Much of the time Pyat is a kind of grotesque babe in the woods, steadily pursuing his own ends with only the vaguest idea of what those around him are up to, or how they are reacting to him. When he undergoes his oral examination at the St. Petersburg Polytechnic, stoked to the gills with cocaine, and delivers a wild science-fictional discourse on the military technology of the future—gatling guns firing poisoned or narcotic needles, vast land leviathans crushing their way through enemy lines—he assumes his professors' stunned silence is due to their being impressed; and when his fellow students hail him as "the great Kryscheff! He's Galileo and Leonardo rolled into one," he modestly assumes they are merely acknowledging his genius.[22] As readers, we are uncomfortably aware that Pyat has made a laughingstock of himself. When the oil magnate "Mucker" Hever puts Pyat on his payroll as Chief Experimental Engineer, Pyat assumes it is because Hever has recognized his brilliance; but we know, from remarks that Pyat has comically misunderstood, that Hever assumes Pyat is blackmailing him on account of his past association with the Ku Klux Klan.[23]

Compounded with Pyat's egotism and impercipience is his more or less constant self-exculpatory relation of events. Pyat, by his own account, is the most put-upon human being since Job. He is repeatedly wronged by others, but never deliberately in the wrong himself; he is repeatedly betrayed by those he trusts, but is himself a tower of virtue. "Mrs Mawgan," Pyat says of the woman who had arranged his cross-country lecture tour for the Klan, accompanied him, and slept with him, "had earned whatever came to her. No one would ever accuse me of betraying her"—even as he signs the affidavit implicating her in as many Klan-related extralegal schemes as he can remember (or imagine), in order to save himself from prosecution.[24]

"I choose to say what is fact and what is fiction," says Pyat, and of course we have access to the "facts" of his adventures only through the words of his own narration.[25] But that narration, we quickly realize, is a consistently inconsistent one: the events Pyat describes, and his interpretation of those events, are at constant odds. If he is one of the most unlikeable narrators in contemporary fiction, he is also one of the most unreliable. There is a kind of grotesque, monstrous glory about Pyat's despicableness, his relentless self-duplicity. We keep following Pyat's narration, continue turning pages and listening to his interminable drone of rancid prejudice and shifty self-exculpation, because we want to know what enormity he will commit next, which ally he will betray, or how, through his consistent idiot's luck, he will be extricated from his latest predicament—smelling, at least to his own impercipient nostrils, like a rose.

Pyat's books aren't really novels, at least in the form into which the genre evolved over the nineteenth century. Rather, they constitute a single huge, picaresque narrative (the *pícaro* is a rogue, though usually far more loveable than Pyat) whose resolution, even as we near the end of *The Vengeance of Rome*, seems to continually recede before us. The Quartet's "plot," if one can call it that, resembles nothing so much as than the cinematic serials of which Pyat is so fond: he moves from place to place, position to position, each new situation involving him in new compromises and dangers, new sexual entanglements, new opportunities to demonstrate his surpassing "genius." In *Byzantium Endures*, we follow Pyat from his childhood in Kiev, through a coming-of-age season in Odessa (where at fourteen he is introduced by a raffish cousin to sex and cocaine, two future mainstays of his life), through his time at the St. Petersburg Polytechnic, then through a rapid series of adventures across the Russian Civil War, where he is progressively involved with Semyon Petylura's Ukrainian nationalist government, the Bolsheviks, Nestor Makhno's Anarchists, and the pro-western Whites. The poles of his consciousness are his longing for his childhood sweetheart Esmé Loukianoff (though he sleeps with uncounted other women in the meantime), his not-at-all platonic love for Prince Nikolai Petroff (though he has nothing but scorn for most practicing homosexuals), and his faith that his own engineering genius, once recognized, will bring about a new technological utopia.

Pyat is reunited with Esmé towards the end of *Byzantium Endures*. She is now a nurse, working selflessly among the Anarchists; she has been raped repeatedly, but has emerged from the experience without cynicism. She has grown up, has become her own woman: self-assured, strong, compassionate, and mature. Therefore, she is as good as dead to Pyat. In *The Laughter of Carthage*, he will "rediscover" Esmé in Constantinople in the person of a thirteen-year-old Romanian prostitute, whom he will rename "Esmé" and carry off to Italy (thereby abandoning the baroness with whom he has been having an affair). *The Laughter of Carthage* takes Pyat over two continents, from Rome and Paris (where he resumes his relations with his beloved Prince Nikolai, "Kolya") to the United States, where he is involved (unwittingly) in a succession of confidence schemes, goes on a lecture tour sponsored by the Ku Klux Klan (whom he feels are the true guardians of western culture in America), manages a travelling theatrical troupe, and eventually settles in Los Angeles. The book's end finds the twenty-four-year-old Pyat in an airplane from California to New York, where he expects to be reunited with Esmé (the younger Esmé, that is, not the original) after a long separation.

This flight dovetails with the formative, Icarus-like flight at the end of the first chapter of *Byzantium Endures*, where the thirteen-year-old Pyat crashes a home-made powered glider into the gorge of Babi Yar. His aspirations throughout the books are tied to the technologies of flying, of transcending gravity. He dreams of giant airships, of vast Laputa-like flying cities that will bear the inhabitants of purified western civilization—heavenly Byzantiums, as it were—high above the earth-bound muck of Carthage and Jerusalem. Pyat's fervent faith in technology is of a piece with that of Hugo Gernsback and the early generations of science fiction writers. Like them, he is a visionary: but his technological vision is inextricably wound up with the virulent ideologies of racism, paternalism, and imperialism.

* * *

Byzantium Endures, the writing of which came to be something of an all-consuming obsession, taxed Moorcock dearly, and he would find the Pyat novels increasingly challenging: the prejudice-soaked midden of Pyat's consciousness was simply too uncomfortable to inhabit for long. Indeed, the Pyat Quartet, which he had originally envisioned as a grand opus which would occupy all his attention but only for a few years, became after *Byzantium Endures* only one of a number of projects. In the interval between finishing *Byzantium Endures* in 1979 and its publication in 1981, Moorcock wrote a third Bastable novel, *The Steel Tsar*, making use of much of the same Russian research that had gone into Pyat, and returned to heroic fantasy with *The War Hound and the World's Pain*. He wrote *The Laughter of Carthage* at the same time as *The City in the Autumn Stars*, the second of the von Bek novels, and the two books share a similar picaresque structure.[26]

In 1982, Moorcock published *The Brothel in Rosenstrasse*, a brief, claustrophobic non-fantasy novel set in Mirenburg, an imaginary Prague-like central European city that would become one of the primary settings of his fantasy works. *The Brothel* has much in common with the Pyat books. Its narrator Rickhardt von Bek is like Pyat elderly and obsessive, given to recounting the events of his youth interspersed with monologues and tirades. But unlike Pyat the old von Bek is consumed by painful self-knowledge, and from the perspective of age is all too aware of how his destructive "erotomania," his passion for the sixteen-year-old Alexandra, has destroyed his own life, a direct parallel to the civil war that tears apart Mirenburg as the lovers pursue their sensuous explorations in Frau Schmetterling's establishment in Rosenstrasse.

Mirenburg, an eighteenth-century version of which would provide the setting for most of *The City in the Autumn Stars*, Moorcock's 1986 fantasy, is a rich and quaint slice of *Mitteleuropa*, recalled through the lens of Rickhardt von Bek's regret and nostalgia in *Brothel*. Similarly, Moorcock had show an increasing deftness and newfound engagement in writerly craft when presenting the urban settings of *Byzantium Endures* and *The Laughter of Carthage*. Kiev, Odessa, St. Petersburg, Constantinople, Paris, Memphis, and Los Angeles (among other cities) come to splendid life in these books, their crowds, quaysides, highways, mosques and churches, sounds, and smells rendered in vivid detail. It is not surprising, then, that Moorcock would turn an affectionate eye upon the city of his own birth in the novel which is perhaps his single greatest achievement, *Mother London* (1988).

Jerry Cornelius is of course a creature of London through and through, and his mother is a kind of personification of working-class London virtue and vice. But the London of *The Final Programme* is a kind of dark parody of "swinging London," especially as represented in such media export vehicles as the television series *The Avengers*, films like *Blowup* (1966) and *Casino Royale* (1967), and the models Jean Shrimpton and Twiggy. The first two Cornelius books present a London of wall-to-wall discotheques, drugs, and rock-n-roll-fuelled sex and violence. *The Condition of Muzak*, especially in its first and last sections, begins to present a more intimate, realistic, and loving vision of the city. It is this vision, of London as a concatenation of millions of ordinary people of a myriad of social classes, races, and ethnic origins, all striving to live their lives in company, that lies at the heart of *Mother London*.

Mother London, one is at first inclined to think, is Moorcock's *Ulysses*, as lavish and comprehensive a portrait of his home city as Joyce's 1922 novel is of Dublin. The two books share a grand ambition, a substantial heft, a similar focus on a single metropolis, and a similar desire to break with the narrative conventions of the nineteenth century novel. Joyce's novel is of course the most famous "difficult" book of the twentieth century, and it affords a remarkable display of its author's structural invention and stylistic virtuosity. Some of its eighteen episodes are written in a mixture of third-person narrative and internal monologue; one episode is in the form of a "catechism," a series of impersonal questions and answers; another, cast in the dramatic form of speeches and stage directions, is a phantasmagorical *Walpurgisnacht* in which it is well-nigh impossible to distinguish what is "actually" happening and what is phantasm; another is written in an evolutionary parade of English prose styles from the Venerable Bede down to Thomas Carlyle.[27]

The innovative structure of *Mother London* is a rather simpler affair, if initially perhaps as bewildering to the reader. Like *The English Assassin* and *The Condition of Muzak*, *Mother London* is a modular novel; each chapter stands on its own, without bridging passages linking it to the ones before and after. The Cornelius books' modularity is complicated by the fact that their individual chapters seem to be drawn from a number of different storylines, to represent fragments of entirely different narratives— even to be set in different versions of the twentieth century. In contrast, *Mother London* tells a single overarching story, one which stretches over almost five decades, from the Blitz of 1940 to the book's moment of composition in the mid 1980s—roughly, that is, the period of Moorcock's own life. The chapters are presented not in chronological order, however, but in what Moorcock thinks of as a "musical" form, reminiscent of the "sonata form" of *The Condition of Muzak*: "Having decided that *Mother London* had to have a non-linear form, I then decided that it had to follow true sonata form, which meant that it had to have the same shifts of mood and pace, slow movements, fast movements, jolly ones and sad ones, that are demanded of a classical symphony."[28] The novel begins with a four-chapter "overture," "Entrance to the City," which introduces the central characters, and ends with a four-chapter "coda," "Departure of the Citizens." Between them are four sections of six chapters each, which run in alternating chronological and reverse chronological order: "High Days," where chapters take their titles from the name of London pubs, runs from 1952 to 1985; "The Unheard Voices"'s six chapters run backwards from 1956 to 1940, while "Fast Days"'s six chapters run forward from 1940 to 1970; "The Angered Spirits," whose chapters are again pub-titled, goes from 1985 back to 1969.

It is entirely possible, then, to reshuffle the chapters, to read them in chronological order as a single narrative. But that's clearly against Moorcock's intentions; he's less interested in the progressive movement of traditional narrative, which drives us onward to answer questions like *what happens next?* or *how does it turn out?*, than he is in counterpointing characters, moods, and revelations from chapter to chapter. The chronological narrative is there as a scaffolding or armature behind the novel as a whole, but the book's real charge lies in the shifts of color and mood as we progress from one chapter to the next, whether we are moving backwards or forwards in time.

In its forty-five-year chronological breadth *Mother London* differs radically from *Ulysses*, which famously takes place on a single day (June 16, 1904). Indeed, while *Ulysses* tracks its characters from early morning straight through to the wee hours of the next day, there are only two chapters in *Mother London* that follow directly upon one another in the manner of a conventional novel: "Late Blooms 1940," the last chapter of Part Three, and "Early Departures 1940," the first of Part Four. These chapters, in which Josef Kiss comes to the Scaramanga sisters' cottage in North Kensington and defuses a German bomb that has fallen on the kennel in their garden, is in Moorcock's words the "pivot" of the book. The experience of the Blitz, the period between September 1940 and May 1941 when London was bombed over seventy times by Hitler's Luftwaffe, "is the core, at the centre of the book."[29] The Blitz deeply marks the novel's central characters: Josef Kiss, who has previously made a precarious living as a stage "mind-reader," discovers that his telepathic abilities can be put to use saving people trapped in bombed buildings; David Mummery, a small child during the war, is whisked out of danger during the bombing by a mysterious "Black Captain"; and the sixteen-year-old Mary Gasalee walks unharmed out of the inferno of her burning house (in which her husband has died) holding her baby, only to lapse into a fifteen-year coma.

These three characters, Josef, Mary, and David—reminiscent of Joyce's trio of Leopold Bloom, Molly Bloom, and Stephen Dedalus, but even more reminiscent of the Holy Family of Joseph, Mary, and Jesus (who, Jeff Gardiner reminds us, is repeatedly referred to as "Son of David" in the Gospels[30])—are first introduced to the reader as members of the same out-patient therapy group, though it will become clear as the novel progresses that their lives are far more closely intertwined. Each of them is afflicted—or blessed—with the same condition, an ability to "overhear" the thoughts of those around them. Josef Kiss makes use of it, as I've noted, during the war; no doubt it comes in handy for David Mummery, who writes books about London. But for the most part Moorcock deploys this inexplicable "psi power," the only substantial element of "fantasy" in an otherwise realistic novel, to seed his narrative with "italicized voices, random unheard voices, in different languages, in patois and in actual London and regional accents." Josef, Mary, and David "are able to hear, often unwillingly, all the voices of the city."[31] This "gift," which pushes Josef and David at least to the brink of madness, makes them extraordinarily sensitive to the totality of the city as a shifting, evolving organism, to the metropolis as a staging-ground in which a myriad of private griefs, joys, triumphs, resentments, and tragedies are forever being played out.

David Mummery and Josef Kiss are in many ways strikingly autobiographical figures. David's early memories of growing up with his mother in the 1940s, of his uncle at 10 Downing Street, his obsession with American cowboys, and of his launching himself as a freelance writer at a very early age, closely parallel Moorcock's own; and Josef Kiss, massive and flamboyant, is as John Clute comments "a redemptive version of the author's well-known public persona."[32] While an extensive study could be written relating Moorcock's fiction to the events of his life—his relationship with his mother as reflected in *Behold the Man*, the destructive personal relationship transformed in *The Brothel in Rosenstrasse*, and so forth—*Mother London*, set in the city in which he grew up and based largely on his own early experiences, is in many ways his most openly self-revelatory book.[33] This is a book, among other things, in which the author tells favorite stories, traces old familiar haunts, and turns over and caresses talismanic memories.

And the ideological arguments of such characters as Mummery, Kiss, and Dandy Banaji closely reflect many of the stances Moorcock has taken in his abundant journalistic writing. Moorcock is healthily averse to myths of a "golden age" from which the present represents a radical and dispiriting "fall," but one of the consistent themes of *Mother London* is that London, a living organism, is constantly changing, and that the changes it has undergone over the almost five decades of the author's life, while healthy in some respects, have come at the cost of much of great human value. In 1985, Josef and Dandy remark on how the "optimism of appreciating capital" is replacing "the old optimism of ideals"; in the wake of the Thatcherite dismantling of the Welfare State, London is gentrifying, is being taken over by upwardly mobile Tories, "timid, prejudiced and mean," from the "damned Home Counties, always London's bane."[34] With them they bring a new racial tension to the city: "Bloody brokers, Dandy," grumbles Kiss, "from Haywards Heath and Beaconsfield who now have the gall to blame the disruptions they cause on black people! Soft-palmed whites, Dandy, are the real cause of London's trouble."[35]

Along with this gentrification, the invasion of the urban center by the suburban elites until only the wealthy can afford to live in the city proper (a phenomenon that Moorcock will lament at much greater length in the 2000 novel *King of the City*), comes a packaging and commodification of London's history, the so-called "heritage industry." When David's cousin George Mummery invites Josef Kiss to buy into his scheme for "The New Ludgate Chop House," an "authentic" old-fashioned dining establishment that would operate on a members-only basis—"The food's absolutely basic chops, steaks, sausages, peas, fried potatoes, the sort of stuff any caff in London's doing for a pound fifty—and I'll get fifteen quid a plate for it"—Josef is appalled. "It's self-deception," he tells Mary Gasalee, "a gigantic charade. It'll be the end of us. A farce." "Better than a tragedy," she replies, perhaps more wisely, for she knows that civilization itself is "a process of self-mythologizing."[36]

Myths are at the heart of *Mother London*, most centrally the myth of London under fire. The book begins with an extract from David Mummery's notebooks: "By means of certain myths which cannot easily be damaged or debased the majority of us survive. All old great cities possess their special myths. Amongst London's in recent years is the story of the Blitz, of our endurance."[37] A society maintains itself, Moorcock would argue, by telling stories to interpret and make sense of its own history, its own experience. Some of those stories—those myths—serve the interests of those in power. Josef Kiss, for instance, has nothing but scorn for the notion of the brave leaders keeping up the spirits of the "valiant, chirping Cockneys": "I hate the Germans but I hated our leaders far more…. They didn't say how they were too scared to let any aristocrat go into the East End for fear they'd be

torn to pieces, how Churchill's life was in danger from the salt of the earth,"
Kiss grouses; "It wasn't Churchill or the King of bloody England who kept
up our morale. It was men and women whose homes and families were
bombed to bits discovering their own resources."[38] This then is Josef Kiss's
myth of the Blitz, a story of people discovering the best in themselves under
fire, a myth of sociality, commonality, and working-class solidarity.

Moorcock reaffirms that story, *in propria persona*, in a comic book
text published after the September 11, 2001, terrorism attacks:

> The Authorities thought we wouldn't be able to stand it.... But we didn't just
> show we could take it.... We took control of our streets, our own defense....
> And the more Hitler hit us ... we grew stronger. The cities which sustained
> these terrible Nazi attacks were called by the Russians—who had known the
> worst of them—"Hero Cities." And every citizen was a hero.[39]

Here, writing directly to address the aftermath of an attack as psychologically damaging for New York City as the Blitz was for London, Moorcock recasts his myth of the Blitz as lived history—"I speak from experience." But if Mary Gasalee is right, civilization itself is no more or less than self-mythologizing, than the crystallizing and perpetuating of narrative structures—myths—that organize and make sense of lived history. If we contrast *Mother London* to the four volumes of the Pyat Quartet that bracket it, the essential benignity of Moorcock's myth of the Blitz is starkly evident, when set against the dark myths of racial struggle, religious intolerance, and technocratic utopia that populate Pyat's imagination—and have populated the imaginations of so many twentieth-century figures, from Hitler and Stalin through the architects of South African Apartheid, Pol Pot, George Wallace, and Enoch Powell.

Myth, in the popular sense—made-up stories, fantasies—shades closely into *miracles*, those stories of moments when the laws of nature are contravened. Apart from the central characters' telepathy (and even here we are left with doubts as to whether it is a real power or a manifestation of their mental illness), the realism of *Mother London* is ruptured by two events, not directly presented but remembered, recalled, that might qualify as miracles: Mary Gasalee's emergence from her burning house, which she doesn't remember but has recounted to her by the traveller Jocko Baines; and David Mummery's rescue by the "Black Captain" (whom he will later know as the African ex-sailor Mombazhi Faysha). "I am however absolutely certain the Black Captain flew," Mummery writes; "if he had not been able to fly he could not have found me before the other bombs went off." Faysha will neither confirm nor deny it: "'If it did occur then it was a miracle,' he told me once."[40]

These two "miracles," tales of miraculous survival amidst destruction and death, are ambiguous, poorly attested; like the "miracles" Karl Glogauer performs for his followers in *Behold the Man*, they are drawn forth from the needs of the multitude. They become a part of the larger myth of London. The enigmatic character Old Nonny, whose shorter name, Old Non, is an anagram of the city's, and who has much in common with Mrs. Cornelius (saving the latter's vulgarity), is a kind of living memory of London: she "can tell the old tales of Brutus, Boadicea and Dick Turpin with the same vivid relish as she recounts the newer legends of the Blitz.... She speaks of David Mummery, rescued by the Black Captain, of Josef Kiss who reads minds and by this means saved a thousand lives, and of Mary Gasalee walking unscathed from the inferno with her baby in her arms."[41] But Old Nonny knows that such hagiographical miracles are less important than the small moments of solidarity, kindness, and affection that go to make a society better. When Josef laments London's decline, she tells him, "A city London's size is everything to everybody.... It's bound to get better." And to his ironical rejoinder—"So you do believe in miracles, Nonny?"—she replies, "Oh, I believe in *small* miracles, you know."[42]

The overall curve of *Mother London* is deftly crafted, especially given the complex and counter-intuitive chronological order in which Moorcock disposes his narrative. As so often, Moorcock likes to center his fiction on great retrospective gatherings—one is reminded of the Peace Talks Ball in *The English Assassin*, the various celebrations in *Gloriana; or, The Unfulfill'd Queen*, and the grand Christmas harlequinade towards the end of *The Condition of Muzak*, among many others. *Mother London* is punctuated by several such gatherings. The last chapter of the fourth section, "Variable Currents 1970," finds most of the major characters celebrating at the Kensington Summer Festival, where Josef and Old Nonny ride the carrousel and David and Mary watch: "If they could they would gladly live this instant forever."[43] This is immediately followed by "The World's End 1985," where the characters have gathered at the Scaramanga sisters' cottage to celebrate the forty-fifth anniversary of Josef Kiss's defusing their bomb. These two chapters, the one an island of transient contentment and the other of retrospection, feel almost like a premature conclusion, coming as they do some sixty-five pages before the "coda" proper, the final "Departure of the Citizens" section. But Moorcock fills those pages with incident: David Mummery recalls the 1977 Notting Hill Carnival race riots and his wartime "rescue" by the Black Captain; Josef Kiss saves the Scaramangas' cottage from a clutch of greedy real estate speculators; Mary Gasalee hears of her miraculous deliverance for the first time from a first-hand witness;

and in 1959 (for these chapters are running in reverse chronological order) Josef Kiss, tormented by sexual hallucinations, beats up a young stranger who has been abusing his wife, and then is shepherded off by Old Non into a kind of originary site—The Old Bran's Head, "London's first pub."[44]

The final section is all dénouement. David Mummery, in despair at the side-effects of the psychiatric drugs he is required to take to avoid institutionalization, has committed suicide. Mary Gasalee and Josef Kiss, in contented, lubricious old age, have gotten married, and the final chapters of the book, like the last bits of a Jane Austen novel, are a celebration of that event. It can all be seen as imbued with what Clute scorns as a "damaging sentimentality,"[45] a sentimentality—perhaps inevitable—that Moorcock risks throughout the novel through his very choice of a fundamentally retrospective mode. But much of that sentimentality, or more precisely *nostalgia*, is skillfully defused by the novel's unconventional structure. And much of it bears a family resemblance to that of another great London novelist, Charles Dickens, who is perhaps the largest influence lurking behind Moorcock's London writings. "People have made comparisons between *Mother London* and *Ulysses*, but it's not true," says Moorcock; "I'm still a popular novelist. My role model can't be James Joyce; it has to be Charles Dickens."[46]

* * *

Mother London, like *Byzantium Endures*, *The Laughter of Carthage*, and the Cornelius books before them, was marketed as a mainstream novel, and it received a good deal of acclaim in the critical press. Moorcock, it seemed, had finally broken out of the ghetto of genre writing, and was to be taken seriously as a "literary" novelist. The book was even shortlisted for the Whitbread Award, one of the most prestigious British prizes (it lost to Salman Rushdie's *The Satanic Verses*, by far the literary sensation of the year).

With *Mother London*, Moorcock established himself prominently among a group of writers concerned with the mythology and "psychogeography" of the city, among them his friends Iain Sinclair and Peter Ackroyd. And writing the book had provided a welcome respite from the Pyat novels, for not merely was inhabiting Pyat's twisted consciousness a considerable psychic strain, but the thematic heart of the novels, the events with which they must deal, was providing almost overwhelming. "For years," Moorcock said in 1991, "I'd been writing about the worst things in the world. What I have to face to write each of the Pyat books is harrowing. I'm staring at Hitler, the Holocaust, all that horror, all the time I'm writing."[47] It is no surprise, then, that whereas only three years separate *Byzantium Endures* (1981) and *The Laughter of Carthage* (1984), it would be another eight before the third volume of the Quartet, *Jerusalem Commands* (1992), was published. In the interim, Moorcock had not only written *Mother London*, but had returned to heroic fantasy with a fresh enthusiasm, writing a third Erekosë novel (*The Dragon in the Sword*, 1986) and two new Elric books.[48] It was as if the "mainstream" critical recognition he had received for the first Pyat books and *Mother London* had given him license to devote part of his energies to entertainments less immediately grounded in actual history. And truth to tell, his fantasies were probably more immediately remunerative: while it might be difficult to persuade the average mainstream novel-reader to tackle a vast, multi-volume picaresque epic narrated by a priapic, anti–Semitic scoundrel or the initially bewildering, fractured episodes of *Mother London*, there were scores of thousands of Elric fans eager to read whatever new adventures Moorcock might invent for the doomed albino.

Clearly, Moorcock was in no hurry to complete the last two Pyat novels. *Jerusalem Commands* came out in 1992; *The Vengeance of Rome* would finally arrive in 2006, a quarter-century after *Byzantium Endures*. The publication of Pyat's "memoirs" had taken almost as much time as the adventures those memoirs chronicle. The books are on one level an extended picaresque adventure, a vast serial in which we as readers are perpetually wondering what absurd situation Pyat will end up in next, and by what combination of turpitude and sheer idiot luck he will be extricated therefrom. But on a more profound level they are an exploration of the European mind "between the wars," an examination of the fears, prejudices, and hopes that drove two of the most "civilized" countries in Europe—Italy and Germany—into the arms of totalitarian regimes, and beyond that, into genocide. The shadow looming over the whole of the tetralogy is that of the Holocaust, which darkens and renders grotesque even the funniest and most light-hearted of Pyat's adventures. In the Pyat Quartet, "everything just keeps moving, rolling on remorselessly towards Auschwitz," commented Moorcock when he was still in the midst of the tetralogy; "Auschwitz figuratively, because I'm not sure it'll be the actual camp. I think it's more likely to be Sachsenhausen or somewhere."[49] With the twentieth century's ultimately horror as his inevitable destination, it is no wonder that Moorcock took as long as he did writing Pyat's fictive journey.

Jerusalem Commands is if anything even more hectic than *The Laughter of Carthage*, and Pyat's adventures even more far-fetched. His flight to New York City to join Esmé ends in disaster; he has been double-crossed by "Mucker" Hever, it turns out, and is forced to return west riding the rails hobo-fashion in the company of Jacob Mix, an amiable African American with far more practical wisdom than Pyat. Mix will stick close to Pyat through much of the book, not out of any Moonglum-like loyalty, but because he recognizes Pyat as "the luckiest bastard in the whole damned universe."[50] In Hollywood, Pyat (as "Max Peters") makes a name as a cinema scenographer, then as an actor, playing "Ace" Peters in a series of dogfight films and "The Masked Buckaroo" in westerns. Reunited at last with Esmé, he takes ship with a group of others (including Mrs. Cornelius, who has become the film star "Gloria Cornish") for Egypt to film a costume epic capitalizing on Tutankhamun-mania.

In Egypt, everything falls apart. The movie project, deserted by its American backers, comes under the control of al-Habashiya, a monstrous transvestite criminal lord, who turns it into a pornographic circus. Pyat is forced to rape Esmé repeatedly on film, but of course convinces himself that he has not betrayed her—indeed, she has betrayed him, having slept with their English producer. Al-Habashiya sells Esmé to the far east white slave trade, and takes Pyat into his harem, a grotesque carnival of mutilation, pederasty, and sadomasochism. Having escaped and crossed much of the Sahara by camel with his old love Prince Nikolai (now a gunrunner), Pyat falls in with the Albanian aeronaut Rosie von Bek, who is ballooning across Africa in the service of Mussolini's Italy. At the end of the novel, Pyat and Jacob Mix are once again in a cattle car, escaping Marrakech and a sentence of death from T'hami el Glaoui, the Pasha whom Pyat has promised to equip with a fleet of up-to-date aircraft of his own design.

There is really a quite astonishing range of incident and setting crammed into *Jerusalem Commands*'s almost 500 pages. The scene shifts from New York to Hollywood to Casablanca, Alexandria, Cairo, Luxor, Aswan, various oases in the Sahara, and Marrakech, with considerable detail devoted to the mechanics of getting from one place to another. If, however, *Jerusalem Commands* is the "scherzo" in the Quartet's overall symphonic structure (to borrow John Clute's musical metaphor), at times it is a very slow-moving scherzo indeed.[51] Slow-paced travel can be boring for the traveller, but all too often Pyat's various transits—from the United States to Alexandria, upriver from Cairo to Luxor, across the Sahara by camel-train—try not merely his own but his reader's patience as well.

Pyat's polymorphous priapism is much in evidence throughout the novel. In Hollywood, he beds a series of starlets and secretaries, all the while pining for the just-out-of-reach Esmé. In transit to Egypt, he is involved with the captain of the *Hope Dempsey*,[52] Maurice Quelch: a "marriage of true minds" like his earlier affair with Prince Nikolai. In Egypt, he resumes relations with Esmé, though it is clear that the bloom is to some degree off the rose of his worshipful love for her. After his horrific experiences in al-Habashiya's harem, Pyat is for some pages rendered uncharacteristically uninterested in sex. But by the time he has reached the Lost Oasis of Zazara (a period during which, it is strongly implied, he has discovered the charms of his "beautiful" female camel, "Uncle Tom"), he has recovered enough to indulge in a whole range of erotic acrobatics with Rose von Bek in the gondola of her balloon.

Each of the volumes of the Pyat Quartet pivots around a scene of violent humiliation. In *Byzantium Endures*, Pyat is mercilessly whipped, his buttocks permanently scarred, by the brutal Cossack Grishenko. In *The Laughter of Carthage*, he is beaten up and left for dead in the desert near Walker, Nevada by a group of Klansmen who have discovered that he is Jewish. Pyat's degradation in *Jerusalem Commands* is far more absolute, and much more painfully protracted. Not merely is he placed in the position of betraying his beloved Esmé and forced to repeatedly violate her on film, but he is made subject to al-Habashiya's degrading sexual demands, which culminate in Pyat's being told that he is to be blinded: because, in a rare access of morality, he has refused to kill one of the children in the harem for al-Habashiya's amusement.

With his typical luck, however, Pyat is rescued the very night before this sentence is to be carried out. What is striking is not the marks that this experience leaves upon his psyche—unsurprisingly, he is reduced to something close to catatonia for many days afterwards—but the extent to which the experience precisely *fails* to bring Pyat to any deeper self-knowledge. When al-Habashiya's demands upon him have reached their most monstrous, Pyat recalls, "I remember I did not blame God" (and here the name "God" is ambiguous, for al-Habashiya has taught Pyat to refer to him always as "God") "for reducing me to this. I blamed Esmé."[53] His flights of fancy will hereafter be inflected from the Egyptian *Book of the Dead*, he will rhapsodize about his flying machines and levitating cities in the language of the ancient Egyptians' sun-boats, and will fantasize about Anubis weighing his heart; in short, he will speak in terms of a descent into the underworld and subsequent rebirth. But Pyat is essentially unchanged, unreborn. Once he has recovered his strength and has access to a steady supply of cocaine, he is once again the egomaniacal dreamer, convinced that he has the future of the human race in his hands, that he has been repeatedly betrayed, without ever betraying.

* * *

4. Reality and Its Bitter Myths 107

In 2000, Moorcock published another "realistic" novel, *King of the City*. The book is by no means a sequel to *Mother London*, but it begins and ends with clear evocations of the earlier novel—its last line, "Myths and miracles, pards. What would we do without them?" is pretty much a restatement of the close of *Mother London*—and its marketing emphasized the two books' commonality as London novels.[54] In narrative terms, however, the two are very far apart indeed. *King of the City* is for the most part a long, rambling monologue by Denny Dover, former rock musician, middling photojournalist, and current paparazzo. Vast tracts of pages are given over to directionless reminiscences of his time in London in the salad days of the sixties and seventies, his association with various figures in the world of music, literature and journalism, his youthful longing for his beautiful and idealistic cousin Rose Beck. In counterweight to Rose is Denny's other cousin, John Barbican Begg, a hugely wealthy real estate developer and financier, personification of all that has gone wrong in English society with the Thatcher revolution and its long neoliberal aftermath. Begg and those like him, unleashed by Thatcher's dismantling of the welfare state, have destroyed what's left of the London of *Mother London*, replacing it with acres of shining high-rises and luxury developments. The old, organic city is no more, and much of *King of the City*'s considerable rhetorical verve is given over the lamenting its demise.

Though I'm not sure I'd go so far as John Clute, who calls *King of the City* "Moorcock's single worst book," it does indeed leave much to be desired.[55] After a promising and amusing opening, its actual action seems to take more or less forever to get underway. Too much of the book's events feels like the self-indulgent fantasies of a middle-aged bookman: Denny reforms his old rock band, the Deep Fix (not coincidentally, the name of Moorcock's own group), they appear on *Top of the Pops* and become an international sensation. And *King of the City*'s ending, in which Rose Beck practically single-handed engineers a new, kinder, and more organic world order, is almost mawkishly happy. On the other hand, one is inclined to indulge Moorcock in some unearned happy endings, given the enormity of the materials with which the Pyat Quartet deals.

The *King of the City* characters Rose Beck and Barbican Begg, and the Albanian aviatrix Rose von Bek in *Jerusalem Commands* are members of the extended clan of von Beks, Becks, Beggs, and so forth Moorcock was developing over the 1990s, and their appearance in these ostensibly "realistic" novels, as well as in far more overtly "fantastic" vehicles such as the von Bek novels proper (*The War Hound and the World's Pain*, *The City in the Autumn Stars*, etc.) or the "Second Ether" sequence, is indicative of how porous the line between "realism" and "fantasy" is in Moorcock's writing.[56] More broadly, the appearance of fantastical (or science-fictional) figures like Rose von Bek and the Cornelius family in the Pyat Quartet, as we shall see, raises questions about the very stance towards reality or history the writer can take in an ostensibly "realistic" work like the Pyat tetralogy.

That tetralogy finally winds to its grim and impressive end in *The Vengeance of Rome*. The title, I take it, is something of a pun, evoking as it does two more stages of Pyat's descent into the maelstrom of prewar European history: *Rome*, the capital Mussolini's Fascist Italy, where Pyat sells *il Duce* on his dream of building vast, army-crushing "land leviathans" that will make possible the rebirth of the Roman Empire; and Ernst *Röhm*, the scarred, canny, and homosexual leader of the Nazi *Sturmabteil* ("Brownshirts"), who takes Pyat under his wing as confidant and lover after Mussolini sends him abroad. *The Vengeance of Rome* is Pyat's journey into the heart of darkness of the twentieth century. But Moorcock chooses, wisely I think, not to send Pyat all the way to Auschwitz, to the death camps.[57]

Instead, after his protector Röhm is murdered in the July 1934 purge known as the "Night of the Long Knives," Pyat finds himself in the Dachau concentration camp, where he rejoices that he is not among the "Jews, gypsies and homosexuals," that he has a violet armband marking him as a "privileged" prisoner.[58] He becomes something of a pet to SS Sturmführer Schnauben, with whom he has extended conversations. One of them, foreshadowing the horror of the gas chambers yet to come, is painfully emblematic of Pyat's mixture of scientific knowledge, naïveté, and idealism. "Do you know anything about eugenics?" the officer asks him; "Exterminating a few failures is easy, but how would you kill a million?"

> I do my best to engage with the problem. He has called me "Herr." I need his approval. "You would doubtless have to gas them."
> "What kind of gas?"
> I find this conversation disquieting. "Some kind of cyanide. Whatever gas worked best in the trenches. Whatever is most easily mass-produced. This is not my area of specialty. I work for peace. I work for humanity."[59]

This is as close as Pyat gets to the Final Solution. To put Pyat himself in Auschwitz would confer too much dignity on his wretched self-delusion; it would push the obscene absurdities of his political and racial ideals over the edge into outright obscenity.

Pyat is, of course, eventually delivered from Dachau through the offices of his old lover Prince Nikolai, now an officer in the Gestapo, and sent to build and then test his one-man airship with the German military supporting Franco's forces in the Spanish Civil War. And from there it is only a short series of misadventures till he is in England, reunited with Mrs. Cornelius, with thirty-five years before him to remember, reinterpret, and suitably embroider his adventures "between the wars."

The Vengeance of Rome is a long, at times slow, majestic conclusion to the Quartet. Its pivotal moments of humiliation and degradation are two: Pyat's long immiseration in the concentration camp; and an earlier, luric episode—the novel's only extended portrait of Adolf Hitler—in which, dressed as a woman, Pyat has an extended session of scatalogical rough sex with the Führer. The motivations for this scene (not to mention its physical mechanics!) are a trifle far-fetched, but it culminates in one of the most horrific moments in Moorcock's fiction: Pyat has defecated and urinated on Hitler's face; he has buggered him with a dildo; now, as he leaves the room, he looks back on "Alf's" visage: "Through the filthy crust those pale, unsouled, unblinking eyes were staring at me, as if to remember me. Only for an instant did they meet mine. They flickered with chilling triumph."[60]

Hitler's eyes will be evoked again at the end of the novel in perhaps the book's—and the Quartet's—most painful passage. It is 1970, and the elderly Pyat has been contacted by Esmé—the real Esmé this time, not some ersatz wish-fulfillment—who has brought his mother to be reunited with him. Mrs. Pyat has survived far worse than her son: she barely escaped the September 1941 Nazi massacres in the Babi Yar gorge (the site, we remember, of the thirteen-year-old Pyat's first abortive flight); she was in Auschwitz when the Allies liberated that camp in 1945; since the war, she has been living in Jaffa. Now, as the old woman hands Pyat a copy of his birth certificate, a document which confirms what he has spent his entire life denying—that he is not Maxim Arturovitch Pyatnitsky but Moise Aaronovitch Peskonechnya, that he is neither Cossack nor Slavic but Jewish—he rejects her out of hand: "Madam, with all respect, I regret that I am not related to you.... I am a Russian Cossack, descended from Russian Cossacks. I am not a fool. I know my own Slavic blood."[61] "Still sobbing she rose and came towards me, trembling arms outstretched," Pyat recalls; "I could stand no more.... I fled that nightmare. Something in the woman's eyes reminded me of Hitler."[62] The eyes, the cliché would have it, are the "windows of the soul." But in others' eyes, Pyat sees only the mirror of his own fears, hatreds, and self-delusions. And Pyat himself, in turn, is a mirror, a distorting funhouse mirror perhaps, in which we can see the roots of many of the horrors of the century just past.

A number of characters from Moorcock's other fictions make appearances in the Pyat Quartet: Rosie von Bek is at once the Rose and member of the multi-branched von Bek/Beck/Begg clan; Captain Quelch, or at least his name, is familiar from the Second Ether books.[63] Most prominent, however, is Mrs. Cornelius, who appears regularly throughout the four novels at the most opportune moments, helping Pyat out of jams and generally being adored by him (from a suitable distance). Major Nye, familiar from *The English Assassin* and *The Condition of Muzak*, also appears at various points in Pyat's wanderings. In *The Vengeance of Rome*, as we are brought up to the present of Pyat's retrospective narration, we meet almost the entire central cast of the Cornelius Quartet in a London pub. Bishop Beesley, whose real name is "Billy the Mouth," is a confidence trickster, newly released from prison; Mo Collier is a barman; Miss Brunner is a former girls' school headmistress, deposed in a scandal; Frank Cornelius "works for Hoogstraten, the property tycoon, and tends to ape his new boss."[64] Later we hear of an earlier year when "Mr Auchinek the impresario" persuaded the Holland Park Comprehensive school to revive a turn-of-the-century harlequinade, with Mrs. Cornelius's children in the leading roles: "Jerry played Pierrot, Frank was Harlequin and Catherine was Columbine. We expected them to go on to successful stage careers in those days."[65] These are the characters as they appear in the final section of *The Condition of Muzak*: stripped of all paraphernalia of technology and high fashion, of time-travel and dimension-hopping, of grand cosmological struggle, Jerry and company are rendered grubby, mundane, "realistic." They are, in Clute's term, "skinned."[66]

The realism of the Pyat Quartet, its grounding in the dark experience and recorded, unavoidable facts of our recent history, has the at least momentary effect of revealing all the rest of Moorcock's writing as airy, lightweight: diversion, even—to use that ambiguous term—*escapism*. But the critique of fiction and fantasy the Quartet implies goes further than that: for what is Pyat himself but a fantasist, a thwarted inventor whose imagination of the future is fundamentally science-fictional? In interpreting his world in terms of race memory, of the struggles between new gods and old, and in looking to "champions" like Mussolini to save the West, Pyat is a composer of heroic fantasy; and when he rhapsodizes about a world of hygienically shining towers and levitating cities, a world cleaned and improved by technology, he is as it were writing science fiction. When set against the brute reality of the past century, fantasies seem either frivolous or, as in Pyat's case, positively morbid—a bent of mind that is one of the roots of the malaise.

But there's an interesting effect in reading the Pyat Quartet in the context of the entirety of Moorcock's fiction. That is, when Pyat gets something historically *wrong*—as when he assumes that Evelyn Waugh is a woman, or that Ezra Pound and Gabriele d'Annunzio were close friends—we are reminded of his fundamental *unreliability* as a narrator. But there is a flicker of a question: what if this is a version of history in which Waugh *was* a cross-dressing woman? And when Pyat quotes the great Victorian poet Ernest Wheldrake (an imaginary creation of Swinburne's), or describes conversing with "Desmond Reid" (whose only existence is as one of Moorcock's pseudonyms), we are reminded that what the books offer is not *the* first four decades of the twentieth century, but a *version* of those decades. An alternate history, as it were: closer to the "real" thing than Oswald Bastable's 1973 in *The Warlord of the Air* is to the 1973 we may have lived through, but nonetheless an alternate, an *other* history.

And such is true of all fiction. In the grand scheme of things, "realism" may be no more than a special, limited category of the fantastic, offering its own pleasures and rewards, but having access to no special, privileged insights either into the human heart, human society, or the machinery of the world's pain. Pyat's worldview, sour, proud, twisted, is built on myths and fantasies; but so are the generous and open-hearted worldviews of Josef Kiss, Mary Gasalee, and the ordinary Londoners of *Mother London*. We make sense of our experiences by telling stories, Moorcock's fiction implies over and over again; and those stories, whether they hew closely to the world we know ("realism"), extrapolate beyond it into the realms of possibility ("science fiction"), or flout its laws with impossibilities ("fantasy"), help us live our lives. It is through fiction that we negotiate the facts.

5

Consolidating the Multiverse

Moorcock had intended *Gloriana; or, The Unfulfill'd Queen* to be a farewell to fantasy, but his hiatus from writing fantastic novels proved rather brief—only three years. The Pyat books, set aside and returned to like a reluctant burden, would weigh upon his imagination for a very long time. He began the tetralogy in early middle age, at thirty-nine; he would be sixty-six when the last volume was finally published. The Pyat Quartet and other large, realistic novels—*Mother London, King of the City*—would be the constant ground base to this quarter-century of his writing career. But for a complex of reasons—financial exigencies, no doubt, and probably a simple desire to escape the nightmarish landscape of Pyat's consciousness for a while—Moorcock returned to writing fantasy in the early 1980s, and has continued to do so ever since (though not, one might add, at the breakneck pace of the 1970s).

It would have been easy enough, one supposes, for a writer of Moorcock's fecund imagination simply to invent a new crop of Eternal Champion avatars. Instead, Moorcock began the 1980s by striking out in a relatively new direction, that of *historical* fantasy, fantasy grounded in and commenting on the history of our own world, rather than that of some invented realm. The von Bek novels—*The War Hound and the World's Pain* (1981) and *The City in the Autumn Stars* (1986)—feature not a new protagonist, but a *family* whose members will play roles in Moorcock's books well into the next century. And their metaphysical backdrop is not the Law/Chaos opposition that underpins the first Eternal Champion series, but a variation on the struggle between that Heaven and Hell that Milton presented in *Paradise Lost*, with that symbol beloved by both medieval romancers and turn-of-the-century aesthetes, the Holy Grail, thrown in for good measure. In *The Dragon in the Sword* (1986), Moorcock gives us another John Daker/Erekosë novel, this one featuring a von Bek as a central character. Like *The Quest for Tanelorn*, *The Dragon in the Sword* provides an ending to the saga of the Eternal Champion; but, as we shall see, it is a conclusion that is purposefully partial and ambiguous, open to new beginnings and alternate endings.

At the end of the decade, Moorcock revived his most popular protagonist, Elric of Melniboné, for a pair of novels, *The Fortress of the Pearl* (1989) and *The Revenge of the Rose* (1991), that fill in blanks in the albino prince's career, flesh out (and revise) his character, and complicate his place in the multiverse, as well as introducing the Rose, a major recurrent character in Moorcock's fiction. By this point in his career, Moorcock had created enough characters, enough worlds and plotlines, that he could afford to play self-conscious musical variations—as in the Cornelius tetralogy—on his earlier work, making his novels echo-chambers of figures, motifs, and narrative turns for the attentive reader to recognize.

* * *

The turn of the decade between the 1970s and 1980s was a time of great personal instability for Moorcock. His marriage to the writer and editor Hilary Bailey, a collaborator on *New Worlds*, had disintegrated at the beginning of the 1970s, and by the end of the decade his second marriage, to illustrator Jill Riches, was also unraveling. After he completed *Byzantium Endures* in July 1979, Moorcock moved to California, initially to visit his dying friend Graham Hall, then to try his hand as a movie screenwriter. It was there he met Linda Steele, whom he was to marry in 1983.[1] The first half of the decade saw him sorting out his personal and financial affairs; in the mid–1990s he and Linda would settle on a ranch outside of Austin, Texas, and divide their time between Texas and London, and later Paris.

Moorcock's return to fantasy with *The War Hound and the World's Pain*, then, was part of a general tidying-up of his affairs. And strikingly, since he composed the book more or less simultaneously with the more ostensibly "literary" *The Brothel in Rosenstrasse*, it is an implicit assertion that there was nothing to be embarrassed about in pursuing "genre" writing. If *Gloriana* was an attempt to emulate Mervyn Peake, the most respectable of "literary" fantasists, in *The War Hound* and the books that followed Moorcock would (with some missteps) return wholeheartedly to the business of writing novels within the formulaic expectations of the genre—the irredeemable villains, the object-centered quests, the acts of heroism and sacrifice—striving now to stretch and complicate those expectations, rather than bypass them altogether.

The German nobleman Ulrich von Bek, the titular "war hound," is a commander of infantry in the Thirty Years War (1618–1648), the protracted, brutal, and nominally religious conflict that devastated Germany more cruelly than any war before the twentieth century.[2] Von Bek has ridden to war out of pious and patriotic convictions, to support the Protestant King Christian of Denmark. By 1631 he finds himself on the Catholic, Imperialist side at the infamous Sack of Magdeburg, where only 5,000 of the city's 30,000 inhabitants survived the two days of fire and plunder.[3] Through his exposure to the unrelenting horrors of war, the symptoms of the "world's pain," von Bek has become a seasoned, cynical professional soldier, a true *Krieghund*, and has lost all religious and political loyalties.

To his surprise, then, von Bek finds himself entrusted by the Devil himself with a quest to recover the cure for the "world's pain"—the Holy Grail. In a neat reversal of Revelation 12.7 ("And there was war in heaven") and *Paradise Lost*, there is war in Hell. The fallen angel Lucifer, weary of his exile, wishes to be reconciled with God (thus his quest for the Grail), and his various subordinate dukes—chief among them Arioch, familiar from the Elric and Corum novels—are in open rebellion, hoping to seize leadership of the infernal realms. Arioch's primary lieutenant, out to sabotage von Bek's quest, is Johannes Klosterheim, a failed "Knight of Christ" who appears first as a fanatic but rather downmarket Jew-hunter, but who by novel's end has become transfigured by his own burning Luciferian ambition. (Klosterheim dies at the end of *War Hound*, but he will reappear in its sequel, *The City in the Autumn Stars*, and take his place among the recurrent antagonists in Moorcock's fantasy novels, like Prince Gaynor the Damned.)

Most of the novel is taken up with von Bek's ultimately successful Grail quest. It is interesting, however, that at this point in his career Moorcock chooses to deal with such a culturally specific artifact. The various numinous objects of his earlier novels—the swords, the Runestaff, the jewels and amulets—are images familiar from folklore, canonical literature, and fantasy in general, and the Chalice in *Phoenix in Obsidian* is certainly reminiscent of various Grail stories. But in *The War Hound and the World's Pain* Moorcock adopts outright the Grail motif, so well known from medieval romances, nineteenth-century literature and opera (Tennyson's *Idylls of the King*, Wagner's *Parsifal*), to twentieth-century culture: T. S. Eliot's *The Waste Land* (1922), Charles Williams's *War in Heaven* (1930), and Robert Frost's "Directive" (1946) are only a few of the very diverse modern grail-texts.[4] But the Grail, as discovered by von Bek after the usual complement of battles, encounters with strange creatures, hair-

5. Consolidating the Multiverse   115

breadth escapes, and hot pursuits, is by no means the shining vessel of traditional Arthurian lore, nor does it have any connection with the Last Supper, Jesus's blood on the cross, or Joseph of Arimathea. Rather, it is a simple clay pot, made by a woman named Lilith, and it embodies not holiness or heavenly redemption but *harmony*, which is the cure for the world's pain. "And the Cure," Lilith tells von Bek, "is within every one of us."[5]

Lucifer, once he has the Grail, is not yet able to effect a full reconciliation with God, but the deity has in essence offered the world a new deal: the Lord has withdrawn from the earth, leaving it from now on in Lucifer's keeping. "Heaven has put the world into my sole charge," says the fallen angel:

> If I help mankind to accept its own humanity, then I, Lucifer, shall be all that I was before I was cast down from Heaven.... I do not rule, as such. I am charged to bring Reason and Humanity into the world and thus discover a Cure for the World's Pain. I am charged to understand the nature of this cup. When I understand its nature and when all mankind understands its nature, we shall both be redeemed!

With God having withdrawn from the world and Lucifer taking only an advisory role, humanity has entered a new phase of self-discovery and self-reliance, of "investigation and analysis."[6] (One might compare the endings of *The Quest for Tanelorn* and *The Sword and the Stallion*, each of which as well ushers in a new era free of the supernatural.) Indeed, Moorcock intends *The War Hound and the World's Pain*, in its very particular setting during the last of the great European wars of religion, to comment upon and perhaps, in the vocabulary of fantasy, to *explain* the "transition from the Age of Religion to the Age of Reason."[7] In his earlier fantasy novels, Moorcock had worked out a vocabulary to describe the large shifts of belief and *Weltanschauung* that marked epochs in the societies of his created worlds; in the historical fantasy of *War Hound*, he extends the method to actual European history.

The War Hound and the World's Pain, in terms of the generic fantasy novels so many of which Moorcock had written in the previous decades, is an almost unqualified success. Its opening third, in which von Bek introduces himself, places us within the terrestrial hell of the Thirty Years War, and comes to accept his charge from Lucifer, is particularly vivid and carefully managed. There is a satisfying unity to the action as a whole, and only a hint of the "speeding-up" effect that besets the final stages of so many of Moorcock's books: all too often in his commercial fantasies Moorcock seems to be cramming several chapters' worth of action into the final pages.

Alas, almost every structural flaw that one can imagine seems to attend upon *The City in the Autumn Stars*, the sequel-of-sorts to *War Hound* Moorcock published five years later. Twice the length of *War Hound*, *The City* is far too long: its first half is disconnected, unfocused, languorous; its second half is crowded with confusing and sometimes pointless incident, a hectic and pell-mell gallop towards the novel's climax. Moorcock is inclined to credit some of the novel's structural failures to his editor, who demanded he cut about a third of his original manuscript (which must have been sprawling indeed); the result is "a book with only a bit of backbone left. There's quite a bit of the body and face, but most of the skeleton's been removed." But Moorcock's also happy to acknowledge that much of what's wrong with *The City* is his own fault, a failure to remember the most basic demands of his genre: "because I hadn't written a commercial fantasy for quite some time, I'd actually forgotten the purpose of *that* form, which is to write a cracking yarn and fill it with wonders, and I was attempting instead to write a literary novel, a philosophical novel."[8]

Where *War Hound* had dealt with the seventeenth-century transition from an "age of faith" to an "age of reason," *The City in the Autumn Stars* sets out to examine the transition from "the Enlightenment ... to the Industrial Age. I wanted to examine that particular form of mechanical rationalism which came out of the Enlightenment." To do so, Moorcock chose to write "in the manner of eighteenth century picaresque"—Henry Fielding's *Tom Jones*, for instance, or any number of Smollett's novels. (Moorcock was simultaneously writing another picaresque—*The Laughter of Carthage*.) The languid, rather undirected form of the picaresque, however, is only sustained through the more or less realistic first half of the novel: the second half plunges into fantasy, with its concomitant chases, searches, discoveries, and pitched battles against supernatural adversaries. By the end of the book, having wandered through a full-length historical-realist narrative that abruptly and unexpectedly switches genres to the most frenetic and outrageous fantasy, the reader is almost as exhausted and bewildered as the protagonist Manfred von Bek, setting down his memoir a quarter-century later in a haze of melancholy nostalgia.

Whatever its structural flaws or its shortcomings as a readerly text, *The City in the Autumn Stars* is a fascinating book. Manfred von Bek, a direct descendent of Ulrich von Bek of *The War Hound and the World's Pain*, has been a courtier to Catherine the Great, a veteran of the American Revolutionary War, and an enthusiastic supporter of the French Revolution, even a delegate to the Revolutionary Assembly, but in 1793 he is fleeing France in dismay at Robespierre's Reign of Terror. He is pursued by

5. Consolidating the Multiverse

the fanatic revolutionist Montsorbier, and in turn finds himself pursuing the mysterious, alluring, and elusive Libussa, Duchess of Crete, whom he has only encountered once, but with whom he has fallen head-over-heels in love, with a strange desire that approaches the supernatural. His destination is Mirenburg, the imaginary central European city Moorcock introduced in *The Brothel in Rosenstrasse* (which revolved around the *fin de siècle* erotic adventures of yet another von Bek). In Mirenburg von Bek becomes involved in a colossal confidence scheme involving a projected navigable balloon, its architect the genial Scottish rogue the Chevalier St. Odhran (who will become another recurrent character in Moorcock's fiction).[9] And then things get strange. Von Bek, St. Odhran, Libussa, and Klosterheim—who has had his soul returned to him by Lucifer since his last appearance in *War Hound*, and who is cursed with eternal life—sail the balloon into the *Mittelmarch* (the "Middle Marches," a sort of border land between worlds), and in an alternate Mirenburg (the titular "city in the autumn stars") become engaged in a frantic and deadly race to find the Holy Grail.

Libussa, it emerges, wants to use the Grail as part of an alchemical ritual in which she and von Bek will merge into a single creature, "Hermaphrodite, self-reproducing, possessing the sum of all knowledge and virtue; an harmonious and immortal creature neither master nor slave; both male and female; the being described in Genesis."[10] Much of this description is closely paraphrased from *The Final Programme*, for the culminatory plotline of *The City in the Autumn Stars* is a refunctioning of the last section of the first Cornelius novel, in which Miss Brunner and Jerry Cornelius are merged together in the womb of the supercomputer DUEL and have "the sum total of human knowledge" fed into their collective mind.[11] Just as in the first two-thirds of *The Final Programme* Moorcock had rewritten the epic fantasy of the first two Elric stories in a kind of science fiction idiom, in the last chapters of *The City in the Autumn Stars* he reworks the later part of that science fiction novel in the idiom of historical fantasy. Libussa is as ruthless as Miss Brunner, if far more attractive, but she is also less successful. She would merge with von Bek—whose family, we remember, has a special relationship with the Grail—to create a new ruling power as the earth enters a moment of alchemical conunction (reminiscent of the Conjunction of the Million Spheres), a power that would be a ruthless "lion" to replace the "lamb" of the Christian dispensation. It is the Grail itself, as personification of Harmony, that rejects the ceremony, recoiling from the "beast" Libussa would unleash on the world. She dies, and a new era dawns, one free of all metaphysical domination. "The Day of the Lion failed to dawn," von Bek reflects, "Today is the Day of the Steam Engine."[12]

Thus von Bek muses during *The City in the Autumn Stars*'s lengthy dénouement, during which his narrative voice resumes the somewhat old-fashioned pace of the novel's opening. (The early part of the novel includes a passage written in imitation of Ann Radcliffe; the ending one in imitation of Jane Austen.[13]) But that sedate, melancholy final stretch fails to make narrative sense of the welter of action that has come before: in the Mirenburg of the *Mittlemarch*, von Bek and Libussa enter an "inner" city within the city, then a "deeper" city within that; they encounter a talking fox, Lord Renyard, who discusses the Encyclopedists with them; a mysterious "goat queen," attended by white apes, is murdered for no clear reason; Lucifer appears to von Bek and gives him the sword of Paracelsus, in whose pommel an eagle is imprisoned; and so forth. And Moorcock is not entirely comfortable with the alchemical business around which the novel's later events revolve. "The problem with that symbolic vocabulary," he comments, "is that I don't believe in it."[14] It is one thing for him to adopt the Holy Grail, strip it of its Christian symbolic freight, and reinterpret it as an emblem of self-discovered human harmony; it is quite another to tackle the system of far-fetched astrological and chemical correspondences that made up the grammar of alchemy.

* * *

Moorcock had originally planned a third von Bek novel, which would follow a member of the family into the twentieth century, the "Age of Politics."[15] In the event, some of the ideas for that unwritten book turned up in *The Dragon in the Sword*, published later the same year as *The City in the Autumn Stars*. *The Dragon in the Sword* is an explicit return to the Eternal Champion mythos; the title page of the first American edition carries the subtitle, "Being the Third and Final Story in the History of John Daker, The Eternal Champion."[16] Readers recalling the end of *The Quest for Tanelorn* could only wonder: hadn't John Daker—as Erekosë—found his Ermizhad in the city of Tanelorn? Hadn't he perished, destroying the Cosmic Balance and returning human destiny into humanity's own hands, and been enshrined in Tanelorn as a statue among the other statues of Champions? And what could be more "final" than that?

Since 1975, when *The Quest for Tanelorn* was published, there had been only minor additions to the Eternal Champion canon: the Elric novel *The Sailor on the Seas of Fate* (1976), which recast *Quest* from Elric's point of view and incorporated the 1973 novella "The Jade Man's Eyes"; the mislaid and rediscovered Elric story "The Last Enchantment" (composed 1962, published 1978)[17]; "Elric at the End of Time"; and the graphic novel *The Swords of Heaven, The Flowers of Hell*, plotted and outlined by Moorcock and written and illustrated by the American artist Howard Chaykin.[18] *The Swords of Heaven* constitutes a bridge narrative between *Phoenix in Obsidian* and *The Quest for Tanelorn*: Urlik Skarsol is drawn away from his ice-world to become the hero Clen of Clen Gar; after various adventures, at book's end he boards the mysterious Dark Ship that will take him and the other Champions to fight Agak and Gagak. In his introduction to *The Swords of Heaven*, Moorcock emphasizes that the series has been brought to a close: "Readers who followed the long Eternal Champion cycle will know that I completed it several years ago with a sequence of books known as *The Chronicles of Castle Brass*. That sequence was designed to bring all the threads together." He has collaborated on *The Swords of Heaven* because of his admiration for Chaykin's work and because it allows him to produce a "third John Daker volume" (something magical about the trilogy form, perhaps); but this is "my final tale of the Eternal Champion."[19]

Seven years later, when he wrote *The Dragon in the Sword*, Moorcock had clearly rethought the "finality" of *The Quest for Tanelorn*, though he was still very much interested in bringing the threads of his various fictive creations together. *Dragon* functions as both the (real) third John Daker novel and as the *de facto* third von Bek novel,[20] and it provides another, alternate ending to the Eternal Champion cycle—one which proves in fact utterly open-ended. The novel begins as something of a "reset" of *The Swords of Heaven*. John Daker-Erekosë is still in the Scarlet Fjord, as Urlik Skarsol, but he is tormented by the inevitable dreams and by his longing for Ermizhad. In fevered visions, he dreams of embarking on the Dark Ship and disembarking repeatedly, in one case as Clen of Clen Gar. In one vision, he encounters the dwarf Jermays the Crooked, who tells him "you must go back aboard.... You disembarked too soon."[21] In another, he meets the Knight in Black and Yellow—clearly Hawkmoon's Warrior in Jet and Gold, and identical in features to Elric's Sepiriz—who counsels him to heed the voices he has been hearing, summoning him under yet another unfamiliar name: "A great and momentous adventure lies ahead of you," the Knight tells him, "it could result in your partial release from this doom. It could produce a beginning and an ending of enormous import."[22] So Urlik—or rather, John Daker, since his "original" identity is of central importance to *The Dragon in the Sword*—boards the Dark Ship, and the blind Captain and his Steersman brother bring him to yet another realm for another round of adventures as the Eternal Champion.

The invented world of *The Dragon in the Sword* is one of Moorcock's most ingenious. It consists of six separate "realms"—not exactly planets, but what Corum would call "planes," which coexist in a wheel-shaped formation but which have intermittent portal-like linkages with one another: Maaschanheem, a nightmarishly marshy world in which the inhabitants mostly live on enormous floating/rolling "hulks"; Draachenheem, sketchily described, but seemingly a standard-issue quasi-medieval fantasy world; Gheestenheem, "Realm of the Cannibal Ghost Women"; Barganheem, whose most prominent inhabitants are a race of wise and super-evolved bears; Fluugensheem, "whose people are guarded by the Flying Island"; and Rootsenheem, "whose warriors have skins of glowing blood."[23] At the "hub" of this wheel lies Alptroomensheem, "Realm of the Nightmare Marches"—a full-blown realm of Chaos, where various Dukes hatch plots to conquer the wheel as a whole.

The plot of the novel is too complex for a brief summary, though its various moving parts, coincidences, and connections fit together rather better than the similar convolutions of *The City in the Autumn Stars*. Suffice it to say that John Daker, who is offloaded from the Dark Ship in Maaschanheem, immediately encounters Ulric von Bek, a refugee from Hitler's Germany of 1939. Von Bek has been able to escape to the wheel worlds because those realms are a kind of Middle March in relation to our own world. Daker has been summoned by the Cannibal Ghost Women, who are in reality Eldren (and not cannibalistic at all), marooned in this particular dimension without their menfold because of a navigational error some ages past, when the Eldren (male and female in separate dragon-led convoys) were migrating from one realm of the multiverse to another to escape the increasing depradations of the Mabden. That of course evokes the Corum novels, and indeed *The Dragon in the Sword* is in large part a self-conscious, at times intentionally parodic collage of motifs and plot twists from earlier works in the Eternal Champion mythos. It's handy that John Daker, the only avatar of the Champion with clear self-consciousness and some memory of his former incarnations, is the protagonist here, for he's able to remain unfazed when, say, Sepiriz (from the Elric stories) pops onto the scene out of nowhere, or when the Eldren women entrust him with a rare and powerful actorios stone like the one Elric wears on a royal ring.

Daker, von Bek, and the Eldren Alisaard must journey to Alptroomensheem, the seat of Chaos, to recover a series of objects to prevent the Princess Sharadim of Draachenheem from conquering all six worlds of the wheel, inviting the Lords of Chaos in, and becoming a Chaos Duchess herself. Her twin brother Flamadin (whose form John Daker has assumed, but who in reality has been murdered by his evil sister) is the local avatar of the Eternal Champion, a kind of pulp-magazine superhero whose exploits are famed throughout the six worlds due to their dissemination in the local equivalent "of our old Victorian penny dreadfuls or dime novels."[24] (The Eldren have summoned him, confusingly enough, under the name "Sharadim," for they assume that a true hero must be *female*.) Von Bek seems to be along for the Grail-handling, since his family has an affinity for that cup. But the central numinous object to be gained is the "Dragon Sword" itself, which at the moment of its forging captured the soul of the dragon leading the Eldren women through the multiverse. When Sharadim and the Chaos Lords have been defeated, Daker breaks the sword, releasing the dragon which will lead the Eldren to their menfolk. Von Bek leaves with them: like Erekosë and Ermizhad or Corum and Rhalina, he and Alisaard have fallen in love.

The Dragon Sword, it would seem, is not merely an analogue to Stormbringer (or the Cold Sword), but Stormbringer itself at an earlier stage of its existence. "The blade," Sepiriz tells Daker, "had been designed to be inhabited." At some later moment, one assumes, it will be reforged and occupied by the demon that springs from it in the last scene of *Stormbringer*. And the Eldren women, reunited with their men on whatever plane they inhabit—Jermays the Crooked strongly implies in the dénouement—will go on to be the ancestors of the Melnibonéans. The events of *The Dragon in the Sword*, then, can be read as a distant prequel to the stories of Elric of Melniboné and the Black Sword.

John Daker boards the Dark Ship in the last pages of the novel, and the Captain puts him ashore in the pre-dawn hours in a vast towered city. It is contemporary London; he has returned to his starting point. But how does one reconcile this ending of the Eternal Champion cycle to that of *The Quest for Tanelorn*? One reconciliation, perhaps over-subtle, revolves around the fact that much of *The Dragon in the Sword* is concerned with John Daker's asertion of his own identity as a specific human being, over and above his role as the Eternal Champion. He has been Erekosë, he has been Urlik Skarsol and Clen of Clen Gar; but he never becomes Flamadin in more than name and features, and at the climax of the novel, when he faces the hosts of Chaos with the Warriors at the Edge of Time at his side, he does so quite self-consciously *as* John Daker, not as a Champion-function. It is by this act of individual self-assertion, by his doing the Champion's work without *becoming* the Champion, rather than by any great feat of heroism or martial valor, that Daker is able to end his own cycle of endless rebirth and struggle. He still longs for Ermizhad, but believes he will soon find her "here, perhaps in this city, in London."

> Though our span of years be that of ordinary human beings, they will be our own years. We shall be free of all cosmic designs, free of destinies and gradiose dooms ... free to be flawed, finite, mortal creatures which from the first was all we ever wished to be.[25]

Somehow, that is, John Daker has "split off" from Erekosë, has discovered his destiny as a "finite, mortal creature," while the Erekosë convinced of his fate as the Eternal Champion, the endless warrior, will go on to fight Agak and Gagak beside Corum, Elric, and Hawkmoon, and will find peace only in death.

But do we need to be so ingenious? This reconciling of the endings of *The Quest for Tanelorn* and *The Dragon in the Sword*—and for that matter the reading of *Dragon* which sees it as a prequel to the Elric stories—might appeal to those of a systematizing bent, to haunters of intenet discussion boards, Hobbit-like genealogists, and descriptive bibliographers. It is one way of "bringing all the threads" of these various narratives together, of making all of them fit into a single whole. But they *need not* fit together. Moorcock's accomplishments as a popular fantasist ought not to make us forget that he is also the editor of the avant-garde *New Worlds*, the admirer of William Burroughs, and the author of the radically discontinuous Cornelius novels and stories. We can strain for a plausible harmonizing of the two endings of the Eternal Champion cycle—like the one I've given above—or we can simply recognize that there are (at least) two separate and possibly incompatible endings to the cycle. It is not a "mistake" on the author's part, but a set of simultaneous alternatives. It is a gesture, like the three endings of John Fowles's *The French Lieutenant's Woman*, which can be read as quite characteristic of the postmodern moment. I prefer to read it in musical terms, as the forms of the Cornelius books and *Mother London* ask to be read: as variations on an absent, unrecoverable theme—no single variation is "truer" than another, no one more "original" than the rest.

* * *

By the late 1980s, nearing the end of his forties and his third decade as a professional writer, Moorcock had every reason to feel satisfied with his accomplishment in a wide range of fields. Of course, his various fantasy series of the 1970s had proved wildly popular, and he was widely recognized as the most important living British fantasist. While *New Worlds* itself had passed on, the insurgent movement of the "New Wave" had indeed effected a transformation in English-language science fiction. The final book of the Cornelius tetralogy, *The Condition of Muzak* (1977), had won the Guardian Fiction Prize, "a literary prize I greatly valued, so I felt as if most of my often experimental work had, one way or another, been accepted by the public."[26] As to Moorcock's forays into "realistic" fiction exploring his own century, *Byzantium Endures* and *The Laughter of Carthage* had been well-received, and *Mother London* had been very widely praised, even short-listed for the Whitbread Prize. With *The War Hound and the World's Pain*, *The City in the Autumn Stars*, and *The Dragon in the Sword*, he had "returned" to fantasy.

In the last part of the 1980s, reluctant to return to the cesspool of Pyat's consciousness and begin writing the third volume of *Between the Wars*, Moorcock realized that while "I thought I had put Elric behind me for good…. I still had not lost my fascination for the crimson-eyed albino…. And so it slowly dawned on me that I might restore my literary wellsprings with a couple of Elric books."[27] There ensued a "second wave" of Elric novels, *The Fortress of the Pearl* (1989) and *The Revenge of the Rose* (1991), which would alter and expand Moorcock's conception of his iconic antihero and his place in the (itself expanded) multiverse.

The Fortress of the Pearl is by far the more straightforward and conventional of these new Elric novels, and indeed Moorcock acknowledges that it is "probably the most formulaic" of the Elric novels.[28] It is set early in Elric's career, after his discovery of the Black Sword but before his return to Melniboné and the destruction of Imrryr. This chronological setting allows Moorcock the opportunity to present another, somewhat less gloomy, side of Elric's character: he is still physically weak, bound in an unwelcome symbiotic relationship to his sword, but not yet weighed down by the burden of remorse at the death of the Cymoril and the destruction of the Bright Empire, nor yet obsessed with his own mournful destiny or (quite as) resentful of his role as a pawn in the struggle between Chaos and Law.

The Elric of *Fortress* is less a Byronic anti-hero than a Candide or Rasselas, travelling the world to gain experience and wisdom to reform and rejuvenate Melniboné, so that "The Bright Empire's brightness would come no longer from the glow of putrefaction but from the light of reason and good will."

> This was his dream and it was why he travelled the world, why he refused the power which was his, why he risked his life, his mind, his love and everything else he valued, for he believed that there was no life worth living that

was not risked in pursuit of knowledge and justice.... It was the logic of one who truly loved the world and desired to see an age dawn when all people would be free to pursue their ambitions in dignity and self-respect.[29]

This youthful idealist, needless to say, is difficult to square with the brutal, ironic cynic we meet at the beginning of "The Dreaming City," even when one takes into account the events of *The Sailor on the Seas of Fate* (which by internal chronology fall between *Fortress* and that story). What Moorcock is up to is a rewriting of Elric, recasting his character in a more humanistic, sympathetic mold. Moorcock had already polished off a few of Elric's harsher edges in earlier revisions of the first wave of stories. In the early text of "The Dreaming City" we are told that "ten thousand years of a cruel, brilliant and malicious culture was behind [Elric] and the pulse of his ancestry beat strongly in his deficient veins. He was a sorcerer and had shed blood in many devious ways in pursuit of his art."[30] In the 1977 appearance of the story in *The Weird of the White Wolf*, Moorcock has omitted that last sentence.[31] Of course, while Moorcock might want to humanize Elric *somewhat*, he has no interest in turning him into Prince Valiant; *Fortress* ends with scenes of sadistic torture and a bloodbath that would do any sword-wielder proud.

The Fortress of the Pearl has a distinctly Middle Eastern flavor, the result of Moorcock's recent travels in North Africa and the Middle East. In structure, it is a double quest into the realm of dreams, in which the search for the imprisoned soul of Varadia, the Bauradim people's "Holy Girl" (note the pun on "Holy Grail") is intertwined with the search for the Pearl at the Heart of the World, which Elric must bring back in order to obtain the antidote for a deadly elixir to which he has been unwittingly addicted. His companion and guide on this eventually successful quest is Oone the dreamthief, who shares both a name and a general air of *savoir faire* with Una Persson, the temporal adventuress. *Fortress* plays with some large ideas, among them the notion that dreams or ideals can become disconcerting or heartening realities, but for the most part it is a sturdy and cunningly constructed formulaic fantasy, with Oone and Elric progressing from one dream realm to another and encountering concomitant shifts of scenery and supernatural dangers. Clearly, as he composed the book Moorcock was looking ahead towards possible further expansions of the Elric mythos. In the novel's epilogue, we learn that Oone and Elric's sojourn in the dream realms has produced more than just a rescue: Oone is pregnant, with "A daughter, I think. Maybe even a brother and sister, if the omens are properly interpreted. More than pearls can be conceived in dreams."[32] She does not believe Elric will ever learn of this daughter (or children); but an omen-interpreting reader should be on the lookout for their appearance in future Moorcock volumes.

If *The Fortress of the Pearl* was a particularly well-wrought instance of the formulaic heroic fantasy—a kind of paradigmatic "Elric novel"— Moorcock was determined to do something new, to alter the terms of the formula in *The Revenge of the Rose*.[33] The results were bound to displease some readers who had been following Elric for two decades now, but the new elements Moorcock introduces in this novel result in a book quite unlike any of the heroic fantasies he had written, and some of them prove central to his fantasy writings for the rest of his career. In the first place, there is *humor*. Laughter in the Elric books is almost always grim, thin-lipped, ironic. "Elric at the End of Time," Moorcock's hilarious displacement of the moody albino prince into the frivolity of Jherek Carnelian's world, had met with some outrage from diehard Elric readers. But while *The Revenge of the Rose* is by no means an out-and-out comedy—it bears the usual complement of damned souls, inhuman cruelties, a world in danger of being overwhelmed by Chaos, a desperate quest for numinous objects, and so forth—the book is shot through with both broad and subtle humor.

Much of this humor is embodied in the person of Elric's companion-for-the-nonce, the poet Ernest Wheldrake, whom readers recognize both from *Gloriana; or, The Unfulfill'd Queen* and the *Dancers at the End of Time* trilogy, where Amelia Underwood frequently quotes his works and refers to him as a Victorian contemporary, something of a more respectable Algernon Swinburne. Small, bird-like, and red-haired (in this like Elric's more frequent companion Moonglum, Moorcock's friend Barrington Bayley [Moonglum's real-life model], and for that matter Swinburne himself), Wheldrake is given to quoting reams of his own poetry, most of it (save for a number of stanzas in imitation of the Border ballads) quite execrable. While he involves himself in Elric's quests gamely enough, Wheldrake seems to be constantly composing their adventures into some mawkish epic poem—that is, when he isn't relating everything to the minor literary squabbles of suburban Putney.[34]

The Phatt family, hereditary clairvoyants and seasoned travellers of the multiverse, also generate a good deal of humor. They are a classic Dickensian household: the feckless Fallogard Phatt, his young son Koropith, beautiful niece Charion, and the matriarch Ma Phatt, whose half-senile ramblings, studded with clairvoyant insights, range in reference from Elizabethan street songs to Edwardian music hall. Wheldrake's passion for Charion Phatt, and his courtship rivalry with the giant toad Khorghakh, are exquisitely awkward. And as if to tease readers who have taken the whole Eternal Champion cycle a bit too seriously, Moorcock peppers his text with jokey references to his earlier books. "Prague!" exclaims Wheldrake at one point, "and do you know Mirenburg, perhaps? Even more beautiful!" A seedy trading boat is named the "*Oona Peerthon*." At one point Prince Gaynor wonders existentially, "are we mere ingredients? Eggs in some mad god's omelette?"[35]

Local humor in *The Revenge of the Rose* shades easily into full-scale Swiftian social satire. In the town Agnesh-Val, Elric and Wheldrake are told by a thin man named Reth'chat that "hospitality" is no more than unearned "charity," and that the Distressed Travellers House is to be privatized: "With luck, it should soon turn a profit." Another tells them that Reth'chat—whose name is an anagram of Margaret *Thatcher*—is "a relic … from an age most of us have only read about. He would have us judged by our wealth and martial glory rather than our good will and tranquility of spirit."[36] Agnesh-Val is in the realm of the ironically named "Gypsy Nation," a vast caravan of mobile villages which roll endlessly, all the way around the world, along a broad concourse walled with refuse. These so-called "free" Gypsy villages are the apotheosis of neo-liberalism, of a triumphant competitive capitalism. Space in the villages is available only to those whose credit is good; once one falls behind, one is consigned with a host of others to the "marching boards" in the bowels of these vast structures, which are rolled ever onward by the unceasing manual labor of this (literal) *under*-class. "Progress" is this society's mantra: the villages must always keep moving, whether they crush stragglers under their wheels or, as when the Chaos Lord Mashabak has severed the high causeway leading them a over a bay, progress leads only to annihilation. Later in the novel, Elric will witness Arioch's creation of a gigantic clock-society, in which every member must strictly adhere to his or her regimented task or risk bringing the whole structure down; this bit of satire—presumably of a totalitarian state—is much less fully developed than the Gypsy Nation.

The clairvoyant Phatts are not the only new characters introduced in *The Revenge of the Rose*, nor is Wheldrake the only figure to enter Elric's ambit from another corner of Moorcock's multiverse. The principal antagonist in the novel, Prince Gaynor the Damned, was introduced in the second Corum novel, *The Queen of the Swords*, where he commanded Queen Xiombarg's Chaos army. Gaynor was once a hero, Jhary-a-Conel explains, a champion of Law, but became a renegade: "He was punished, some say, by the power of the Balance. Now he may never serve Law or know the pleasure of Law. Now he must serve Chaos eternally," being sometimes

5. Consolidating the Multiverse

defeated and immediately shifted to another realm to continue his fight: for Gaynor is immortal, unable to die.[37] He is something of an anti–Champion, even, it is implied, a renegade Champion, now being eternally punished. Gaynor appears only briefly in *The Queen of the Swords*, but he is the dominant evil figure in the second Corum trilogy, and it is not surprising to find him turning up in *The Revenge of the Rose*, for Moorcock is able to use him as a kind of counterpart, an evil *Doppelgänger*, to his Eternal Champion figure Elric. Indeed, Gaynor is portrayed with considerable sympathy in *Revenge*; Elric even feels, at one point, a "close affinity" with Gaynor.[38] For a while he and Elric pursue their similar quests cooperatively, though towards novel's end it is clear that Gaynor's deathless predicament has warped him beyond redemption.

The central adjustment to Gaynor's character in *The Revenge of the Rose* is that Gaynor is no longer a fallen champion of *Law*, but of the *Balance*: "I was once a Prince of the Balance," he tells Elric, "a Servant and Confidant of that Unordinary Intelligence that tolerates, celebrates and loves all life throughout the multiverse and yet which both Law and Chaos would overthrow if they could."[39] In this Gaynor as anti–Champion, we see the consolidation of the gradual shift in Moorcock's conception of the relationship among Law, Chaos, the Balance, and the Eternal Champion. Where Corum had seen himself as serving Law against Chaos, and Elric as well had found himself betraying his ancestral loyalties to Chaos in order to further Law's ends, it is now clear that the Champion's role is never fixed to one or the other force, but his (or her) central duty is to serve the Balance between them. Indeed, with Arioch's regimented clockwork-universe in view, it's evident that the end-result of Chaos can look very much like an excess precisely of Law.

While Gaynor the Damned is a familiar face (or rather, a familiar helm, since he never reveals his features), the character of the Rose is unlike anyone in Moorcock's earlier fiction. She is clearly a product of his desire to introduce more strong female characters into his novels. His early books sometimes partook of the sexism pervasive within the heroic fantasy genre, with female characters principally serving as love interests or prizes, crouching in fear as the heroes hacked away, or as mysterious priestesses or sorceresses. But even in the earliest Elric stories, one encounters figures like Yishana of Jharkor, strong-minded, self-willed, and assured in their own sexuality; and even the love interests in series like the Corum or Hawkmoon books are more than willing to take up arms beside the male protagonists. Una Persson is clearly the dominant figure of the Cornelius books, and Amelia Underwood is a character of some depth and complexity. With Oone the dreamthief Moorcock begins to present wholly independent female characters in his heroic fantasy, and to that extent, the Rose is an extension of a project already underway.

But the Rose is more: Though she is a clearly defined character with her own history, her own sense of humor, and her own heroic quest, she is also something of an archetype. Indeed, it is unclear whether she is human at all. She is one of the "daughters of the Garden,"[40] whose race has been wiped out by Gaynor—thus the revenge she seeks. At the climactic battle with the Chaos-army, she summons the Tangled Woman, a vast beneficent force whose arms are "of a million rose-branches," whose faces are "of knotted rosewood," and who addresses the Rose as "her daughter."[41] A sturdy and not at all ethereal figure, the Rose is a skilled wielder of her sword Swift Thorn and her dagger Little Thorn. She is no benign garden-dweller. But when Gaynor is defeated and she comes to take the revenge she has sought for so long, that revenge does not wholly, or even primarily, consist of punishing Gaynor and his Chaos-masters, but takes a constructive form. "We shall use the power of Mashabak," the Rose says, now that the Chaos Lord has been imprisoned, "We shall force the Count of Hell to restore everything we loved. And so, by turning this evil into good, we redeem the past! And that is the *only* way by which we mortals may redeem our past! It is the only positive revenge."[42]

The Rose, a creature half-human and half-plant, represents a new ecological consciousness in Moorcock's writing, and the figure of the Rose, in various avatars and variations, will begin to populate Moorcock's fiction through the 1990s and the first part of the 2000s, even coming to displace that of the Eternal Champion, a protagonist-function who, after four decades of service, may have begun to show its age.

Perhaps the most radical aspect of *The Revenge of the Rose*, however, is a newly open and flexible conception of the multiverse, the cosmological structure that has underpinned all of Moorcock's fantasy novels. In the first wave of Eternal Champion fictions, the various realms of the multiverse coexist, occasionally impinge upon one another, but can be traversed only on unusual occasions and through very specific "portal" devices (the "summonings" to which John Daker and Corum respond, the Dark Ship which sails between the worlds, etc.). With the device of the Middle Marches (introduced in *The War Hound and the World's Pain*), realms which lie between various worlds, the multiverse has become more porous, more easily travelled. Multiverse-hopping is even easier in *The Dragon in the Sword*, where portals from world to world have been regularly calculated and mapped, and where the Eldren can follow a convenient dragon across the boundaries between realms. In *The Revenge of the Rose*, travelling through the multiverse has become almost an everyday occurrence, and—and this is key—has been to some degree conflated with time travel, the journeying among the various possibilities of the time streams that is the forte of Una Persson and the Guild of Temporal Adventurers.

Elric feels little surprise when the dragon Scarsnout carries him from the road to Elwher to Melniboné in its distant past. Wheldrake, plucked out of Albion's court by Doctor Dee's alchemical machinations, has lived in both Victorian and Elizabethan England, and has become so accustomed to shifting from one realm to another that he's not unduly astonished to find himself in Elric's world and later in that of the Gypsy Nation. Other characters traverse the multiverse at their own volition. "I travel the time streams," says the Rose, "in search of my revenge."[43] The Phatts are experienced travellers between the worlds; they expect one day to

> learn the plan of the entire multiverse and travel at will from Sphere to Sphere, from realm to realm, from world to world, travel through the great clouds of shifting, multicoloured stars, the tumbling planets in all their millions, through galaxies that swarm like gnats in a summer garden, and rivers of light—glory beyond glory—pathways of moonbeams between the roaming stars.[44]

The family's clairvoyance spans the realms. His son, Fallogard says, "has found pathways through the realms that I had not even heard rumoured. And the girl [his niece Charion] can seek out an individual through all the layers of the multiverse. She is a bloodhound, that child."[45]

And realm-travelling, now, involves time dislocation. When Elric meets Wheldrake after the destruction of the Gypsy Nation, it has been a matter of hours since he has seen the poet, but Wheldrake has lived through a year of wandering, and a number of years seem to have passed for the Phatts: Charion has grown from a sullen girl into a self-sufficient young woman. The multiverse fascinated Moorcock early in his career by proposing a myriad of alternate universes, echoing and ringing variations on one another. Now, he finds himself increasingly fascinated with the narrative potentialities of a *traversable* multiverse, of a multiverse in which travel between realms also involves travel across time, and of characters who can easily tread the webs of "moonbeam roads" from one realm, one age, to another.

* * *

Moorcock had asserted that he had brought the tale of the Eternal Champion to a close with *The Quest for Tanelorn*, then provided another ending for the cycle in *The Dragon in the Sword*; he had made scant reference to the Champion in *The Fortress of the Pearl* and *The Revenge of the Rose*, and none at all in the von Bek novels. Nevertheless, he would revive the concept in a big way over the 1990s, as he oversaw the collection of the bulk of his fantasy and science fiction novels in two series of uniform "omnibus" editions, under the titles "The Tale of the Eternal Champion" (in the UK) and "The Eternal Champion" (in the U.S.). The omnibuses, assembled by Moorcock with his editor and bibliographer John Davey, are a crucial moment of consolidation in Moorcock's writing career. By presenting the vast majority of his fiction under the collective title of "Eternal Champion," Moorcock asserts that his fiction has a unity of theme, a central continuity that goes beyond its having been produced by a single author. And much of this work Moorcock had never properly proofread, much less extensively revised. These omnibus publications gave him the chance to revisit his work, in some cases substantially altering texts so that they refer more directly to other works in his now-coalescing canon.

In 1992 and 1993, Millennium Books, one of the UK's foremost science fiction and fantasy publishers, issued a fourteen-volume set of Moorcock omnibus volumes under the title "The Tale of the Eternal Champion."[46] Many of the volumes were named after their central protagonists. *Von Bek* collected both von Bek novels, plus the 1965 short story "The Pleasure Garden of Felipe Sagittarius." *The Eternal Champion* included the John Daker/Erekosë/Urlik Skarsol novels. *Hawkmoon* and *Count Brass* collected the seven Hawkmoon novels, while the Elric stories (including *The Fortress of the Pearl* and *The Revenge of the Rose*) were arranged by internal chronology in *Elric of Melniboné* and *Stormbringer*. Corum's two trilogies appeared as *Corum* and *The Prince with the Silver Hand*. Other volumes, not so obviously parts of the Eternal Champion mythos, included two volumes collecting the End of Time novels and stories; *A Nomad of the Time Streams* (the Bastable trilogy); *Earl Aubec* (a heterogeneous collection of short stories); and *The New Nature of the Catastrophe*, Jerry Cornelius stories by Moorcock and various others—but not including the principal Cornelius tetralogy. *Sailing to Utopia* collected *The Ice Schooner* and two other science fiction novels, *The Black Corridor* (with Hilary Bailey) and *The Distant Suns* (with James Cawthorn), as well as the short story "Flux" (1963).

The Millennium "Tale of the Eternal Champion" was complete by December 1993, and the following year the American firm White Wolf—which was far better known as a publisher of role playing games than of fiction, but which had taken its name from one of Moorcock's epithets for Elric—began to issue a very similar omnibus series under the title "The

Eternal Champion." White Wolf was unable to print the material in *The New Nature of the Catastrophe*, as rights were already held by another American publisher, but it added two collections that Millennium did not include: *Kane of Old Mars*, the trilogy of Burroughs pastiches Moorcock published in 1965; and *The Roads Between the Worlds*, three of Moorcock's science fiction novels from the 1960s: *The Wrecks of Time* (1965–66), *The Winds of Limbo* (1965), and *The Shores of Death* (1966).[47] The White Wolf series also adds *The Sundered Worlds*, the book in which Moorcock first introduced his multiverse, to its own version of the *Eternal Champion* volume; to make room, *The Dragon in the Sword* is shifted to the *Von Bek* volume.

The White Wolf omnibus series "The Eternal Champion," whose last volume was published when Moorcock was sixty, collects something over forty-five separate previously published books, and in putting it together Moorcock is not merely *collecting* his disparate works, but actively *consolidating* them under the aegis of the figure of the Eternal Champion. Other authors' collected fictions have had more contingent titles: Sir Walter Scott's books were the "Waverley Novels" only because *Waverley* happened to be the title of the first one published, and the title of his "Magnum Opus" edition of 1829–1833 simply indicated the edition's size (forty-eight volumes). The title of Henry James's "New York Edition" of 1907–1909 reflected the home of James's youth and the setting of some of his stories, but mostly the place of the edition's publication. And while Honoré Balzac eventually came to see most of his novels and stories as part of a vast interlinked work, the "Comédie Humaine," that very title (the "human comedy," along the lines of Dante's *Divine Comedy*) is all-encompassing, rather than specific. But "The Eternal Champion" as a collective title actively implies that the protagonists of these books are all manifestations of that figure, all participate somehow in the eternal struggle between Law and Chaos.

One suspects that Moorcock has gone too far, that a number of characters who have pretty much nothing in common with his more long-established Eternal Champion avatars have suddenly found themselves sailing under Champion's colors. That is, there is a clear "core set" of four Champions, those who came together to fight Agak and Gagak in *The Sailor on the Seas of Fate* and *The Quest for Tanelorn*: John Daker/Erekosë, Elric, Dorian Hawkmoon, and Corum. Beyond that, there are the figures who are recognizable transmutations of those Champions: Jerry Cornelius, for instance, the 1960s-model updating of Elric, or Jherek Carnelian, the naïf version of Jerry. But then there are a range of protagonists who never, in the context of their own stories, give any hint of Champion-like representativeness: Michael Kane of the Old Mars novels, a stalwart warrior in the Burroughs mode, but in no perceivable way a partisan of Law, Chaos, Balance, or anything else; or Oswald Bastable, less an actor in his own stories than a kind of human hockey puck, bounced from one set of loyalties to another. Or the protagonists of Moorcock's science fiction novels of the 1960s, a heterogeneous group if ever there was one: Alan Powys of *The Winds of Limbo*, Clovis Marca of *The Shores of Death*, Faustaff, the burly, ribald world-engineer of *The Wrecks of Time*, Ryan, the hanging-by-a-thread space-emigrant of *The Black Corridor*.

The concept of the Eternal Champion, as it first emerges in "The Eternal Champion" and as it is developed through the Elric, Corum, Hawkmoon, and further John Daker novels, is firmly rooted in the narrative and moral universe of heroic fantasy, and beyond that the structural conventions of popular adventure fiction, even of medieval romance. A "champion" is a champion *of* something, and by definition struggles on behalf of one side, coded "right," against another, coded "wrong." Moorcock rightly avoids the overtly moral vocabulary of "good" and "evil," but the basic structure of a heroic protagonist battling malevolent antagonist(s), remains in place through the majority of his fantasy writing. At first glance, then, it seems incongruous for Moorcock to collect narratives of a far more ambiguous structure—whether the seriocomic moral quest of Jherek Carnelian, who (unconsciously) seeks a deeper moral foundation for his experimental infatuation he has found blossoming into actual *love*, or the desperate wanderings of Oswald Bastable, who like Stephen Dedalus finds history (or in Bastable's case *histories*) "a nightmare from which I am trying to awake"[48]—under the totalizing, even simplying, sign of the "Eternal Champion."

But I think that Moorcock, rather than shoehorning a miscellaneous cast of protagonists into a heroic fantasy hero-position, is suggesting that the term "champion" might be a bit more elastic than it initially appears. After all, while they may not be battling commanders of Chaos at the heads of mutant armies, there is something quite admirable, humane, and perhaps even heroic about Jherek Carnelian's willingness to renounce his utopian End of Time, even to acquire a *conscience*, in order to win Amelia Underwood's love; or Ryan's desperate struggle to maintain his sanity in the pitiless solitude of deep space in *The Black Corridor*; or even Jephraim Tallow's quixotic pursuit of an ideal-saturated golden barge that forever eludes him (in *The Golden Barge*, Moorcock's oldest surviving novel, collected in *Earl Aubec*). Tanelorn, after all, is as much a possibility in each of our minds as it is a city in (fictive) reality. To struggle for resolution in one's life, one might venture, is as much a mark of a Champion of the Balance as the most spectacular feats of sword-play.

* * *

Collecting one's life's works—even in admittedly incomplete form, since neither of the Moorcock omnibus editions includes the Cornelius novels, the three Pyat novels already published, the comic Jerry Cornell novels, or anything like a comprehensive assembly of his short fiction—is inevitably an opportunity for retrospection and reassessment, perhaps for revision. Scott went to considerable pains to revise the Waverley novels for his "Magnum Opus" edition; in the case of *The Bride of Lammermoor*, he went so far as to shift the action of the novel from before the 1707 Act of Union (between Scotland and England) to some two or three years *after* that act, in order to mend a legal improbability in his original plot.[49] James was even more radical in his revisions for the "New York Edition" of his fiction, rewriting his earlier works on a sentence-by-sentence level so that they conformed more closely to his later, super-subtle prose style.

The majority of Moorcock's novels had gone straight from his typewriter to the publisher, in more or less first-draft form. His books were written according to the ethos of the popular market, and while the omnibus versions—some of them—show evidence of stylistic revision here and there, for the most part Moorcock allows them to retain their hot-off-the-typewriter freshness. Of the Michael Kane books, Moorcock writes, "I somehow feel that they should appear as they were written: flaws, internal jokes, enthusiasms, respect for genre conventions, and all, so you'll find hardly a word changed here."[50] The Runestaff tetralogy was "written rapidly in the mid-sixties and I think I'm wise enough, these days," writes Moorcock, "not to interfere too elaborately with work which, if it lacks polish, carries the unmistakable mark of a time when we all, young and old, seemed to have more energy and a perhaps naïve belief that we could swiftly improve the world for everyone."[51] Of the science fiction novels collected in *The Roads Between the Worlds*, Moorcock writes, "I have, with John Davey's help, made the few revisions necessary for inclusion here, but have otherwise had the sense not to begin tinkering with them. Whatever vitality they possess has not been refined to extinction."[52] It's fairly safe to say, then, that actual *revision*, the correction, reworking, rewriting of the previous texts, has not played a large role in the consolidation of Moorcock's work in "The Eternal Champion" omnibus series. Except in two cases: one of them a matter of nomenclature, of a rather pervasive series of name-changes that extend across a broad swathe of

Moorcock's fiction, long and short; and the other a case of wholesale rewriting, that of the last section of *The Steel Tsar* (1981), the third Oswald Bastable novel.

In much of his early writing, Moorcock bestows names on people and places with mixed success: "Elric," "Melniboné," and "Imrryr" are splendid (even if "Elric" seems to come from a Poul Anderson-Lord Dunsany box of standard-issue Elven names—compare Dunsany's Alveric and Anderson's Alfric and Imric[53]), but the contiguous countries of Jharkor and Dharijor are too sketchily described to be distinguished one from another, especially by name, and Lin Carter is surely right to deride the name of Moorcock's lost city of R'lin K'ren A'a as apt to give a reader "indigestion."[54] The names of Moorcock's invented cities, countries, and minor characters seem all too often hastily cast-off snarls of semi-pronounceable graphemes. But from at least the end of the 1960s, he grows more and more interested in the possibilities of tying the various domains of his imagined universes together by the device of repeated, altered, or anagrammatized names.

There are any number of examples, and I won't even go into the moments when Moorcock has introduced himself or his literary and musical associates into his fiction by putting their names (anagrammatized, reversed, or punned upon) into his stories—his friendly "in-jokes," as it were. But it is only a small step from *Elric*, for instance, to *Urlik* Skarsol, another avatar of the Champion, and the difference between the two names is split in that of *Ulrich* von Bek (another *Ulric* von Bek will appear later). Una Persson of the Cornelius stories will reappear in the Bastable books, and her name will be echoed in the similar characters of Una Countess of Scaithe (*Gloriana; or, The Unfulfill'd Queen*) and Oone the dreamthief (*The Fortress of the Pearl*).

By far the most name-play is generated by "Jerry Cornelius." The name, which Moorcock borrowed from a "local greengrocer" back in 1965, is one of his happiest *trouvées*: it marries the familiar ("Jerry") and the exotic, foreign ("Cornelius"), the Hebrew prophetic ("Jeremiah") and the Classical.[55] If Cornelius was a Champion for the Age of Entropy in the late 1960s, his name almost immediately began appearing in diverse variations in Moorcock's other books. The seedy spy of *The Chinese Agent* and *The Russian Intelligence* is Jerry Cornell, his perpetually embarrassing family an over-the-top parody of Cornelius's. A slightly more serious variation on the Cornelius character is Jherek Carnelian, and the name has its versions among the minor characters and Companions of the Champion mythos: Jhary-a-Conel is Corum's sidekick, and the dwarf Jermays the

Crooked appears in *Stormbringer*,[56] *Phoenix in Obsidian*, and *The Dragon in the Sword*. The boy who is the spirit of the Runestaff in the fourth Hawkmoon novel is Jehamia Cohnahlias. The full name and title *Corum Jhaelen Irsei*, the Prince in the Scarlet Robe, is an anagram of *Jeremiah Cornelius*, as *Jerry Cornelius* can be rearranged to make the unpronounceable *J'osui C'reln Reyr*, the Creature Doomed to Live in "The Jade Man's Eyes."

The name that had come to most occupy Moorcock by the 1990s, when he was compiling the "Eternal Champion" volumes, was not Cornelius but *Bek*. The Eternal Champion was a singular figure, if he appeared in a myriad of different avatars. But "Bek" names not a person but a family—Graf Ulrich von Bek of *The War Hound and the World's Pain*, Manfred von Bek of *The City in the Autumn Stars*, Rickhardt von Bek of *The Brothel in Rosenstrasse*, Ulric von Bek in *The Dragon in the Sword*.[57] And while some von Beks might be identified with the Eternal Champion, and the family as a whole has a certain guardianship relation with the Holy Grail, the Bek name is as likely to cast up wastrels and nonentities as any other family.

From the turn of the 1980s/1990s, Moorcock was busily expanding the Bek franchise, inventing new family members and cognate branches of the family—Beggs, Becks, even Bekovs. In 1995 he released *Lunching with the Antichrist, A Family History: 1925–2015*, a collection of stories published over the previous two decades, all of them concerned with various Becks (or Beggs, etc.). These characters' individual quests for the Grail are not necessarily mystical, Arthurian endeavors, as in *The War Hound*: "The Grail has occasionally turned out to be a rather spectacular cup with magical properties," Moorcock writes in his introduction, "but more often it has taken the form of relationships, sexual fulfillment, spiritual revelation." These stories "are mostly about people looking for some kind of resolution or meaning to their lives."[58] Of these stories, perhaps the most striking is "Lunching with the Antichrist," an elegiac tale of a disgraced London clergyman, Edwin Begg, and his strange love affair with the Rose, a "sentient flower," and how together they give birth to "a new human creature, neither male nor female but self-reproducing, a new messiah, and it set us free at last to dwell on that vast multiplicity of the heavens, to contemplate a quasi-infinity of versions of ourselves, our histories, our experience."[59] The story is an index of where Moorcock's focus was turning in the mid-nineties: although some of the motifs are familiar from earlier works—the hermaphroditic messiah-figure, most notably, from *The Final Programme* and *The City in the Autumn Stars*—Moorcock is much more interested in the intersection between this humble Begg's message of humanity and common decency and the glimpse of transcendence afforded to him by the Rose.

The two oldest stories in *Lunching with the Antichrist*, "Dead Singers" (1974, as "A Dead Singer") and "Crossing into Cambodia" (1979, part of the sequence *My Experiences in the Third World War*), seem on their face quite unrelated to the Bek-Begg-Beck mythos Moorcock had begun with 1981's *The War Hound and the World's Pain*. And indeed, Moorcock has made them into Bek stories by the simple expedient of changing their protagonist's names. "A Dead Singer" revolves around Shakey Mo Collier, a minor character in the Cornelius novels and stories; in the *Lunching with the Antichrist* "Dead Singers," he has become "Mo Beck."[60] "Crossing into Cambodia"'s originally nameless narrator, a Russian intelligence agent assigned as liaison to a Cossack unit fighting in Vietnam, is brought into the family with a single line inserted in the 1995 edition: "You're the intellectual, Bekov."[61] Moorcock has made a disparate collection of twenty years of his short fiction—some fantastic, some futuristic, some slightly uncanny, and some baldly realistic—into a "family history" by changing his characters' names, much as he's made Michael Kane and Oswald Bastable "Eternal Champions" by reprinting their adventures under that title.

What Moorcock does for a few of his stories in *Lunching with the Antichrist*, he does on a rather larger scale in a number of the novels reprinted in the Eternal Champion omnibuses. When he includes *The Sundered Worlds*, his first science fiction novel (and his first exploration of the multiverse) in *The Eternal Champion*, the opening volume of the White Wolf series, Moorcock is careful to frame its somewhat anomalous appearance there. It is placed between *The Eternal Champion* (the 1970 novel, that is) and *Phoenix in Obsidian*, interrupting the continuity of those two John Daker novels; but Moorcock supplies a brief bridge passage in which John Daker dreams of the "Warriors on the Edge of Time" (who will appear in *The Dragon in the Sword*) and of Renark of the Rim, the protagonist of the first half of *The Sundered Worlds*.[62] More crucially, Renark, who is merely "Jon Renark," former Warden of the Rim in the 1965 first edition of the novel, has become "Renark von Bek, Count of the Rim," in the 1994 omnibus.

The White Wolf edition of *The Eternal Champion* is a rather more heterogeneous volume than the identically-titled Orion/Millennium version, which simply serves up the three John Daker novels—*The Eternal Champion, Phoenix in Obsidian*, and *The Dragon in the Sword*—in order of composition. The White Wolf edition also adds the Elric-world story "To Rescue Tanelorn…," which like *The Sundered Worlds* has no clear continuity with the Daker novels. But renaming Renark serves to tie him in both with the Eternal Champion mythos and the von Bek family, and by gathering these four texts (*The Eternal Champion*, *The Sundered Worlds*, *Phoenix in Obsidian*, and "To Rescue Tanelorn...") Moorcock is able to present four of his central motifs—the Eternal Champion, the multiverse, the Black Sword, and Tanelorn as ideal of balance and moderation—in a single volume, the introduction or overture to his works as a whole.

The White Wolf *Eternal Champion*, then, gives us the major leitmotifs of Moorcock's subsequent work, and a foretaste of the Bek "countermelody," as it were. The second volume of the series, *Von Bek*, collects *The War Hound and the World's Pain*, *The City in the Autumn Stars*, and *The Dragon in the Sword* (which is, after all, both a John Daker *and* a von Bek novel), and adds the 1965 short story "The Pleasure Garden of Felipe Sagittarius," which Moorcock regards as a "key" work, presumably because it's one of his earliest successful ventures into the realms of alternate history and scrambled timelines.[63] The story, which is a kind of hard-boiled *noir* mystery, is set in a ruined, temporally unidentified Berlin, where Otto von Bismarck is the Chief of Police, Adolf Hitler a minor police official, Kurt Weill a nightclub musician, and Albert Einstein a barfly. The narrator, in the story's first version, is "Minos Aquilinas, top Metatemporal Investigator in Europe"; in the omnibus *Von Bek*, he has become "Minos von Bek."[64] Similarly, the protagonist Max File of the 1963 short story "Flux," has his name changed to "Max von Bek" in the omnibus *Sailing to Utopia*.

The densest cluster of Bek-namings, however, occurs in the sixth volume of the White Wolf series, *The Roads Between the Worlds*, which has no counterpart in the Orion/Millennium series. The pattern ought to be clear by now: Moorcock has been given the opportunity, rare enough for a "mainstream" author and almost unheard of for a "genre" writer, to collect the vast majority of his work in uniform editions; the science fiction potboilers he wrote in the early-to-mid-sixties seem extremely difficult to assimilate to the figure of the "Eternal Champion," but they can be woven into the grand tapestry of his interconnected fictive multiverse by making them part of the loosely-woven Bek mythos—by rechristening their characters. So in *The Winds of Limbo*, the protagonist Alan Powys becomes "Alain von Bek," his father Simon Powys "Simon von Bek" (thereby losing, alas, Moorcock's gentle homage to the great novelist John Cowper Powys). In *The Shores of Death*, Clovis Marca becomes Clovis Becker. Moorcock is understandably reluctant to give up the Marlovian and Shakespearean resonances in the name of Doctor Faustaff, the protagonist of *The Wrecks of Time*, but the Doctor's principal antagonist, "Steifflomeis" in the early editions, becomes "Klosterheim," familiar to readers of *The War Hound and the World's Pain* and *The City in the Autumn Stars*, and a minor character, Gordon Ogg, becomes "Gordon Begg."

In *The Roads Between the Worlds*, Moorcock ties together these really very disparate science fiction adventures, not merely through a bit of name-changing among their characters, but by a series of frame passages introducing each novel, and featuring "Renark von Bek, Count of the Rim."[65] This Renark is a seasoned, experienced traveller of the multiverse, a kind of interdimensional Allan Quatermain presented in prose that echoes Victorian adventure-exploration stories. And his multiversal travels are described in the language and concepts of Moorcock's Second Ether books—*Blood* (1995), *Fabulous Harbours* (1995), and *The War Amongst the Angels* (1996): the realms of the multiverse are matters of "scale," Renark carries a Purdy rifle loaded with angel-shot, he encounters the *Now The Clouds Have Meaning*, "perhaps best known of all the famous Chaos Engineers' ships."[66] Each of the three novels of *The Roads* is presented as one of Renark's memories of a previous adventure, and thereby Moorcock embeds the oldest of his science fiction writings in the framework of his most recent conception, the high-spirited, hyperbolic, not-quite-serious world of the Second Ether. But the last of the frame narratives, and the ending of the volume as a whole, seeks to bring together all of these conceptual strands: the Second Ether, the Bek family, the Eternal Champion mythos—not to mention Tanelorn, The Holy Grail, and the motif of the "moonbeam roads":

> Renark von Bek, Count of the Rim, turns from where the tail of the Chaos ship vanishes down-scale. He eases the strap of his Purdy on his shoulder, takes off his hat and runs his hands through his pale hair. Then he prepares to continue his long walk along the moonbeam roads, to pursue his eternal quest for that lost treasure of antiquity, the stewardship of which his family had undertaken in its earliest centuries; that Grail which he has sworn to restore to Bek. And, as he walks, all his descendants, all his ancestors, walk with him, an eternal champion, eternally reincarnated, eternally destined to destroy all that comforts him, to restore justice and virtue to the multiverse, to seek the peace of fabled Tanelorn, to walk the roads between the worlds.[67]

* * *

Of all of the changes Moorcock made to his books for the Eternal Champion omnibuses, his revisions to *The Steel Tsar* are the most far-reaching. *The Warlord of the Air* (1971) was a success, in his words "a nice little Edwardian pastiche, and a rehearsal for later Cornelius books."[68] The next Bastable book, *The Land Leviathan* (1974), was frankly "a commercial sequel." And Moorcock wrote the third volume, *The Steel Tsar* (1981), under both financial and personal pressures—he needed the money, and was in the middle of a disintegrating and physically violent relationship; indeed, he settled for half of his promised advance on the book, seeing how disappointed his publisher Donald Wollheim was with the finished product.[69] (Twenty thousand words of *The Steel Tsar* came as "seed" material from leftover misplaced drafts of *Warlord*: "my daughter Kate found it under her bed, so I used it!"[70])

The Steel Tsar uses the same alternate history framework as the two previous Bastable books. Where *The Warlord of the Air* contemplated British imperialism and *The Land Leviathan* race relations and post-colonialism, *The Steel Tsar* explores, in an admittedly rather tired and half-hearted fashion, the history of twentieth-century Russia, where the utopian ideals of anarchism and Marxist socialism fell afoul (in both our world and Bastable's) of the ruthless opportunism of a series of authoritarian leaders. But Moorcock recognized, when first drafting the book, that this was the point at which he could provide Bastable with an "out"— that here he had the opportunity to give his longsuffering protagonist some measure of peace, by allying him to a group of congenial time travellers, the League of Temporal Adventurers, represented by Una Persson.[71] The first version of *The Steel Tsar* is indeed a "crude" book, as Colin Greenland comments: its final section, in which the reader meets an alternate version of Josef Stalin and witnesses his betrayal of the heroic anarchist Nestor Makhno, is huddled together and rushed through in an almost painfully transparent manner.[72]

But when he came to collect the Bastable novels for the Eternal Champion omnibus series, Moorcock saw the opportunity to mend some of the flaws of that first version, and to bind the trilogy as a whole more closely in with his other works. In part this involves renaming minor characters: In *The Warlord of the Air* "Lieutenant Allsop" become "Lieutenant Begg," and "Major General Fry" becomes "Major General Nye," a name shared with two military characters in the Cornelius novels, while the revolutionary "Count Rudolph von Dutchke" ("Count Rudolfo Guevara" in the 1978 DAW edition) becomes "Count Rudoph von Bek." "Captain Harding" becomes "Captain Quelch," a familiar figure in the Second Ether series. In *The Land Leviathan*, the racist provisional U.S. president's name has been changed from "Penfield" to "Beesley," thus associating him with the Cornelius novels' Bishop Beesley. In *The Steel Tsar*, "Greaves" has become "Nye," and "Shawcross" has become "Underwood," perhaps tying him to Amelia Underwood of the Dancers at the End of Time trilogy.

More notable is Moorcock's rewriting and expansion of the novel's final section. In part he fleshes out the character of Djugashvili, the "Steel Tsar" of the title; more importantly he adds far more material regarding Bastable's initiation into the League of Temporal Adventurers. In the first edition of the novel, Bastable's initiation is rather perfunctory: Una Persson mentions the League to him some fifteen pages from the end of the novel, and at the conclusion he bids farewell to the reader as a full-fledged member.[73] In the revised version of *The Steel Tsar*, in company with Una Persson and Cornelius Dempsey[74] (a character whose experience mirrors his own in *Warlord*) Bastable suddenly has insights into the structure and workings of the multiverse, and begins to recognize his own identity as an avatar of the Eternal Champion. Una introduces him to Max von Bek—not present at all in the 1981 version—a red-eyed albino who also identifies himself as "Monsieur Zenith," a metatemporal traveller alternately visible and invisible to the other characters. This von Bek clearly evokes Elric, but also evokes Zenith the albino, a long-running villain in the Sexton Blake detective series, which Moorcock edited and wrote for at the very outset of his career.[75]

It is easy to see why Moorcock regarded the rewriting of *The Steel Tsar* as a "pivot"[76] around which the whole consolidating enterprise of the Eternal Champion omnibuses would revolve, for any number of the elements of his various fictive structures are presented in this new-modeled *Nomad of the Time Streams*: the von Bek and Eternal Champion *mythoi*; the newly open, traversable conception of the multiverse; and most importantly, the continual struggle for human dignity, autonomy, and toleration of difference that has been the constant ground-bass of Moorcock's fiction. Intriguingly, Moorcock's revisions—and here I'm thinking as well of *The Roads Between the Worlds*—also serve both to point forward to his current imagined worlds of the Second Ether, and to gesture back toward the genre writing—Sexton Blake, Victorian adventure stories, the Western—of his childhood, which he would soon begin to draw upon for inspiration in a larger and more explicit way.

* * *

It's an open question what difference this vast effort of consolidation and filiation represented in the Orion/Millennium and White Wolf omnibuses makes in a *reading* of Moorcock's fiction. The effect of most of the name changes, for instance, is fairly nugatory: we have a small chuckle when we encounter Gordon *Begg* in *The Wrecks of Time* (in *the Roads Between the Worlds*), but the change of name doesn't make him any more or less significant than when we met him as Gordon Ogg in *The Rituals of Infinity* (the book's title in its 1978 U.S. paperback edition). And the overarching conception of the "Eternal Champion," while it provides a useful umbrella for much of Moorcock's early fantasy, and is complicated and subtilized in interesting ways for his mid-period work, still proves very difficult to relate to much of his miscellaneous science fiction.

The collected writings of any author show a series of family resemblances from work to work. But Moorcock, consciously and unconsciously, has been writing new variations on his basic motifs—his themes, his characters, his plot structures—from the very beginning. The work as a whole coheres as a complex musical edifice, with or without the aid of a series of tellingly-similar name-tags, or an overarching specific title like "The Eternal Champion." I think it significant that the most recent, "definitive" collection of Moorcock's work by the UK publisher Gollancz, which incorporates practically *everything* except the Pyat novels and the two London books, *Mother London* and *King of the City*, was to be launched under the title "Moorcock's Multiverse." But even that seems perhaps a bit too confining. Now it stands as "The Michael Moorcock Collection"—a collection which is, in Alan Moore's words, an "intertextual and organic whole"; or in John Clute's, "a 100 books that make up one book."[77]

6

The Second Ether, the Moonbeam Roads and Beyond

It's hard to know what part the great mass of fantasy novels Moorcock produced at white-hot speed over the late 1960s and early1970s will play in his long-term reputation. Those tales of the Eternal Champion were written rapidly—in three to ten days apiece—and very consciously formulaically, but they were not written cynically. "I have always believed, somewhat puritanically," Moorcock reflects, "in giving the audience good value for money. I enjoyed writing them, tried to avoid repetition, and through each one was able to develop a few more ideas."[1] Readers have certainly enjoyed these books: for better or worse, much of Moorcock's popular reputation rests on the adventures of Hawkmoon, Corum, and of course of Elric.

Moorcock gave up writing three-day epics by the 1980s, however, and by the mid–1990s, having established himself with *Mother London* and the first three volumes of the Pyat Quartet as a writer of non-fantastic fiction, and having established a kind of canonical order to his fantasy novels with the "Eternal Champion" omnibus volumes, he settled down to writing fantasy unapologetically: no more renunciations. The fantastic fiction Moorcock has written over the last two decades—and I will intentionally avoid the question of whether these books should be classified as "fantasy," "science fiction," or some hybrid of the two—quite deliberately extend and complicate the various conceptual structures and *mythoi* of his earlier books. The "Second Ether" books—*Blood* (1995), *Fabulous Harbours* (1995), and *The War Amongst the Angels* (1996)—reimagine the multiverse and the eternal struggle between Law and Chaos in terms derived from Moorcock's reading in chaos theory. As strikingly, they present a pair of richly imagined universes: the one, a kind of racially-inverted post-apocalyptic American South, the other a constantly shifting overlay of differently "scaled" planes of existence, navigated by motley crews of adventurers who pay high-spirited homage to the space operas and pirate stories of Moorcock's youth. The figure of the Rose, the plant-human hybrid first introduced in the Elric novel *The Revenge of the Rose* (1986) is central to these books.

The three long novels of the Moonbeam Roads trilogy (2001–2005) are in effect a major reboot of the Elric franchise; more accurately, these books extend the von Bek mythos, incorporating Elric, the Rose, and various Elric-avatars as central figures therein. The final volume of the trilogy, *Son of the Wolf* (2005, as *The White Wolf's Son*), provides yet another "ending" for the Eternal Champion saga. Of course, Moorcock had "ended" the saga at least three times previously, in *The Quest for Tanelorn* (1975), *The Dragon in the Sword* (1986), and *The War Amongst the Angels*. This ending is no more definitive, no more "final" than any of the previous ones, though it does form a rather neat conceptual loop. But Moorcock has asserted—definitively this time, it would seem—that he will write no further Elric novels, that he is no longer interested in embroidering the adventures of the Eternal Champion. Instead, in his latest project, "The Sanctuary of the White Friars" (first volume *The Whispering Swarm*, 2015), he has begun writing in a mode of juxtaposed autobiography and portal fantasy, mining the genre fiction of his youth to produce a vivid allegory of the fiction-making process itself.

* * *

"Science fiction" is a fundamentally oxymoronic term, putting side-by-side the names we use for the pursuit of true knowledge about the world ("science") and the art of making up untrue stories ("fiction"). Early in the twentieth century, SF periodicals eagerly asserted their scientific *bona fides*; *Amazing Stories* bore the slogan "Extravagant Fiction Today.... Cold Fact Tomorrow," *Science Wonder Stories* "Prophetic Fiction Is the Mother of Scientific Fact." Hugo Gernsback's magazines occasionally ran contests awarding prizes to readers who could find scientific or logical errors in their stories.[2] But science fiction writers have always used the plausibility of the scientific as a rationalization for the counter-factuality of the worlds and situations they create, and some of them more cavalierly than others. Moorcock's work has often been influenced by contemporary developments in scientific thought and technological innovation—the concept of "entropy," as mediated (probably) by Norbert Wiener, in the *New Worlds*-period fiction, or the rise of supercomputing as reflected in

The Final Programme. But it's in his Second Ether books of the mid–1990s that he most enthusiastically, if playfully, adopts the images and vocabulary of a particular scientific development: the so-called "Chaos theory" that had been explored by mathematicians, physicists, economists, meteorologists, and others since the early 1970s, and which had begun filtering into the popular media by the mid- to late 1980s.

Chaos theory is the science of turbulence, of seeming disorder: a search for the underlying mathematical and physical principles of phenomena—the shifting movements of clouds, the behaviour of liquid particles in a waterfall, the curlicues and whorls into which the smoke from a cigarette breaks after its initial vertical ascent—that seem on their face random. The theorists of chaos, in the words of James Gleick, "believed that simple, determinist systems could breed complexity; that systems too complex for traditional mathematics could obey simple laws; and that, whatever their particular field, their task was to understand complexity itself."[3] It's understandable why a writer with a well-developed interest in the opposition between Chaos and Law would be interested in a scientific discourse that aims precisely to investigate the relationship of order and disorder, to explore how "the simplest systems ... create extraordinarily difficult problems of predictability. Yet order arises spontaneously in these systems—chaos and order together."[4]

Perhaps most importantly, chaos theory—specifically the fractal geometry of the French mathematician Benoit Mandelbrot—offered Moorcock a new and more vivid way to conceive and to visualize his multiverse. "Mandelbrot," he says in one interview, "supplied me with a map of my own brain."[5] Fractals are shapes, generated by mathematical equations, that display an equal degree of ornamented complexity at whatever resolution we observe them, what Mandelbrot calls "self-similarity": "Self-similarity is symmetry across scales. It implies recursion, pattern inside pattern."[6] Mandelbrot found fractal patterns in the fluctuations of cotton prices, in electronic transmission noise, in the pattern of river floods. He came to believe that the overall geometry of nature was fractal.

In exploring the details of the collection of points known as a "Mandelbrot set," researchers found that

> any segment—no matter where, and no matter how small—would, when blown up by the computer microscope, reveal new molecules, each resembling the main set and yet not quite the same. Every new molecule would be surrounded by its own spiral, and flame-like projections, and those, inevitably, would reveal molecules tinier still, always similar, never identical, fulfilling some mandate of infinite variety, a miracle of miniaturization in

6. The Second Ether, the Moonbeam Roads, and Beyond 145

which every new detail was sure to be a universe of its own, diverse and entire.[7]

This passage serves as a splendid description of the multiverse itself, as Moorcock conceives it in his Second Ether books.

Moorcock's earlier tales had presented the various realms of the multiverse as separate but to one degree or another similar; characters travelled from one realm to another by various means: the Eternal Champion might be summoned to a given realm by the inhabitants' incantations (*The Eternal Champion, Phoenix in Obsidian*); the Black Ship ferries Champions and heroes between the realms (*The Sailor on the Seas of Fate, The Quest for Tanelorn*); the Eldren sail, following a dragon, through a momentary "portal" to another world (*The Dragon in the Sword*). In more overtly science-fictional tales—that is, novels which make more of a show of rationalizing their fantastic elements—Renark leads humanity through the realms of the multiverse using alien technology (*The Sundered Worlds*), while Una Persson, Catherine and Jerry Cornelius, Oswald Bastable, and other members of the League of Temporal Adventurers move between different realities by switching "time-streams," moving from one alternate history to another.

In the fractal multiverse of Moorcock's Second Ether books, however, travel between realms is a matter of moving up and down dimensions, or "scales." This "Mandelbrotian" conception of the multiverse is handily laid out in Moorcock's short story "Through the Shaving Mirror." "Millions of different versions of our reality are separated by size," explains his character Monsignor Cornelius;

> Each version, though scarcely different in terms of the multiversal compass, is as invisible to us as if we were only seeing a single magnified pixel out of a complex computer image. We never see the whole. It is either too small or too large. We coexist in the same space through scale. Each alternative world has greater or lesser density and is invisible to the others.[8]

In Moorcock's 1995 novel *Blood: A Southern Fantasy*, we are told how the "wild-eyed Chaos Engineers, who cruise the Second Ether for adventure, curiosity and massive profit," "using the principles of *self-similarity*, pilot their peculiar craft up and down the scales. They call this process 'folding,' a kind of blossoming movement which enables their ships to progress in a series of 'folds' in which they 'lock scale' with a number of proscribed multiversal levels." As Professor Pop, deputy to Captain Billy-Bob Begg of the chaos ship *Now The Clouds Have Meaning*, explains, "we are dissipating and concentrating mass in ratio to size and so on—we can go 'up' scale or 'down' scale."⁹ The multiversal realms of the Second Ether through which the Chaos Engineers travel are mostly extraordinarily alien, inimical to human life. Our own corner of the multiverse, the "First Ether," is dominated by the culture of the "Singularity," which seeks to impose its linear reality upon the ever-shifting chaos of the Second Ether as well, and is opposed by the Chaos Engineers. The names of each party's ships are emblematic, and humorous: Singularity ships include *The Linear Bee, The Statement of Truth, Definitely Sagittarius, The Straight Arrow, The Only Way*; Chaos Engineers' are *I Don't Want to Go to Chelsea, Plum Blossom Local, Ruby Dances, My Memories, The Blue Gardenias*.

The ongoing adventures of the Chaos Engineers and their rivals, the captains of the Singularity (both groups in quest of the universe-sized sentient ship the *Spammer Gain*, who seeks her lost fishlings), are embedded within the text of *Blood* as a series of brief chapters from *Corsairs of the Second Ether*, a long-running serial adventure by "Warwick Colvin Jnr." They are fast-moving, high-spirited, and trashy, and are avidly read by Sam Oakenhurst, one of the principal characters of the overarching narrative of *Blood*. *Blood* takes place in an alternative, racially inverted American South—people of color dominate, while whites ("whities," "blancos") are treated as childlike inferiors and relegated to subservient positions—a world which is technologically advanced but energy-starved. The appearance of "colour spots," " a source of free apparently limitless energy," is greeted as a godsend. But in drilling into a mass of colour off the coast of Mississippi, wildcat engineers unwittingly open the "Biloxi Fault," an opening into "'ultra-reality,' the Source Matter of the universe," which has the effect of hastening the planet's descent into entropy.¹⁰ Oakenhurst and his friend Jack Karaquazian are gamblers—"jugadors," "mukhamirim"—adepts at games that range from the familiar poker to forbiddingly complex role-playing and world-building contests that take place in virtual reality. They travel this entropic world like a pair of high-tech riverboat gamblers, living from game to game. To some degree, *Blood* is a love story, narrating Karaquazian's guilt-sullied passion for the adventuress Colinda Dovero and Oakenhurst's love—and eventual sacrifice—for the Rose, the same half-human, half-plant hybrid readers had encountered in the Elric novel *The Revenge of the Rose*. Their major antagonist, at least in the early part of the novel, is Paul Minct, a grotesque masked figure who, it will become clear, is essentially identical to Prince Gaynor the Damned (from the Corum novels, and the object of the Rose's vengeance in *Revenge*).

The action of the first half of *Blood* takes place in this alternative South, with the adventures of the Chaos Engineers and the Singularity occasionally popping up as a kind of counterpoint in the magazines Sam Oakenhurst reads. In the latter part of the novel, however, we realize that the "primary" frame narrative—Biloxi, the jugadors, the colour spots—is actually contained *within* that pulpish story of the endless war of Plurality and the Singularity. The Rose leads Sam and Jack into the Second Ether, where they directly engage in that struggle, either as themselves or as incorporated into the identities of the famous Chaos Engineers: they play the *zeitjuego*, the great "Game of Time." It is all very fast-paced, high-spirited, and great fun: and even at times quite funny, as is up to this point unheard of in Moorcock's numerous grand facings-off between the forces of Chaos and Law. But Moorcock is able to strike a delicate balance between the pathos of his love relations (Jack-Colinda, Sam-the Rose) and the frenetic, cartoonish action of the struggle in the Second Ether, and ultimately endows both his Chaos Engineers and Singularity captains with a kind of ideological dignity.

Fabulous Harbours (1995) is not really a sequel to *Blood*, though it does fall neatly between that book and *The War Amongst the Angels*, a more expansive novelistic treatment of *Blood*'s cosmology.[11] *Fabulous Harbours* is a collection of short stories, framed as a series of fireside tales related among Jack Karaquazian, Colinda Dovero, the Rose, and a motley collection of Beks and Beggs. Like *Lunching with the Antichrist*, published the same year, this is a "Bek" book, a family portfolio of sorts.[12] Perhaps most notable are a brace of stories featuring the detective Sir Seaton Begg, Moorcock's version of the long-established English crime franchise Sexton Blake (he had edited the Sexton Blake Library some thirty-five years before),[13] and Begg's encounters with his distant cousin Ulrich von Bek, an albino European nobleman—from Mirenburg, of course—who bears a sentient black sword and has a special relationship with the Holy Grail. Von Bek is also known as "Monsieur Zenith"—Zenith the Albino, a memorable antagonist in the Sexton Blake tales—and his moral position is ambiguous at best. Frankly, one can almost sense how much *fun* Moorcock is having with these stories: he has combined his most famous creation, Elric the doomed albino, wielder of the Black Sword, with a more recent invention, the moody, Grail-bearing von Bek(s), and put the combination in orbit around Sexton Blake, a familiar commodity of British popular culture.

Avoiding the medievalist settings and plot clichés of heroic fantasy (except in the Elric story "The Black Blade's Summoning," which manages to rope in Renark von Bek and the Second Ether's Captain Quelch), the stories of *Fabulous Harbours* draw upon a range of the genre fictions with which Moorcock grew up: the pirate stories that inform "The White Pirate" (and indeed, the whole *Corsairs of the Second Ether*); the hard-boiled crime fiction of "The Girl Who Killed Sylvia Blade"; the desert adventure of "No Ordinary Christian." In *The War Amongst the Angels* (1996), Moorcock extends his revivification of popular genre even further, to the American Western tale—Buffalo Bill Cody and Wild Bill Hickok appear here, alongside Jack Karaquazian, Sam Oakenhurst, Colinda Dovero, and the Rose—and the seventeenth- and eighteenth-century highwayman narrative: in *Angels*, semi-legendary highwaymen Dick Turpin and Claude Duval are refigured as "tramway tobymen," robbers of the trolleycars which criss-cross Britain and America in an alternate twentieth century.

If *Blood* was a bold new departure for Moorcock, *The War Amongst the Angels* is an outright triumph, one of his most complex and satisfying fantasies. It is subtitled "An Autobiographical Story," and the autobiography is that of its principal narrator, Margaret Rose Moorcock—or, since she has been married to Rickhardt von Bek (of *The Brothel in Rosenstrasse*), Rose von Bek.[14] Rose is a creature of London (where her actress mother lives; in later years her mother will become "radio's 'Mrs Cornelius,' offering Cockney wisdom to afternoon listeners"[15]) and Yorkshire (where her father resides, and where Moorcock himself had a house for some years). Her "poor Texas cousin Michael" wrote serial stories featuring scores of heroes, until after a mental breakdown he retired to the "family ranch" and took up a local career as a "honky-tonk singer."[16] Rose herself, it becomes rapidly clear, is an "eternal," one of those who can roam the time streams at will; as "Captain Hawkmoon" she has robbed trams with Dick Turpin; she has lived among the Gypsy Nation with Elric and Ernest Wheldrake (*The Revenge of the Rose*); she has had an affair with the defrocked pastor Edwin Begg ("Lunching with the Antichrist"); she has explored the multiverse with Sam Oakenhurst; she has had who knows how many adventures across time and space.

The angelic war of the book's title is a continuation of the same struggle we saw in *Blood*, that between the Chaos Engineers and the lords of the Singularity, led by Old Reg—Lucifer, who reveals himself at the novel's climax in his full awful glory to Ulrich von Bek. (Von Bek ought by family tradition to be of the Devil's party, rather than fighting alongside the Chaos Engineers, Dick Turpin, the Rose, her father and uncle, the *jugadors* Sam and Jack, and a roll-call of others.) These travellers of the Second Ether manifest as "angels" when they intrude upon our own world, and it is in such scenes that Moorcock achieves his most striking effects: the angels,

6. The Second Ether, the Moonbeam Roads, and Beyond 149

whether singular or chaotic, are repulsive creatures, vast, misshapen, covered in shining carapaces, and stinking very, very badly.

The Second Ether books are quite unlike anything that's come before them in Moorcock's fantasy writing. Not merely do they boldly juxtapose and then integrate two wholly new fictive worlds—the alternative present of mixed technology, racial inversion, and "colour" and the shifting fractals of the Second Ether itself—but in their structure they step beyond the linear storytelling that had up to this point characterized Moorcock's fantasy. *Blood*, as I've noted, has an internal narrative which displaces and inverts its seemingly primary frame narrative. In *War*, not merely does Rose's storytelling jump backwards and forwards in time, but the narrative voice unexpectedly (and without notice) shifts to other characters; chapters from *Corsairs of the Second Ether* break into the narrative; and the final long sequence—the "battle scene," as it were—is told in a series of abrupt jump-cuts, shifting from focus to focus, narrator to narrator. In his mid-fifties, Moorcock has reached an enviable pitch of storytelling and world-evoking power, and deploys his skills in as virtuosic a manner as possible, at the same time never losing sight of the comic potentialities of his material.

* * *

Comics, of course—graphic storytelling—had been one of the media in which Moorcock had gotten his earliest start. His characters had by the 1990s been well represented in the graphic medium: there were adaptations by various hands of Elric, Hawkmoon, and Corum. But Moorcock had himself done relatively little work in comics since the early 1960s. Between 1969 and 1970 Moorcock and M. John Harrison wrote a comic strip, *The Adventures of Jerry Cornelius* (art by Mal Dean and R. Glyn Jones), for *International Times*. In 1972 Moorcock and James Cawthorn furnished the plot for two issues of the fantastically popular *Conan the Barbarian*, in which Elric is temporarily introduced into Conan's Hyborian world.[17] And Moorcock provided an outline for Howard Chaykin's Eternal Champion story *The Swords of Heaven, The Flowers of Hell* in 1979.

When Moorcock returned wholeheartedly to the graphic medium in 1997, he did so with a bang. *Michael Moorcock's Multiverse*, published first by DC Comics in twelve issues, then collected as a graphic novel in 1999, is an intricate and dazzling production, a kind of *summa* of Moorcock's fictional work to date.[18] It jumps among three different narratives, each drawn by a different artist in a radically different style, before finally making its separate storylines converge into a final, familiar struggle between Law and Chaos, ending with a restored Balance. "Moonbeams and Roses" (drawn by Walter Simonson) takes place in the universe of *Blood* and the Second Ether, and features the Rose, Jack Karaquazian, Sam Oakenhurt, Colinda Dovero, and the whole crew of Chaos Engineers and proponents of the Singularity—as well as Moorcock himself, a bemused and reluctant gambler at the gaming tables of Biloxi. "The Metatemporal Detective" (art by Mark Reeve) follows Sir Seaton Begg and sidekick "Taffy" Sinclair (modeled on Moorcock's friend the novelist Iain Sinclair), in company with the enigmatic albino Count Zodiac, through an alternative Nazi Germany and the London underworld in a quest for the Holy Grail that will eventually lead them to the mysterious "Silverskin"—seemingly Jerry Cornelius himself. "Duke Elric" (drawn by John Ridgway) sets the Melnibonéan prince, with little explanation, in Dark Ages Europe, from which he must travel to Africa, also in search of this Silverskin.[19]

The Silverskin, it finally emerges, is "every aspect of the Eternal Champion—in an agony of consciousness," embodied in a single form. It speaks to Elric in the accents of Arioch, his patron demon—"Come, sweetest of my selves—Come into my yearning heart"[20]—but Elric refuses to be absorbed, and instead plunges the Black Sword into Silverskin's heart; more or less simultaneously, the Chaos Engineer Professor Pop reverses the polarities of the First and Second Ether, freeing Pearl Peru from her imprisonment by the Singularity, and the *Spammer Gain* discovers her lost fishlings. The Balance in restored.

The three plots of *Michael Moorcock's Multiverse* are of remarkable intricacy, and shot through with ironic references to Moorcock's earlier books. At the same time, there is a refreshing looseness to the overall conceptual structure of the book, which moves forward like a jellyfish trailing dangling plot lines and unexplained events. The early Eternal Champion romances had sometimes threatened to collapse under the weight of their metaphysical stakes, the perpetual Law-Chaos struggle in which the world was perpetually in danger of annihilation. The stakes are of course the same in *Michael Moorcock's Multiverse*—and, for that matter, in *Blood* and *The War Amongst the Angels*—but Moorcock has come to handle them with a much more playful touch, to approach the fate of the multiverse as a game to be played, as seriously or as lightheartedly as one sees fit, rather than as an inevitably grim and mordant struggle.

* * *

One suspects that the three novels of the Moonbeam Roads sequence—*Daughter of Dreams* (2001, as *The Dreamthief's Daughter*),

Destiny's Brother (2003, as *The Skrayling Tree*), and *Son of the Wolf* (2005, as *The White Wolf's Son*)—will be Moorcock's last venture into heroic fantasy, the genre he did so much to define in the early sixties with his first Elric stories. He has said as much. In the introduction to a 2006 French omnibus, *Le Cycle d'Elric,* Moorcock writes, "with the publication of the last Elric book in the US, *The White Wolf's Son,* I resolved to write no more fantasy novels, convinced that I did not want to risk 'thinning' him out as I have seen happen to too many of my favourite series heroes. I have laid not only Elric to rest, but also the Eternal Champion."[21] These three novels, then, are written with the unmistakable intention of "wrapping up" the vast series of loosely interwoven fictions Moorcock had begun forty-four years earlier with "The Dreaming City"—or even earlier, when at seventeen he had drafted the first version of "The Eternal Champion."

The Moonbeam Roads novels outbulk most of what has come before in Moorcock's fantasy: each of them is over twice as long as one of the Eternal Champion novels he produced back in the seventies. This expanded length—along with, frankly, a far more generous writing schedule—allows Moorcock to mount more complex and carefully dovetailed plots; it allows him to present somewhat more detailed settings and descriptions; it allows his characters and narrators, for better or worse, to indulge in sometimes lengthy passages of philosophical, metaphysical, and moral speculation. There are perhaps too many moments in these three novels when the reader feels as though she is listening to a lecture on the nature of the multiverse, the relative merits of Law and Chaos, or the extent to which the human imagination not merely shapes, but *makes* reality. Moorcock, it seems, is writing a conceptual *summa,* laying out at length and in detail the metaphysical underpinnings of his fantasy.

Even as they present the theory of the multiverse in its more expansive form, these novels also draw in and (to some degree) harmonize the elements of a half-dozen different fictional sequences: Elric, the von Bek stories, the Oswald Bastable books, Hawkmoon, John Daker/Erekosë, Una Persson and the Guild of Temporal Adventurers. In the "first wave" of Eternal Champion romances back in the 1970s, Moorcock had staged moments of crossover, near-repetition, and coincidence among his different universes. In the omnibus editions of the 1990s, he had asserted the unity of his fiction as "Eternal Champion" writings through selective revision and bibliographical presentation. Now, in the Moonbeam Roads trilogy, he writes an explicit account of the machinery of the recurrent hero and his (or her) place in the eternal struggle.

The Moonbeam Roads books, however, are by no means merely recapitulation and summary, for in them Moorcock introduces a range of new settings, characters, and thematic materials, and experiments with several new narrative modes. *Daughter of Dreams* introduces us to the underground realm of Mu-Ooria, which borders the "deeper city" of Mirenburg (*The City in the Autumn Stars*) and is the home of the gentle, wise, and scholarly Off-Moo, who are rather like etiolated Eldren or Vadhagh. Much of *Destiny's Brother* takes place in a pre–Columbian North America, and makes constant reference to Native American culture; the Iroquois leader Ayanawatta, whom Longfellow romanticized in *The Song of Hiawatha* (1855), is a central character. *Daughter of Dreams* and *Son of the Wolf* bring the Eternal Champion and his struggle into the contemporary moment and the recent past: the former begins in immediately pre-war Germany, while the latter takes its initial setting in twenty-first-century Yorkshire.

Moorcock makes much play with narrative voice in these novels, for each of them shifts among narrators and points of view. *Daughter of Dreams* is told in the first person, but that first person shifts between Ulric von Bek, the latest descendent of the von Bek line, and his alter ego Elric of Melniboné (with whom, indeed, he merges for a while, sharing consciousness and memories). The first third of *Destiny's Brother* is narrated by Oona von Bek (Ulric's wife, and the daughter of Elric and the dreamthief Oone—see *The Fortress of the Pearl*); the middle section is a third person narrative constructed by Moorcock from his conversations with Una Persson, the temporal adventuress; and the last third is narrated in the first person by Ulric. Most strikingly, the bulk of *Son of the Wolf* is told in the voice of Oonagh Beck, Oona and Ulric's twelve-year-old granddaughter, whose narration is spangled with references to TV, cell-phones, e-mail, and other paraphernalia of the contemporary. One cannot help suspecting that Moorcock, seeing the enormous success of series like J. K. Rowling's seven Harry Potter novels (1997–2007) and Philip Pullman's trilogy *His Dark Materials* (1995–2000), thought he might himself explore the possibilities of adopting the perspective of an adolescent protagonist for a while.

Daughter of Dreams is in essence the third von Bek novel, an alternate version of *The Dragon in the Sword*, with the twentieth-century German nobleman Ulric von Bek on the run from the Nazis: in *Dragon*, they sought to wrest from him the location of the Grail; in *Daughter*, they're after his hereditary sword Ravenbrand, which is easily recognized as an analogue to Elric's Stormbringer. In the first part of *Daughter of Dreams*, Ulric is visited several times by the apparition of Elric, until finally the albino is able to break through into the world of Mu-ooria where Ulric finds himself, and the two merge themselves into a single figure. All is facilitated by Oona, who is not herself a dreamthief but the daughter of one, and who is an experienced traveller of the "moonbeam roads," the paths between the various realms of the multiverse. Like her father Elric, and like Ulric, Oona is a white-skinned, red-eyed albino, though she and Ulric show no hint of the physical weakness that plagues Elric.

For antagonists, the trio face the recurrent Klosterheim and Ulric's cousin Gaynor Paul von Minct, who combines in a single character Gaynor the Damned (first introduced in the Corum books) and Paul Minct (from *Blood*). Klosterheim and Gaynor are Nazis in the twentieth century; in Elric's world (a parallel storyline), they have enlisted the power of a senile and aggressive Lord of Law, "the famous Duchess Miggea of Dolwic,"[22] in order to isolate Tanelorn and seize Elric's black sword. In the Moonbeam Roads novels, the spiritual stakes of the eternal struggle are rather higher than the usual domination of the world by Law or Chaos. Instead, in each book Gaynor and Klosterheim, driven by the desire for absolute power and by a profound nihilism, seek to fundamentally alter or even destroy the structure of the multiverse as a whole. In each case, they are thwarted by Elric and his various associates. At the end of *Daughter of Dreams*, memorably, Elric leads a brace of *Phoorn*—Melnibonéan dragons—to scatter their inflammable venom among massed squadrons of Nazi warplanes, thereby turning the tide of the Battle of Britain.

Oona, Elric's daughter, while herself a traveller of the moonbeam roads, is not a dreamthief like her mother Oone. Indeed, it's unclear whether Oone herself still pursues that profession; as Oona explains to Elric, "Her interests are no longer in these worlds, although she occasionally visits the End of Time, I understand"[23]—thereby suggesting that Oone, the dreamthief of *The Fortress of the Pearl*, is one and the same with Una Persson of the Cornelius and Bastable books. Those more or less science-fictional *mythoi* are considerably in evidence in the Moonbeam Roads books: Bastable appears regularly, first introducing himself as "Captain Oswald Bastable, GTA"—Guild of Temporal Adventurers—and Prince Lobkowitz is one of the central characters of *Son of the Wolf*.[24] But there is little talk of "time-streams" or mechanical time machines here; instead, characters are able to walk the moonbeam roads between realms by talent or training, or they travel between realities in *dreams*.

Elric's presence in *Destiny's Brother* and *Son of the Wolf* is a dream-presence, though he has corporeal form and can suffer physical injury and death. That is, he can be present in pre–Columbian North America (*Des-

tiny's Brother), early twentieth-first-century Europe (*Son of the Wolf*), and all periods in between, because he is on an extended "dream-quest," an alternate existence entered into by Melnibonéan adepts. "In Melniboné," Elric himself explains in the prologue to *Destiny's Brother*, "we were trained to enter dreams in which we lived whole and very long lives, gaining the experience such realities brought. I had lived over two thousand years before I reached the age of twenty-five."[25]

In the hours before the disastrous sea battle that forms the culmination of Book Two of *Stormbringer*, Elric, having lost Stormbringer in a struggle with the Chaos Lords, has been secured to the mast of his enemy Jagreen Lern's flagship to watch the battle unfold.[26] In *Stormbringer*, Elric's sleep is brief indeed before he is roused by the noise of battle preparations. But in *Destiny's Brother*, we learn that during the night Elric has dreamed the "Dream of a Thousand Years," a dream during which he has arrived in Dark Ages Europe, fought in the Crusades, sailed with the pirate Barbary Rose in the Mediterranean—in short has lived a millennium of adventures. In *Destiny's Brother*, he will journey to North America with the Viking renegade Gunnar the Doomed (an avatar of Gaynor the Damned) and will join forces with his daughter Oona, Ayanawatta, his alter ego Ulric von Bek, and the mysterious young albino Native American warrior White Crow to thwart Gunnar and Klosterheim's plans to poison the multiverse-tree. White Crow seems at first kin to Elric; only in the last pages of the book does Ulric realize that he *is* Elric—a younger Elric, on another dream-quest: "White Crow was neither son nor brother nor nephew nor twin. White Crow was completing his own dream-journey, part of his apprenticeship, his training as an adept, his preparation for his destiny, to become Sorcerer Emperor of Melniboné."[27]

The extended dream-experience, in which the dreamer lives out long stretches of experience in an objective "instant," is by no means an original fictive device. The dilation of subjective time is central to Ambrose Bierce's "An Occurrence at Owl Creek Bridge" (1890) and Jorge Luis Borges's "The Secret Miracle" (1943), and dream-adventures are something of a staple of fantasy literature, from Langland's *Piers Plowman* to William Morris on. By means of such "dream-work," Moorcock can avoid some of the implausibilities inherent to his continued writing of Elric as a "series hero." How much adventure, after all, can be crammed into one objective lifetime? The twelve volumes of Conan's adventures, as presented in the Lancer/Ace editions of the 1960s and 1970s, already strained credibility. But when other publishers began issuing Conan pastiches—at least forty-five volumes of them between 1978 and 1996[28]—and Conan's exploits pro-

6. The Second Ether, the Moonbeam Roads, and Beyond 155

liferated in hundreds of comic book issues, films, and even Saturday morning cartoons, it was clear the Barbarian was no longer a single character with a lifespan to be detailed (as L. Sprague de Camp had conceived him when he engineered the first paperback series), but a franchise figure, much like Doc Savage, Sexton Blake, or Batman.

This is at least in part the "thinning out," I take it, that Moorcock wants to avoid with Elric. By allowing Elric to experience adventures while in a dream state, he avoids overburdening the "real" Elric's lifespan, which can be clearly traced from *Elric of Melniboné* to *Stormbringer*, with an excessive, implausible crowd of incident. And since upon waking Elric has few memories of what he has encountered in his dreams—only a vaguely-defined mastery of new aspects of sorcery or the elements—what happens in the dream realms pretty much stays in the dream realms, does not contaminate the "real" world.

Between *Destiny's Brother* (2003) and *Son of the Wolf* (2005), Moorcock made further use of both the dream-motif and Native American imagery in *Elric: The Making of a Sorcerer*, a graphic novel published in four parts in 2004–2006, then collected as a single volume in 2007.[29] This story is set during Elric's youth, when his father Sadric is still emperor of Melniboné, and follows the young prince through a series of four dreams, in each of which he journeys to Melniboné in an earlier period of its history and participates in decisions that will determine the future development of the Bright Empire as well as his own destiny. He learns the origins of the Black Sword, and forges a connection between it and the members of his own bloodline; he makes compacts with earth god Grome, the sea god Straasha, and the wind elemental Shaarnasaa, some of whom will "reappear" in the "canonical" Elric texts; most memorably, he commits Melniboné to an alliance with Arioch of Chaos, a relationship which will be the defining trait of the island empire.

It is all an exercise, on one level, of very well-done "backstory," but more interesting is the extent to which Moorcock takes advantage of the graphic medium to "restyle" Elric and his world, to get away from the quasi-medieval, distantly sub-pre–Raphaelite visual idiom in which they had been depicted by artists ranging from James Cawthorn and Barry Windsor-Smith to Robert Gould and John Ridgway. Instead, Moorcock wants a fantasy realm untouched by Tolkienian medievalism, drawing its visual vocabulary from North America. In a "note on style" to the illustrator Walter Simonson, he describes his desired Melniboné thus:

> Make towers very elongated wigwams—cowled rather than roofed. The design and dominant styles—braided hair or shaven scalp with single lock—

as Plains and forest Indians, as if these early Americans had risen to the skills of building a huge city like this and practising advanced metallurgy. No feathers as such, but some have crowns of metal feathers and so on. The colours are native American.[30]

Simonson has not consistently followed this "style-sheet"—there are lots of echoes of Conan-style iron age in some episodes—but the book as a whole is a striking visual defamiliarization and reimagining of the Elric mythos.

Elric's "Dream of a Thousand Years," which began in Europe in AD 900, comes to an end in 2001, at the conclusion of *Son of the Wolf*.[31] He has not been idle over the millennium, but has lived under a number of names and guises; indeed, we learn, Sir Seaton Begg's antagonist "Count Zodiac" *is* Elric. As befits a novel intended to "wind up" the saga of the Eternal Champion, *Son of the Wolf* brings onstage a motley carnival of characters from various corners of Moorcock's multiverse: Oswald Bastable; Prince Lobkowitz; Lieutenant Fromental, a minor figure from the Pyat books; the Chevalier St. Odhran and the talking fox Renyard, fan of the Encyclopedists, from *The City in the Autumn Stars*; and of course the inevitable antagonists Klosterheim and Gaynor the Damned. Oona the dreamthief's daughter is much in evidence, but the plot largely revolves around her granddaughter (by adoption) Oonagh, in whose breathless adolescent voice much of the action is narrated. The novel shifts settings abruptly and frequently, from contemporary Yorkshire, to Mu-ooria, various versions of Mirenburg, and Europe and Londra under the Dark Empire of Granbretan. This is not *quite* the Dark Empire of the Hawkmoon books, but an alternative version, in which Hawkmoon has refused the Warrior in Jet and Gold's aid and Kamarg has been conquered.

The various plot- and timelines—too complex to summarize—come together in a cavernous amphitheater beneath Londra, "the capital of the world's pain, the land of perpetual torment,"[32] where Klosterheim and Gaynor are decisively defeated and Monsieur Zodiac/Elric recovers Stormbringer, which he (in his waking life) will use to free himself from Jagreen Lern's flagship. Bastable, reprising his actions at the end of *The Warlord of the Air*, drops an atomic bomb on Londra, wiping out the beast-lords of Granbretan. Oonagh is returned to her parents in twenty-first-century Yorkshire; with her is a blind albino youth who has been the focus of Klosterheim and Gaynor's search for much of the book. The young man is Elric's son Onric, Oona's twin brother, stolen away in his childhood and blinded by Dark Empire "scientists." He has grown accustomed to the name Jacques D'Acre—or, as it will be anglicized, Jack Daker. At novel's end he has had his eyesight surgically restored, and he and Oonagh, now

6. The Second Ether, the Moonbeam Roads, and Beyond 157

some years older, are happily married. We have returned to the very beginning point of the whole Eternal Champion saga—John Daker in contemporary London—a saga which has the form, in one of its aspects at least, of a never-ending, repeating cycle.

But in only *one* of its forms. The novel ends with the hopeful/ominous "An End and a Beginning," and Oonagh may worry that "lately, Jack's been having some bad nights"—evoking how John Daker begins his own narrative with the voices that called to him in his sleep—but they are also considering a move from London to Yorkshire, and they have at least two children, in contrast to Daker's vague memory of "a woman. A child. A city."[33] Is Jack Daker the John Daker of *The Eternal Champion*? The *shape* of the situation is the same, the name is similar, but the details do not precisely match. And this is key: What constitutes Moorcock's fictive multiverse is not a series of precise repetitions across works and across worlds, but a series of resemblances, of isomorphisms, near-repetitions, and correspondences. "Repetition," Lobkowitz tells Renyard, "is very much a norm in the multiverse. It's a sign of order, as in music. Our lives, personalities, and stories all tend to repeat themselves, as do the composition and arrangements of the stars and planets."[34] But such "repetition" is not *identical* recurrence; there is always alteration, progression, variation—in life and in the multiverse as in music. Gaynor the Damned is almost but not entirely Gunnar the Doomed, and the two are almost but not entirely Paul Minct. Jherek Carnelian is a version of Jerry Cornelius, just as Jerry is a version of Elric, but they are not identical; nor, for that matter, is the Jerry Cornelius of *The Condition of Muzak* quite the same as the Jerry Cornelius of *The Final Programme*.

In *Son of the Wolf* the saga of the Eternal Champion comes to an end, as it has come to an end several times before: with Erekosë's destruction of the Balance in *The Quest for Tanelorn*; with John Daker's return—no longer as Erekosë—to London in *The Dragon in the Sword*; with the great pitched battle of angels at the end of *The War Amongst the Angels*, which Oonagh and her family witness from their tower house in Ingleton in the last pages of *Son of the Wolf*. Each of these endings seems final, conclusive, but no two of them are identical. More importantly, these endings are always "An Ending and a Beginning," for each of them leaves an opening for the saga to start up anew. Prince Lobkowitz is quoted at the beginning of *The Warlord of the Air*—a passage which is echoed and repeated, in various forms, in probably a dozen of Moorcock's books: "The War is ceaseless. The most we can hope for are occasional moments of tranquility in the midst of the conflict."[35] The Balance itself is constituted by the ceaseless struggle of Law and Chaos, the unceasing desire in each individual and in society as a whole either to unify reality into an unchanging order, or to throw off the trammels of order and surrender to the torrent of change and innovation. The world's pain is rooted in the excess of either principle; the cure for the world's pain, the harmony embodied in the little clay cup Lilith gives Ulrich von Bek at the end of *The War Hound and the World's Pain*, lies in the attempt to remold our personal and social reality into forms in which neither Law nor Chaos predominates.

The multiverse, as it is presented in the Moonbeam Roads trilogy, is a model of how we as human beings give form to reality through our hopes and desires, and how we create different worlds though our conscious and unconscious choices—choosing and rejecting alternatives, forever creating new branches ("branes") in an endless network of alternative existences. But of course it is more immediately a model to describe and structure the body of Moorcock's fiction, which has over five decades exfoliated and proliferated in so many directions, creating so many disparate yet similar worlds.

* * *

Moorcock turned sixty at the end of 1999, but he has remained busy indeed in the new millennium. Some of his writing has been quite outside of his established realms of heroic fantasy; other pieces have lovingly revisited the genre fiction of his youth: a foretaste, as it were, of the retrospective explorations of his current major project, "The Sanctuary of the White Friars," which promises to be a trilogy as expansive and complex as anything he has ever written.

In 2000, Moorcock published *Silverheart*, a fantasy novel written in collaboration with Storm Constantine, best known for her gender-bending Wraeththu novels. Moorcock provided a "scenario" for Constantine to flesh out—a scenario which ended up being "some 45,000 words of manuscript"—and he reckons the book "pretty much a fifty-fifty collaboration."[36] But neither the book's premise nor its execution live up to one's hopes. Perhaps because Moorcock and Constantine were working with an eye towards the computer role playing game format (Moocock had been "asked to provide a scenario for a [computer] game"[37]), the book's invented world seems overly schematic and mechanical, and its unfolding action is deeply dependent on "plot coupons," goals to be met before the protagonist Max Silverskin can progress to the next "level." Of course, he manages to overcome all difficulties and defeat all foes, and of course the multiverse is saved; but the reader is not tempted to return to the console for another play-through.

6. The Second Ether, the Moonbeam Roads, and Beyond   159

Silverheart is clearly a work of the left hand, pursued while Moorcock had larger projects on his platter, central among them planning and executing the Moonbeam Roads novels and completing the Pyat Quartet. Once *The Vengeance of Rome* was published (2006) and he had bidden farewell to the Eternal Champion saga, Moorcock spent some time reacquainting himself with his "cultural roots," the "PG Wodehouse, Edgar Rice Burroughs and Sexton Blake stories I enjoyed as a kid."[38] Truth to tell, he had never lost touch with his roots, especially those in various adventure genres. He had paid homage to the westerns of his youth and to his adopted home in *Tales from the Texas Woods* (1997), a miscellaneous collection of essays and stories, including the early cowboy tale "Johnny Lonesome Comes to Town," which had appeared in *Searchlight: Adventure Stories for Boys* in 1961.[39] In 2007 he published *The Metatemporal Detective*, a collection of stories featuring Sir Seaton Begg, his own skewed, multiversal version of Sexton Blake.[40]

Moorcock was already well into mapping out his next project—"a series of autobiographical novellas and stories in which I examine my taste for romance and fantasy"—when he was offered the chance to write an original Doctor Who novel. Like so many Britons of his generation, Moorcock had watched *Doctor Who* for much of his life, and as chance would have it, having finished bingeing on Wodehouse, Burroughs, and Sexton Blake and curtailed his reimmersion in such film and TV favorites as *Hopalong Cassidy* and *The Prisoner*, *Doctor Who* had become "almost the only escapism I allowed myself."[41]

The BBC had launched the television program *Doctor Who* in 1963, and it ran for a quarter century with a number of different actors playing the mysterious "Doctor," a Time Lord from the planet Gallifrey who travels across time and space in his police box-resembling TARDIS (Time and Relative Dimension in Space). BBC Wales officially rebooted the series to great popular and critical acclaim in 2003. Moorcock's recent immersion in P. G. Wodehouse's comic novels is very much in evidence in *Doctor Who: The Coming of the Terraphiles; or, Pirates of the Second Aether!!*, for the book is an extended *comic* transposition of Doctor Who into the cosmological framework of Moorcock's Second Ether. The "Terraphiles" of the title are a galaxy-wide society of fifty-first-thousandth century hobbyists interested in the history, culture, and above all sports of "ancient" earth—the earth, that is, of roughly the Middle Ages through 1940. Their records of the period being exceedingly spotty, their misunderstanding of pretty much everything about Old Terra is a source of constant hilarity. (One is strongly reminded of the denizens of Moorcock's End of Time—

or for that matter, the version of the middle ages one sees at the local renaissance fair.) But mostly, the Terraphiles are a set of characters straight out of Wodehouse: the henpecked, fabulously wealthy industrialist (his fortune comes from terraforming) and his overbearing wife; the beautiful but perpetually exasperated daughter (her fashionably retro nickname is "Flapper"); and a bevy of handsome, sporty, and irremediably *dim* young men.

Moorcock strikes a fine Wodehouseian note with these characters, and excellently captures the latest occupants of the TARDIS: the eleventh Doctor, as played by Matt Smith, a gangling, bow tie-wearing bundle of awkwardness, mastery, and non-sequitur; and his companion Amy Pond (played by Karen Gillan), an impetuous, stubborn, and shrewd red-haired Scot. The book is alight with references to Moorcock's earlier works, and indeed takes us back to the very earliest moment in his career, *The Sundered Worlds* (1962). The climactic sporting tournament of the novel takes place on the planet Miggea of the Ghost Worlds, the mysterious dimension-travelling "Shifter" that launched Moorcock's entire exploration of the multiverse. *The Coming of the Terraphiles* is by no means another entry in the Eternal Champion saga (even though its plot hinges on the imbalance between Law and Chaos, the imminent destruction of the multiverse, and so forth), but it does contain some of Moorcock's latest and most thoughtful formulations on the multiverse and on the way fiction, in the end, structures reality. "This isn't just physics we're talking about," says the Doctor:

> It's metaphysics. It's the only way we can understand reality. And both are represented by mythology, by legends, by the shamanistic power of humanity to tell a story that is an absolute lie beneath which hides an absolute truth. Life and death, Law and Chaos, Matter and Antimatter. What a species! A poem creates a formula. A formula becomes material. And so it goes on.[42]

* * *

The Whispering Swarm was published early in 2015, shortly after Moorcock's seventy-fifth birthday. It is the first volume of a projected trilogy, "The Sanctuary of the White Friars." Moorcock is no stranger to the trilogy form: the six Corum books were written as two trilogies, and the Dancers at the End of Time and the Moonbeam Roads novels were quite consciously planned in three-volume form; other sequences—the Michael Kane books, the Bastable novels, and the Second Ether books—seem to have arrived at their trilogy status through more contingent pressures. Of course, there is no shortage of trilogies in contemporary fantasy writing,

6. The Second Ether, the Moonbeam Roads, and Beyond   161

and this is no doubt the most lasting *formal* influence of Tolkien's *The Lord of the Rings*. As one of Tolkien's editors puts it, "*The Lord of the Rings* is often erroneously called a trilogy, when it is in fact a single novel, consisting of six books plus appendices, published for convenience in three volumes"[43]; nonetheless, that "convenient" division of Tolkien's work would set the three-volume format as a kind of template for works of heroic fantasy for at least a half century to come.

The Whispering Swarm is quite unlike any of Moorcock's previous works of fantasy. Its protagonist is a young writer named Michael Moorcock, and for much of the book he recounts the events of his own life and early career—events which are, so far as one can tell, pretty much identical to those of the life and career of *The Whispering Swarm*'s author. That is, the course of the narrator's life (and for convenience's sake I will refer to him as "Michael," in contradistinction to his author)—his birth in wartime London, his upbringing by a single mother, his early writing and editing of fanzines and pulps, his creation of Elric of Melniboné and Jerry Cornelius, his editorship of *New Worlds*—are told here in a manner perfectly congruent with what Moorcock has recounted in autobiographical essays, memoirs, and interviews. Much of *The Whispering Swarm* is straightforward autobiography, narrated in a rambling, genial manner, with a few names altered in fairly transparent ways: J. G. Ballard has become "Jack Allard," Thomas M. Disch has become "Rex Fisch," Moorcock's first wife Hilary Bailey has become "Helena Denham."

It is a fascinating memoir, saturated with vivid recollections of postwar London and punctuated with amusing personal anecdotes. It makes clear how Moorcock found his way to the forefront of contemporary fantasy and science fiction largely by accident, and how he pursued his gift for genre-based yarn-spinning while always desiring to do something larger, something more ambitious: "While I hammered out scripts and features and novellas and novels for money I also studied form and narrative method.... I wanted to write novels of character dealing with important social issues." "Balzac was one of my heroes," Moorcock writes of the period when he was planning the Cornelius tetralogy, "because he did reams of hackwork before doing reams of ambitious, innovative fiction."[44]

But while it is a memoir of the first thirty years of Moorcock's life, *The Whispering Swarm* is also a portal fantasy. At the age of seventeen, Michael (already a seasoned writer) first finds his way into the "Alsacia," a chunk of Thames-side London centered around a Carmelite monastery (the Carmelites are the "White Friars" of the title) which between the fifteenth and seventeenth centuries was a legally established "sanctuary," and thereby became a haunt of debtors, thieves, and other criminals.⁴⁵ The Alsacia into which Michael enters is still a sanctuary of sorts, a pocket of time outside of mid-twentieth-century history, and there he meets a range of characters from his childhood reading: the western heroes Jim Bowie, Pecos Bill, Kit Carson, Buffalo Bill Cody; the seventeenth-century highwayman Claude Duval; and the eighteenth-century highwayman Dick Turpin. And there he meets the beautiful red-haired, violet-eyed Moll Midnight, who takes him as her companion on an expedition to hold up and rob the mail-bearing electric tram to Hackney. The tram is an anachronism, of course—the last London trolleys were decommissioned in 1952—but more jarring is the anachronism of a tram being held up by horse-riding, flintlock-wielding "tobymen."⁴⁶

Alsacia, it seems, is a fantasy realm made up of elements from Michael's youthful reading and imaginings, an alternate reality in which Moll figures as the woman of his unrecognized dreams. While it will be some years before he revisits Alsacia after that first immersion, Michael will profit from his experience, writing a highly successful series of pulp stories featuring the highwaywoman "Meg Midnight," based on Molly, even as he is creating Elric of Melniboné and writing his first science fiction stories. Over the next decade or so he gets married, has two children, becomes editor of *New Worlds*, and becomes relatively famous. But he is called back, both by a messenger from Brother Isidore, the Carmelite friar who first brought him into the sanctuary, and by the pressure of the "Whispering Swarm," a crowd of voices only he can hear, and which only fall silent when he enters Alsacia. For a while he leads a double life, shuttling between contemporary London, where he sees to his literary responsibilities and his increasingly fraught marriage, and Alsacia, where he can write his "Meg Midnight" thrillers at speed and enjoy a blossoming romantic and sexual relationship with Molly. These two lives inevitably collide, with predictably painful consequences.

The denizens of Alsacia this time around, when Michael resumes visiting in the late 1960s, are less temporally heterogeneous if equally famous and incongruously assorted. Michael learns from Father Grammaticus, the abbot of the monastery, that unbeknownst to himself he has the gift of seeing and walking the moonbeam roads, the paths between alternate realities. On the basis of this gift Michael is invited—nay, drafted—to join a group of ardent Royalists in a plot to save King Charles I from being beheaded by substituting a noted scoundrel and wastrel in his place on the scaffold.⁴⁷ They are led by the dashing Prince Rupert of the Rhine, and the conspiracy includes not only Claude Duval but all four of Alexandre

6. The Second Ether, the Moonbeam Roads, and Beyond   163

Dumas's famous musketeers—Porthos, Athos, Aramis, and D'Artagnan.[48] Michael becomes a participant in this plot not out of any sympathy for the King's cause—he is a fervent opponent of absolute monarchy, a stalwart supporter of the representative democracy that Parliamentary victory in the Civil War seemed (to some) to promise—but because he is enchanted by the daring and idealism exemplified in Rupert and his followers. They are opposed by various grim Puritans, but most significantly by the crafty and ambiguous figure St. Claire, whom the habitual Moorcock reader is inclined at first to identify with Iain Sinclair until he is revealed to be Milton's friend Andrew Marvell, the poet and MP who managed to pursue a successful career through both Protectorate and Restoration.

So far as the fantastic elements of *The Whispering Swarm* go, Moorcock is writing as though he were to a large extent inventing anew the genre in which he has carried out so many explorations, created so many conceptual palaces, over the past fifty years. Moorcock's earlier fantasy novels and sequences had seemed inevitably to build upon what he had already written, to work another variation on the Eternal Champion, the conflict of Law and Chaos, the permeable multiverse; with *The Whispering Swarm*, almost all that weight of precedent is absent. The novel's characters are drawn from history—Rupert, Marvell, King Charles—or from the adventure stories of Moorcock's youth—Duval, Turpin, the four musketeers. Only the sour Puritan Corporal Love bears a certain resemblance to Klosterheim. While the "cosmolabe" Father Grammaticus shows Michael in his study and the similar but more complex instrument Prince Rupert has installed in the basement of the pub The Swan With Two Necks can be read as three-dimensional models of the "multiverse," that particular term—so central to Moorcock's imagination that one can find multiple instances in the omnibus editions of it replacing an earlier "universe"—is almost entirely absent. The occult machinery of the plot involves neither the Lords of Chaos and Law, nor the alchemical elements that play a role in some of Moorcock's books, but the Tarot deck. Of all of the vocabularies of fantasy he has developed over the years, in *The Whispering Swarm* Moorcock firmly retains only a single resonant term, the "moonbeam roads."

The Whispering Swarm as a whole has a strangely languid narrative rhythm: long stretches go by with scarcely a hint of the imbalance and tensions to which one is accustomed in reading fantasy adventure. There is however a great deal of action in the latter part of the novel, jumping back and forth between London of 1649 and the timeless Alsacia, some parts of it more skillfully managed than others. The deepest tension in the book is within Michael himself, the tension between his desire for the a temporal, fantasy-tinged life in Alsacia—a life in which Molly plays only a part, and a diminishing one as the book progresses, but towards which the Whispering Swarm is always pressing him—and his longing for normalcy in twentieth-century London, his desire to be present as a father for his daughters, to mend bridges, if possible, with Helena. At novel's end, Michael has turned his back on Alsacia, and despite the Swarm's continuing noise in his ears, has resolved to return no more.

Given the autobiographical nature of so much of the book, one is tempted to read this resolution and what has preceded it as a disguised version of Moorcock's own life up to this point, including the disintegration of his first marriage.[49] Or, for that matter, as a kind of allegory of the attraction heroic fantasy, and genre fiction as a whole, has held for him, periodically drawing him away from the "serious" task of writing realistic novels; an allegory, perhaps, of the fraught relationship between "fantasy" and "reality," and Moorcock's ongoing project of attempting to reconcile the two, to figure out how to narrate human truth through imaginative fiction.

I suppose there may be a good deal of validity in both of these readings. At the same time, however, Moorcock has presented his readers with a text of rather stunning audacity in *The Whispering Swarm*. The autobiographical material is presented with an almost artless straightforwardness, and so much of it is a matter of verifiable public record (with the sort of name changes that one might expect from any memoirist, to spare the feelings or avoid the legal teams of interested parties or their survivors, and a very few alterations of date and circumstance—Michael's birthday is at the beginning of 1940, while Moorcock was born on December 18, 1939). There is an almost Montaignesque candor in his recollections: but at the same time, we know that much of what he is recording *could not have happened*.

Two of the central figures of twentieth-century literature, Marcel Proust and James Joyce, created major works by transmuting their own experience[50]; a later modernist, Vladimir Nabokov, would do something akin to what Moorcock is up to in his autobiographical parody *Look at the Harlequins!* (1974). In that book Nabokov constructs a narrator who is both a parody of Nabokov himself and a doppelgänger of various Nabokovian characters (notably Humbert Humbert, from *Lolita*). What is most striking and audacious about *The Whispering Swarm* is its block-like juxtaposition of unbuttoned, straightforward autobiography and sheerest fantasy. Nabokov cunningly weaves, stretches, and alters, blurring the boundaries between fact and fiction; Moorcock sets the fact and the fiction side by side, and leaves it to the reader to work out their ultimate, just-out-of-reach relationship. If *The Whispering Swarm* is not a wholly satisfying or achieved work, there are two further volumes of "The Sanctuary of the White Friars" in which Moorcock can make good on its promise. After all, as he told Colin Greenland twenty-five years ago, there is "always the chance to do better tomorrow."[51]

Conclusion

Since at seventy-five Michael Moorcock is still busily writing away, hard at work on one of the largest projects of a career punctuated by large projects, I'm tempted not to conclude this book at all—simply to close with one of those "To Be Continued..." notices that wound up each installment of the serials he used to read as a kid. But I'm afraid my own writerly preference for conclusive form wouldn't stand for that, and it's worth picking up a few dropped threads from what's gone before and attempting a bit of summing-up.

There's a lot that I've barely touched on or left out entirely, both about Moorcock's career and concerning the wider impact of his work. I've scarcely mentioned his relationship with music—his own band the Deep Fix, his numerous collaborations with the "space-rock" outfit Hawkwind, with Blue Öyster Cult, with Robert Calvert—or the way his books have been echoed in the popular music arena, from Hawkwind's *Chronicle of the Black Sword* (1985, a kind of rock opera of Elric's adventures), to the name of the British group Tygers of Pan Tang, to countless references in songs by uncounted (mostly) heavy metal bands.[1]

I've only said a little about Moorcock's relationship with graphic media. His books have been a godsend to several generations of cover artists and illustrators now. Even a *very* partial list of Moorcock cover artists reads like a roll-call of the most prominent names in fantasy art: James Cawthorn, Frank Frazetta, Robert Gould, Jeffrey Catherine Jones, Michael William Kaluta, Rodney Matthews, John Picacio, Boris Vallejo, Michael Whelan, Patrick Woodroffe. There have been many graphic adaptations of his books, some of them very good indeed. Moorcock's friend James Cawthorn did versions of *The Jewel in the Skull, The Mad God's Amulet,* part of *The Sword of the Dawn,* and *Stormbringer* back in the 1970s; most recently, a French team of writers and artists has produced a dark and brutal new adaptation of *Elric of Melniboné*, while Americans Chris Roberson and Francesco Biagini have brought out *Elric: The Balance Lost*, a three-volume series that brings together Elric, Hawkmoon, Corum, and "Eric Beck," their own contemporary avatar of the Eternal Champion.[2]

There are traces of Moorcock's influence in many corners of the comics universe. Neil Gaiman read *Stormbringer* when he was nine and "it changed my life"—and Gaiman freely acknowledges how many aspects of Moorcock's work can be found in his ground-breaking *Sandman* series.[3] Alan Moore, whose *V for Vendetta* (1982–1988) and *Watchmen* (1986–1987) are at the center of any canon of contemporary graphic novels, has been deeply influenced by Moorcock: the various volumes of his *League of Extraordinary Gentlemen* are shot through with references to Moorcock's fictions. Moorcock's relationship with DC Comics writer Grant Morrison has not been a comfortable one—Moorcock has repeatedly accused Morrison of "borrowing" ideas, and of outright plagiarism—but it is difficult not to find Moorcock's fingerprints all over Morrison's *The Multiversity*, his grand harmonizing of the fifty-two alternate realities of DC's "Multiverse."

Strangely enough, Moorcock's creations have yet to be translated to film, aside from Robert Fuest's largely unsuccessful version of *The Final Programme* (1973). There are periodic rumors of an Elric adaptation in the works; one can only wait and see.

* * *

Moorcock's status as a *popular* writer certainly seems assured, if publishers' willingness to issue and reissue his books is any index. The Gollancz Michael Moorcock collection has returned all of his major works of fantasy and science fiction to print, and includes a number of ancillary e-books of his minor works. Wiedenfeld & Nicholson, a related imprint, will shortly be publishing new editions of *Mother London*, *King of the City*, and *London Bone*. In the United States, Tor has reprinted the Hawkmoon tetralogy, and Titan Books has begun a major project of reissuing his various fantasy series, the Cornelius tetralogy, and a number of the graphic adaptations of his books.

His reputation in his chosen genres is now a matter of record. In its special issue celebrating Moorcock's seventy-fifth birthday, *Locus* magazine ran tributes from such science fiction and fantasy luminaries as Harlan Ellison, Norman Spinrad, Alan Moore, and Jeff VanderMeer.[4] When it reissued the Elric stories between 2008 and 2010, Del Rey Books printed them with forewords by such major figures as Moore, Neil Gaiman, and

Tad Williams—as well as such important "crossover" writers as Walter Mosley and Michael Chabon.

While the London *Times* may have named Moorcock as one of the "fifty greatest" British writers since 1945, and while his work has received praise from such figures as Peter Ackroyd, Angela Carter, Iain Sinclair, and Angus Wilson, his status within contemporary "mainstream" writing is still very much in question—at least in the United States, where the distinctions between "generic" and "literary" fiction have historically been more jealously maintained than in the UK. But then again, in this new century the seemingly established relationship between "mainstream" and "genre" fiction is itself in question.

Soon after the publication of *Gloriana; or, The Unfulfill'd Queen* in 1979, in an introduction to the first full edition of his 1958 novel *The Golden Barge*, Moorcock looked back on the first two decades of his writing career. It is something of a formal statement of his (temporary) farewell to fantasy, and a reflection on his relationship to genre writing. Moorcock wonders what direction his work might have taken, starting from the Peakean allegory of *The Golden Barge*, if Ted Carnell had not commissioned the Elric stories, "and thus started me on a long career of adventure story writing, which produced a score at least of fantasy romances and several science fiction novels." The ultimate payoff is unclear: while Moorcock is sure he has "benefited from the apprenticeship in popular storytelling," "I regret the time 'lost' in writing books which never, frankly, stretched my talents very far."[5] Despite the kindness of the many readers who have enjoyed the tales of the Eternal Champion in all his guises, and who would welcome "further fantastic romances," "with *Gloriana*, I am resolved to write no more, feeling that it's high time that I flexed my muscles and looked to new tasks. I love writing, but I could not go on writing in one particular mode for long. Generic writing is too limited." "My ambition," Moorcock continues, "is to combine the 'epic' story with the 'psychological' novel, as, it seems to me, my favorite Victorian and Edwardian writers could do so masterfully…. Thus crude allegory"—as in *The Golden Barge*, or the Elric stories—"must give way to ironic naturalism."[6]

"Ironic naturalism" is perhaps a fair description of a number of the works Moorcock would go on to write in the next quarter-century—the Pyat books, *Mother London, King of the City*—but he has been repeatedly drawn back to the attractions of genre fiction, and has repeatedly fused elements of the "generic" and the "naturalistic." In this, he has not been alone. Any number of celebrated "mainstream" writers, among them Peter Ackroyd, Margaret Atwood, Angela Carter, Doris Lessing, Cormac

McCarthy, Thomas Pynchon, Salman Rushdie, and more recently Michael Chabon, Michael Cunningham, Junot Díaz, and Jonathan Lethem, have also written fantasy or science fiction, and have blurred the lines between "genre" and "mainstream" writing. ("Slipstream" is one of the terms of the moment for such writing.) These writers' relatively prominent critical status in the United States, in contrast to Moorcock's ambiguous one, has much to do with where they started—*within* mainstream writing. Whatever shifts the landscape of twenty-first century fiction may be undergoing, it remains difficult to grasp the brass ring of "literary" reputation if one has begun in the disreputable Grub Street of genre fiction.

Prophesying a writer's future reputation, whether or not his work will make it into some kind of "canon," is as the critic Harold Bloom puts it "a mug's game."[7] But I would imagine that Moorcock's reputation among readers of "serious" fiction will continue to fluctuate, that the rather amazing achievement of such "realistic" works as *Mother London* and the Pyat Quartet will continue to be overshadowed by the enduring popularity of the Hawkmoon, Corum, and Elric books, and by the sheer *mass* of works that Moorcock has written.

It would be a mistake, however, for Moorcock to be eventually recognized as the author of a few works of "mainstream" originality whose merits were temporarily obscured by the great morass of his "genre" works. In the final analysis, Moorcock's writings constitute a deliberate whole, an exploration in various genres, tones, and modes of the roots of human misery—the "world's pain"—in human imbalance. To stand for moderation, a "golden" or Horatian mean in politics, in aesthetics, in personal relations, has not been a particularly fashionable stance in the second half of the twentieth century. But neither has Moorcock, since his salad days of long hair, scarves, feathers, Frye boots, and floppy hats in the early 1970s, been much interested in fashion, intellectual or otherwise. With a persistent, kind, and remarkably *humane* intelligence, he has sought over the past fifty-odd years, in "100 books that make up one book,"[8] to diagnose the "world's pain" and to suggest some possible remedies; and to do so while telling stories that will move, entrance, and above all *entertain* his readers. In the latter aim at least he has succeeded abundantly.

Appendix

The Eternal Champion Omnibus Editions

As discussed in Chapter 5, between 1992 and 2000 the bulk of Moorcock's previously published fantasy and science fiction novels (and a number of his short stories) appeared in two similar but separate series of omnibus volumes published in the United Kingdom and the United States. The books were prepared by Moorcock's bibliographer John Davey, with Moorcock's active participation. The clear intention, most fully realized in the first (Orion/Millennium) series, was to present the stories of the Eternal Champion in a "suggested reading order."

The following is a listing of the volumes of each of those series, in order of publication, with a précis of each volume's contents and some brief indications of the differences between the British and American series.

The Tale of the Eternal Champion, Orion/Millennium (UK)

1. **Von Bek** (1992): *The War Hound and the World's Pain, The City in the Autumn Stars*, "The Pleasure Garden of Felipe Sagittarius"
2. **The Eternal Champion** (1992): *The Eternal Champion, Phoenix in Obsidian, The Dragon in the Sword*
3. **Hawkmoon** (1992): *The Jewel in the Skull, The Mad God's Amulet, The Sword of the Dawn, The Runestaff*
4. **Corum** (1992): *The Knight of the Swords, The Queen of the Swords, The King of the Swords*
5. **Sailing to Utopia** (1993): *The Ice Schooner, The Black Corridor, The Distant Suns*, "Flux"
6. **A Nomad of the Time Streams** (1993): *The Warlord of the Air, The Land Leviathan, The Steel Tsar*

7. **The Dancers at the End of Time** (1993): *An Alien Heat, The Hollow Lands, The End of All Songs*

8. **Elric of Melniboné** (1993): *Elric of Melniboné, The Fortress of the Pearl, The Sailor on the Seas of Fate,* "The Dreaming City," "While the Gods Laugh," "The Singing Citadel"

9. **The New Nature of the Catastrophe** (1993): Edited by Langdon Jones and Michael Moorcock, this volume contains Cornelius stories by Michael Moorcock and various others; it is an expanded version of *The Nature of the Catastrophe*, ed. Langdon Jones and Michael Moorcock (London: Hutchinson, 1971)

10. **The Prince with the Silver Hand** (1993): *The Bull and the Spear, The Oak and the Ram, The Sword and the Stallion*

11. **Legends from the End of Time** (1993): *Pale Roses, White Stars, Ancient Shadows, Constant Fire,* "Elric at the End of Time." This edition was seriously flawed, lacking virtually the whole of one novel and the key end of a story. These were restored in the US White Wolf edition (vol. 13 below).

12. **Stormbringer** (1993): *The Sleeping Sorceress, The Revenge of the Rose,* "The Stealer of Souls," "Kings in Darkness," "The Caravan of Forgotten Dreams," *Stormbringer*

13. **Earl Aubec** (1993): stories

14. **Count Brass** (1993): *Count Brass, The Champion of Garathorm, The Quest for Tanelorn*

The Eternal Champion, White Wolf (US)

1. **The Eternal Champion** (1994): *The Eternal Champion, The Sundered Worlds, Phoenix in Obsidian,* "To Rescue Tanelorn..."

2. **Von Bek** (1995): *The War Hound and the World's Pain, The City in the Autumn Stars, The Dragon in the Sword,* "The Pleasure Garden of Felipe Sagittarius"

3. **Hawkmoon** (1995): contents as Orion 3

4. **A Nomad of the Time Streams** (1995): contents as Orion 6

5. **Elric: Song of the Black Sword** (1996): contents as Orion 8

6. **The Roads Between the World** (1996): *The Wrecks of Time, The Winds of Limbo, The Shores of Death*

7. **Corum: The Coming of Chaos** (1997): contents as Orion 4

8. **Sailing to Utopia** (1997): contents as Orion 5

9. **Kane of Old Mars** (1998): *City of the Beast, Lord of the Spiders, Masters of the Pit*

Appendix 173

10. **The Dancers at the End of Time** (1998): contents as Orion 7
11. **Elric: The Stealer of Souls** (1998): contents as Orion 12
12. **Corum: The Prince with the Silver Hand** (1999): contents as Orion 10
13. **Legends from the End of Time** (1999): contents as Orion 11, but corrected and restored
14. **Earl Aubec and Other Stories** (1999): contents similar to Orion 13, but adds "Sir Milk-and-Blood" and omits "To Rescue Tanelorn..."
15. **Count Brass** (2000): contents as Orion 14

Chapter Notes

Introduction

1. John Davey's *Michael Moorcock: A Reader's Guide* (London: Jayde Design, 1992) includes a suggested reading order for those new to Moorcock's work. The Orion/Millennium (1992–1993) and White Wolf (1995–2000) omnibus editions of Moorcock's novels are intended to present most of his works in such a reading order (though neither one is based in any way slavishly on Davey's arrangement). See the Appendix for a summary of these editions' contents.

2. A useful (if counter-intuitively organized) early bibliography is Richard Bilyeu, *The Tanelorn Archives: A Primary and Secondary Bibliography of the Works of Michael Moorcock 1949–1979* (Manitoba: Pandora's Books, 1981); Davey's *Michael Moorcock: A Reader's Guide* is indispensable; the closest to an up-to-date and relatively—but only *relatively*—reliable Moorcock bibliography can be found at "Moorcock's Miscellany": http://www.multiverse.org/wiki/index.php?title=Bibliography. There is also an uncounted and probably uncountable number of early, uncollected stories and articles.

3. *Into the Media Web: Selected Short Non-fiction, 1956–2006*, ed. John Davey (Manchester: Savoy, 2010) and *London Peculiar and Other Nonfiction*, ed. Michael Moorcock and Allan Kausch (Oakland, CA: PM Press, 2012).

4. From Moorcock's 1981 novel, *The War Hound and the World's Pain*.

Chapter 1

1. Michael Moorcock, "Michael Moorcock, 1939-" (an entry for the *Contemporary Authors Autobiography Series*), *Into the Media Web: Selected Short Non-fiction, 1956–2006*, ed. John Davey (Manchester: Savoy, 2010) 17.

2. Moorcock, "Michael Moorcock, 1939-," *Into the Media Web* 24–25.

3. Colin Greenland, *Michael Moorcock: Death Is No Obstacle* (Manchester: Savoy, 1992) 143.

4. Michael Moorcock, Introduction to *The Eternal Champion*, *Into the Media Web* 577, 575. In addition to these various versions, the story's plot supplies the narrative basis for a 1976 screenplay (never filmed), "Stormbringer," published in *Elric: Swords and Roses* (New York: Del Rey, 2010) 245–329.

5. Michael Moorcock, *Elric: The Sleeping Sorceress and Other Stories* (London: Gollancz, 2013) 3 (italics in original). I quote from the 1962 novella; the novel-length version is reprinted in *The Eternal Champion* (London: Gollancz, 2013) 1–189.

6. Moorcock, *Elric: The Sleeping Sorceress and Other Stories* 6.

7. Moorcock cites *Three Hearts and Three Lions* on a number of occasions; see for instance "The Elric Stories" (1963) (*Into the Media Web* 177) and the dedication of *Elric of Melniboné* (1972), *Elric of Melniboné and Other Stories* (London: Gollancz, 2013) 177.

8. Poul Anderson, "A Logical Conclusion," *Fantasy* (New York: Tor, 1981) 83; originally published in *Fantastic Universe* in 1960.
9. Moorcock, *Elric: The Sleeping Sorceress and Other Stories* 62. Erekosë's moral ambiguity—or blindness—is the focus of Michael Hoey's "Disguising Doom: A Study of the Linguistic Features of Audience Manipulation in Michael Moorcock's *The Eternal Champion*," *Imagining Apocalypse: Studies in Cultural Crisis*, ed. David Seed (Basingstoke: Palgrave Macmillan, 2000) 151–65.
10. Poul Anderson, *Three Hearts and Three Lions* (New York: Berkley, 1978) 163.
11. Moorcock, *Elric: The Sleeping Sorceress and Other Stories* 5 (italics in original).
12. Moorcock, *The Eternal Champion* 8 (italics in original).
13. Moorcock, *Elric: The Sleeping Sorceress* 25.
14. Moorcock, *Elric: The Sleeping Sorceress* 42.
15. John Clute, "Introduction to *The Michael Moorcock Collection*" x; this introduction appears at the beginning of each of the 2013–2015 Gollancz volumes.
16. Greenland, *Death Is No Obstacle* 24.
17. Michael Moorcock, *Moorcock's Multiverse* (London: Gollancz, 2014) 25.
18. Moorcock, *Moorcock's Multiverse* 191.
19. Cited in *Oxford English Dictionary*, "Multiverse" 1.a.
20. *Oxford English Dictionary*, "Multiverse" 1.b., quoting Moorcock, *Moorcock's Multiverse* 172.
21. Moorcock, *Into the Media Web* 579.
22. J. R. R. Tolkien, "On Fairy-Stories," *Tree and Leaf* 46–55, in *The Tolkien Reader* (New York: Ballantine, 1966).
23. Greenland, *Death Is No Obstacle* 8.
24. Farah Mendlesohn describes these as "portal fantasies," while worlds such as Tolkien's are "immersive fantasies." The whole of her *Rhetorics of Fantasy* (Middletown, CT: Wesleyan University Press, 2008) provides a useful taxonomy of fantastic worlds.
25. On the term "epic fantasy," see Moorcock, "Putting a Tag on It," *Elric: The Stealer of Souls* (New York: Del Rey, 2008) 5–8, originally published in the fanzine *Amra* in May 1961; Leiber first suggested "sword-and-sorcery" in *Ancalagon* in April 1961, and again in *Amra* in July 1961.

In this discussion of the early Elric stories, I will be quoting mostly from the 2008 Del Rey volume *Elric: The Stealer of Souls*, since it has the advantage of presenting the first nine Elric tales in order of their first publication (though not, as I will discuss later, in their first *texts*); the most recent Gollancz reissues, like earlier paperback and omnibus repackagings, present the stories according to the internal chronology of Elric's life, which obscures their publication history.

26. Samuel R. Delany, "Sword & Sorcery, S/M, and the Economics of Inadequation: The *Camera Obscura Interview*," *Silent Interviews: On Language, Race, Sex, Science Fiction, and Some Comics* (Hanover, NH: Wesleyan University Press, 1994) 129.

27. The most comprehensive overview of sword and sorcery remains L. Sprague de Camp's *Literary Swordsmen and Sorcerers: The Makers of Heroic Fantasy* (Sauk City, WI: Arkham House, 1976). There is much historical information and amusing anecdote in Lin Carter's introductions to his anthologies *Flashing Swords! #1* (New York: Dell, 1973) and *Flashing Swords! #2* (New York: Dell, 1973).

Perhaps the most negative assessment of sword and sorcery as subgenre is that of Hans Joachim Alpers, in "Loincloth, Double Ax, and Magic: 'Heroic Fantasy' and Related Genres," trans. Robert Plank, *Science Fiction Studies* 5.1 (March 1978): 19–32; Alpers's reading, which finds that "heroic fantasy" propogates ideologies of force that add up to fascism, is so ideologically unsubtle that it barely rises to the level of "vulgar" Marxism, but is nonetheless uncomfortably plausible in the face of much that has been written in the genre.

Among the more probing and subtle commentaries on the ideologies inherent in the sword and sorcery subgenre are Samuel R. Delany's remarks in his essay on Joanna Russ, "Alyx," *The Jewel-Hinged Jaw: Notes on the Language of Science Fiction* (New York: Berkley, 1977) 196–203. He amplifies and complicates these remarks in "Sword & Sorcery, S/M, and the Economics of Inadequation" 127–135.

28. There have been several biographies of Howard and a number of collec-

tions of commentary and scholarship on Conan; a handy (and relatively reliable) introduction to Conan in general is Paul M. Sammon's *Conan the Phenomenon: The Legacy of Robert E. Howard's Fantasy Icon* (Milwaukie, OR: Dark Horse, 2007), to which Moorcock contributes an introduction.

29. At least ten million copies, according to Sammon, *Conan the Phenomenon* 45. Their sales were no doubt helped by the fact that most of them sported Frank Frazetta cover paintings.

30. On early sword and sorcery, see de Camp, *Literary Swordsmen and Sorcerers* 270–289 and Lin Carter, *Imaginary Worlds: The Art of Fantasy* (New York: Ballantine, 1973) 65–69.

31. Moorcock, "The Secret Life of Elric of Melniboné," *Elric: The Stealer of Souls* 446.

32. Moorcock, "Introduction," *Elric: The Stealer of Souls* xxiv.

33. Moorock, *Elric: The Stealer of Souls* 11–12.

34. I quote from the earlier version of the story in *The Stealer of Souls* (New York: Lancer, 1967) 40. Moorcock excises this passage from later versions of "The Dreaming City," and by 2008 he will assert that "Elric does not, of course, exhibit human albinism but an alien condition that occasionally produces a 'Silverskin' of Melnibonéan royal blood" ("Introduction," *Elric: The Stealer of Souls* xxii).

One key inspiration for Elric's albinism, Moorcock has noted on several occasions, is the character Zenith the Albino, a recurrent antagonist in the long-running (1893–1978) "Sexton Blake" series of detective adventures. Moorcock wrote for the Sexton Blake Library in the early 1960s. See Moorcock, "Introduction," *Elric: The Stealer of Souls* xxiii; also reprinted in that volume is "The Zenith Letter" (1924) by Sexton Blake author Anthony Skene, describing his own inspiration for the character of Zenith (457–8).

35. Moorcock, *Elric: The Stealer of Souls* 11.

36. Moorcock, *Elric: The Stealer of Souls* 41.

37. Anderson would name the sword in his 1971 revision of *The Broken Sword*, identifying it as the dwarf-forged Tyrfing, cursed to bring death every time it is drawn, and finally to cause its wielder's own death.

38. Moorcock, *Elric: The Stealer of Souls* 10–11.

39. Moorcock, "Conan: American Phenomenon," Sammon, *Conan the Phenomenon* xi-xvii.

40. Moorcock, *Elric: The Sleeping Sorceress* 28.

41. Moorcock, *Elric: The Stealer of Souls* 94.

42. Michael Moorcock, *Corum: The Prince in the Scarlet Robe* (London: Gollancz, 2013) 12.

43. The identification among Vadhagh, Eldren, Melnibonéans, and elves is made explicit in the 1971 Corum novel *The King of the Swords*, where Corum finds himself in early modern/late medieval Cornwall and learns that "In this land [the Vadhagh] are sometimes known as Elves—sometimes as devils, djinns, even gods, depending upon the region"; Moorcock, *Corum: The Prince in the Scarlet Robe* 397.

44. Poul Anderson, *The Broken Sword* (1954; London: Gollancz, 2014) 5–6.

45. Anderson, *Three Hearts and Three Lions* 40.

46. Elric first summons the wind elementals in "The Dreaming City"; he invokes the cat-god Meerclar in "The Flame Bringers" (1962).

47. Moorcock, *Elric: The Stealer of Souls* 25–26.

48. Moorcock, *Elric: The Stealer of Souls* 68.

49. Moorcock, *Elric: The Stealer of Souls* 78.

50. Moorcock, *Elric: The Stealer of Souls* 80.

51. Michael Moorcock, "Elric," *Elric: The Stealer of Souls* 444.

52. Moorcock, *Elric: The Stealer of Souls* 422.

53. Moorcock, *Elric: The Stealer of Souls* 433.

54. Michael Moorcock, "About My Multiverse," *Into the Media Web* 45.

55. As I read over these pages, the *New Statesman* has just published a lengthy and otherwise nuanced overview of Moorcock's career by Andrew Harrison: its attention-grabbing headline reads "Michael Moorcock: 'I think Tolkien was a crypto-fascist'": http://www.newstatesman.com/culture/2015/07/michael-

moorcock-i-think-tolkien-was-crypto-fascist.

56. Humphrey Carpenter, *Tolkien: A Biography* (Boston: Houghton Mifflin, 1977) 226–31.

57. Edward James, "Tolkien, Lewis and the Explosion of Genre Fantasy," in *The Cambridge Companion to Fantasy Literature*, ed. Edward James and Farah Mendlesohn (Cambridge: Cambridge University Press, 2012) 72–74. For an insider's account of the Ballantine Adult Fantasy imprint, see Carter, *Imaginary Worlds* 268–72.

58. Edward James reads Elric as a character created deliberately in an anti–Tolkienian mode ("Tolkien, Lewis and the Explosion of Genre Fantasy" 73); as will become clear, I think he is mistaken.

59. Brian Attebery, *Strategies of Fantasy* (Bloomington: Indiana University Press, 1992) 14.

60. Michael Moorcock, "Tolkien Times Two" (2003), *Into the Media Web* 638.

61. Most notably Stephen R. Donaldson's Thomas Covenant trilogy and Terry Brooks's Shannara books, the first volumes of each of which appeared in 1977; there would be many, many more.

62. "Epic Pooh" was included in revised form as a chapter in Moorcock's *Wizardry and Wild Romance: A Study of Epic Fantasy* (1987), and again in that work's most recent revised publication (Austin, TX: Monkeybrain Books, 2004). I quote from the 1978 text of "Epic Pooh," in *Into the Media Web* 693.

63. Moorcock, *Into the Media Web* 695.

64. Moorcock, *Into the Media Web* 694.

65. Moorcock, *Into the Media Web* 695.

66. Both Ruskin's and Morris's politico-cultural projects were profoundly backwards-looking, but it should be noted that while what Ruskin proposed amounts to a return to feudalism, with its ideals of absolute social hierarchy, obedience, and responsibility, Morris looked to the middle ages' artisanal guilds for models of cooperative labor and self-governance. Ruskin and Morris both—and by implication, Tolkien as well—can be classified among the thinkers Michael Löwy and Robert Sayre name "restitutionist romantics"; see *Romanticism Against the Tide of Modernity* (Durham: Duke University Press, 2001) 59–63, 127–46. On Tolkien and Lewis in the context of modernity, see Meredith Veldman, *Fantasy, the Bomb, and the Greening of Britain: Romantic Protest, 1945–1980* (Cambridge: Cambridge University Press, 1994) 37–111.

67. "I cordially dislike allegory in all of its manifestations, and have always done so since I grew old and wary enough to detect its presence"; J. R. R. Tolkien, *The Lord of the Rings: Collector's Edition* (Boston: Houghton Mifflin, 1994) 5.

68. Tolkien, "On Fairy-Stories" 68, 70–71.

69. Tolkien, "On Fairy-Stories" 60.

70. Tolkien, "On Fairy-Stories" 67.

71. China Miéville, "Tolkien—Middle Earth Meets Middle England," *Socialist Review* 259 (January 2002), http://socialistreview.org.uk/259/tolkien-middle-earth-meets-middle-england. This statement Miéville attributes to Moorcock, whether quotation or paraphrase, has achieved wide circulation; I've been unable to locate its source. Miéville contributes an introduction to the latest edition of *Wizardry and Wild Romance*, in which he praises "Epic Pooh" as "a *tremendous* piece of work" (Moorcock, *Wizardry and Wild Romance* 13).

72. John Clute, "Introduction to *The Michael Moorcock Collection*" xi.

73. Walter Benjamin, "Conversations with Brecht," trans. Anya Bostock, in Theodor Adorno, Walter Benjamin, Ernst Bloch, Bertolt Brecht, and Georg Lukács, *Aesthetics and Politics* (1977; London: Verso, 1980) 99.

Chapter 2

1. The first of them was "Peace on Earth" in 1959. *New Worlds: An Anthology*, ed. Michael Moorcock (London: Fontana, 1983) contains a very useful index of the contents of the periodical from 1946 to 1979.

2. Michael Moorcock, "Play with Feeling," *Into the Media Web: Selected Short Non-fiction, 1956–2006*, ed. John Davey (Manchester: Savoy, 2010) 358–59.

3. Colin Greenland, *The Entropy Exhibition: Michael Moorcock and the British "New Wave" in Science Fiction* (London: Routledge & Kegan Paul, 1983) 16. Greenland's excellent book presents

Notes—Chapter 2

the best handy overview of *New Worlds*'s history (13–22).

4. Michael Moorcock, "*New Worlds*: A Personal History," *Into the Media Web* 343.

5. Moorcock, *Into the Media Web* 340–41.

6. Michael Moorcock, "A New Literature for the Space Age," *Into the Media Web* 364.

7. On Gernsback and the early self-definition of the SF genre, see Edward James, *Science Fiction in the Twentieth Century* (Oxford: Oxford University Press, 1994) 51–53.

8. Brian W. Aldiss, *The Detached Retina: Aspects of SF and Fantasy* (Syracuse: Syracuse University Press, 1995) 25.

9. Michael Moorcock, Introduction to *The New Nature of the Catastrophe*, ed. Langdon Jones and Michael Moorcock (1993; London: Orion, 1997) viii.

10. Moorcock, *Into the Media Web* 346.

11. Greenland, *The Entropy Exhibition* 17.

12. I borrow the rough "taxonomy" which follows from Greenland, *The Entropy Exhibition* 23–68.

13. J. G. Ballard, "Which Way to Inner Space?," quoted in Greenland 44.

14. David G. Hartwell, *Age of Wonders: Exploring the World of Science Fiction* (1984; rev. ed., New York: Tor, 1996) 110.

15. Michael Moorcock, *Travelling to Utopia* (London; Gollancz, 2014) 359.

16. Greenland, *The Entropy Exhibition* 49.

17. Quoted in Greenland, *The Entropy Exhibition* 51.

18. The Second Law was very much in the popular scientific imagination in the 1950s and early 1960s, in part because of the role it plays in Norbert Wiener's "cybernetics"; see *The Human Use of Human Beings: Cybernetics and Society* (Boston: Houghton Mifflin, 1950).

19. The Jones, Harrison, and Zoline stories are reprinted in Moorcock, *New Worlds: An Anthology*; "Entropy" can be found in Thomas Pynchon, *Slow Learner: Early Stories* (Boston: Little, Brown, 1984) 79–98.

20. The thumbnail sketch of *New Worlds*'s history which follows draws on Greenland, *The Entropy Exhibition* 13–22,

and Moorcock, *Into the Media Web* 338–55.

21. Michael Moorcock, "Aspects of the Author 1: *New Worlds*—Jerry Cornelius" (1972), *Into the Media Web* 70.

22. Moorcock, *The New Nature of the Catastrophe* vii.

23. Michael Moorcock, Introduction to *Elric: To Rescue Tanelorn* (New York: Del Rey, 2008) xviii.

24. Michael Moorcock, *The Cornelius Quartet* (London: Gollancz, 2013) 35.

25. Moorcock, *The Cornelius Quartet* 124–25.

26. Moorcock, *The Cornelius Quartet* 46.

27. Michael Moorcock, *Elric: The Stealer of Souls* (New York: Del Rey, 2008) 42.

28. Moorcock, *The Cornelius Quartet* 184.

29. Moorcock, *The Cornelius Quartet* 21–22.

30. Moorcock, *The Cornelius Quartet* 146–48; the action is dated "196-" on 17.

31. Moorcock, *The Cornelius Quartet* 188.

32. Michael Moorcock, *The Final Programme* (New York: Avon, 1968).

33. Moorcock, *The Cornelius Quartet* 406–7.

34. Moorcock, *The Cornelius Quartet* 427.

35. Moorcock, *The Cornelius Quartet* 460.

36. The phrase is Robert Frost's, from "The Figure a Poem Makes," *Collected Poems, Prose, and Plays*, ed. Richard Poirier and Mark Richardson (New York: Library of America, 1995) 777.

37. Michael Moorcock, "Behold the Man" [introduction to a 1996 reprint], *Into the Media Web* 77.

38. Michael Moorcock, *Breakfast in the Ruins and Other Stories* (London: Gollancz, 2014) 297–98.

39. Moorcock, *Breakfast in the Ruins and Other Stories* 305.

40. Moorcock, *Breakfast in the Ruins and Other Stories* 322; Mark 15.34.

41. Moorcock, *Breakfast in the Ruins and Other Stories* 303.

42. Moorcock, *Into the Media Web* 80, 83. The most extensive additions to *Behold the Man* are in the first half, fleshing out the account of Glogauer's child-

hood. Moorcock considers the shorter version of the story superior to the novel.

43. Michael Moorcock, *The Retreat from Liberty: The Erosion of Democracy in Today's Britain* (London: Zomba Books, 1983) 20.

44. Moorcock, *Into the Media Web* 72.

45. Most of these texts were collected in *The Nature of the Catastrophe*, ed. Langdon Jones and Michael Moorcock (London: Hutchinson, 1971), later expanded as *The New Nature of the Catastrophe*. John Davey's "Jerry Cornelius: A Reader's Guide" (*The New Nature of the Catastrophe* 485–98) provides a fairly comprehensive bibliography of Jerry Cornelius texts to date; Moorcock's own short-form Cornelius works are collected in *Jerry Cornelius: His Lives and His Times* (London: Gollancz, 2014).

46. Norman Spinrad, author's note to "The Last Hurrah of the Golden Horde," in *SF: Author's Choice 3*, ed. Harry Harrison (New York: Berkley, 1971) 268.

47. See Moorcock, *Into the Media Web* 71.

48. Moorcock, *The Cornelius Quartet* 595.

49. Greenland, *The Entropy Exhibition* 151.

50. Moorcock, *The Cornelius Quartet* 563–66, 580–83.

51. Moorcock, *The Cornelius Quartet* 528–30, 547–50.

52. Quoted in Greenland, *The Entropy Exhibition* 152.

53. Richard Ellmann, *James Joyce*, 2d ed. (Oxford: Oxford University Press, 1982) 521.

54. Quoted in Greenland, *The Entropy Exhibition* 158.

55. Colin Greenland, *Michael Moorcock: Death Is No Obstacle* (Manchester: Savoy, 1992) 98.

56. Greenland, *Death Is No Obstacle* 100.

57. Greenland, *Death Is No Obstacle* 99.

58. Una Persson—or at least characters bearing that name—does appear in currently available editions of *The Final Programme* and *A Cure for Cancer*, but in the first edition of *The Final Programme* the character now called "Una Persson" was "Maj-Britt Sandström," while in the first *A Cure for Cancer* "Captain Brunner," rather than Una, appears at the end to rescue Jerry. Moorcock made the name changes, as well as inserting a number of references to Mrs. Cornelius and other characters from the latter two books of the tetralogy, for the 1979 Fontana reprints of *The Final Programme* and *A Cure for Cancer*. See Chapter Five for a discussion of name changes and other revisions Moorcock makes in the 1990s omnibus editions of his novels.

59. Greenland, *Death Is No Obstacle* 96.

60. Moorcock, *The Cornelius Quartet* 11.

61. Moorcock, *The Cornelius Quartet* 1033.

62. *The Selected Writings of Walter Pater*, ed. Harold Bloom (1974; New York: Columbia University Press, 1982) 55, 57, italics original. *The Renaissance: Studies in Art and Poetry* was first published in 1873 under the title *Studies in the History of the Renaissance*; the chapter from which I quote, "The School of Giorgone," was added to the second, retitled edition in 1877.

63. Moorcock, *The Cornelius Quartet* 792, 791.

64. Moorcock, *The Cornelius Quartet* 805–06; on Jerry's pubic hair, see 249.

65. Moorcock, *The Cornelius Quartet* 931, 932, 934.

66. Moorcock, *The Cornelius Quartet* 961, 963.

67. My reading of *The Condition of Muzak*, and indeed the entire *Cornelius Quartet*, is deeply indebted to John Clute's brilliant essay "The Repossession of Jerry Cornelius," first published as an introduction to Michael Moorcock, *The Cornelius Chronicles* (New York: Avon, 1977) and reprinted in *The Cornelius Quartet* 1–9. It remains a definitive statement, as well as a remarkably sensitive piece of literary criticism.

68. The Cornelius novels and novellas outside of the principal tetralogy are gathered in Michael Moorcock, *A Cornelius Calendar* (London: Gollancz, 2015).

69. Michael Moorcock, Introduction to *The Opium General and Other Stories* (1984; London: Grafton, 1986) 9.

70. See Chapter 3.

71. Moorcock, *The Opium General and Other Stories* 10.

72. See Michael Moorcock, "Memorial [Andrea Dworkin]," *Into the Media Web* 710–12; "The Case Against Pornography," *Into the Media Web* 109–13; "Andrea Dworkin," *Casablanca* (1989; London: Gollancz, 1993) 133–36; and "What Feminism Has Done for Me," *Casablanca* 166–68.

73. Moorcock, *The Retreat from Liberty* 82–3.

74. Moorcock, *The Opium General and Other Stories* 13.

75. Moorcock, *A Cornelius Calendar* 612.

76. Moorcock, *A Cornelius Calendar* 615.

77. Moorcock, *A Cornelius Calendar* 662. This merger of course evokes that of Jerry Cornelius and Miss Brunner at the end of *The Final Programme*; a similar (but abortive) alchemical merger was attempted at the climax of *The City in the Autumn Stars* (1986); see Chapter 5.

78. Moorcock, *A Cornelius Calendar* 674, italics mine.

79. Jerry Cornelius has also appeared in two volumes of Alan Moore's graphic novel series *The League of Extraordinary Gentlemen*. The most notable recent entry in the Cornelius "apocrypha" is a full-length novel by Carter Kaplan, *Tally-Ho, Cornelius!* (Hyde Park, NY: Mustard Lid Press, 2008).

80. Samuel R. Delany, "Reflections on Historical Method," *Starboard Wine: More Notes on the Language of Science Fiction*, rev. ed. (Middletown, CT: Wesleyan University Press, 2012) 216.

81. For a fine overview of the controversies, with special emphasis on their fannish dimension, see Rob Latham, "New Worlds and the New Wave in Fandom: Fan Culture and the Reshaping of Science Fiction in the Sixties," *Extrapolation* 47.2 (2006): 296–315.

82. Quoted in Greenland, *The Entropy Exhibition* 167.

83. I except Rob Latham's long series of very scrupulous articles on the New Wave, which represent work toward a sophisticated overview of the whole cultural moment.

84. "The same is true of Damon Knight's *Orbit* anthology series"; Delany, *Starboard Wine* 217.

85. Lester Del Rey, *The World of Science Fiction: 1926–1976, The History of a Subculture* (New York: Ballantine, 1979) 252; the bulk of Del Rey's account of the New Wave (249–62) is mostly an unfortunate index of resistance and reaction.

Chapter 3

1. Michael Moorcock, "Michael Moorcock, 1939-," *Into the Media Web: Selected Short Non-Fiction, 1956–2006* (Manchester: Savoy, 2010) 28.

2. Moorcock discusses the details of his novel-writing formulas in some detail with Colin Greenland in Greenland, *Michael Moorcock: Death Is No Obstacle* (Manchester: Savoy, 1992) 6–12.

3. Moorcock, Introduction to *Kane of Old Mars* (1997), *Into the Media Web* 589.

4. Moorcock, *Into the Media Web* 589.

5. There is a perspicacious—and quite humorous—discussion of the issue of technological incongruities in planetary romance among the writers L. Sprague de Camp, Poul Anderson, and Leigh Brackett in *The Blade of Conan*, ed. de Camp (New York: Ace Books, 1979) 327–47.

6. Michael Moorcock, *Kane of Old Mars* (London: Gollancz, 2015) 9.

7. Moorcock later rewrote two of these thrillers, *Somewhere in the Night* and *Printer's Devil* (both 1966, as by "Bill Barclay"), and published them as *The Chinese Agent* (1970) and *The Russian Intelligence* (1980), "comic capers" featuring the down-at-the-heels MI6 agent Jerry Cornell, a kind of downmarket James Bond (and a seedy transformation of Jerry Conelius).

8. The latter three volumes appeared under slightly different titles in their original U.S. appearances from Lancer Books.

9. Michael Moorcock, Introduction to *Hawkmoon* (Stone Mountain, GA: White Wolf, 1995) vii.

10. Michael Moorcock, *Hawkmoon: The History of the Runestaff* (London: Gollancz, 2013) 18.

11. Moorcock, *Hawkmoon: The History of the Runestaff* 17.

12. Moorcock, *Hawkmoon: The History of the Runestaff* 539.

13. *Selected Writings of Walter Pater*, ed. Harold Bloom (1974; New York: Columbia University Press, 1982) 60.

14. John Clute, "Moorcock, Michael (John)," *The Encyclopedia of Fantasy*, ed. John Clute and John Grant (New York: St.

Martin's P, 1997) 767; the description of "plot coupons," a term invented by critic Nick Lowe, is from David Langford, "Plot Coupons," *The Encyclopedia of Fantasy* 658.

15. Greenland, *Death Is No Obstacle* 6.
16. Moorcock, *Hawkmoon: The History of the Runestaff* 509.
17. Moorcock, *Hawkmoon: The History of the Runestaff* 516.
18. Moorcock, *Hawkmoon: The History of the Runestaff* 626.
19. Moorcock, *Hawkmoon: The History of the Runestaff* 627.
20. Michael Moorcock, *The Secret of the Runestaff* (New York: Lancer Books, 1969) 192; Moorcock, *Hawkmoon: The History of the Runestaff* 627.
21. See Greenland, *Death Is No Obstacle* 64–5. The term "fix-up" was coined by the science fiction writer A. E. van Vogt; see Peter Nicholls, ed., *The Science Fiction Encyclopedia* (Garden City, NY: Doubleday, 1979) 10.
22. Michael Moorcock, *The Eternal Champion* (London: Gollancz, 2013) 308; italics in original.
23. Moorcock, *The Eternal Champion* 244, 281–4.
24. Moorcock, *The Eternal Champion* 220.
25. Moorcock, *The Eternal Champion* 265.
26. Moorcock, *The Eternal Champion* 308–9, italics in original. The Sword of the Dawn fits uneasily in this company, and Moorcock will later make clear (in *The Quest for Tanelorn*) that in the Runestaff tetralogy the Black Sword's manifestation is actually the black jewel in Hawkmoon's forehead.
27. Moorcock, *The Eternal Champion* 310.
28. Michael Moorcock, *Elric: To Rescue Tanelorn* (New York: Del Rey, 2008) 63.
29. Moorcock, *Elric: To Rescue Tanelorn* 76.
30. Moorcock, *Elric: To Rescue Tanelorn* 95. At least one other reference in the story to the eternal or ideal nature of Tanelorn (*Elric: To Rescue Tanelorn* 85) was added after the 1977 publication of the story in *The Bane of the Black Sword* (New York: DAW, 1977).
31. Moorcock, *The Eternal Champion* 246.
32. Moorcock, *The Eternal Champion* 342.
33. Michael Moorcock, *Corum: The Prince in the Scarlet Robe* (London: Gollancz, 2013) 447.
34. Michael Moorcock, "Introduction," *Corum: The Coming of Chaos* (Clarkston, GA: White Wolf, 1997) 5.
35. Never one to take himself too seriously, Moorcock parodies the whole business of a hero outfitted with supernatural add-ons and carrying sentient weapons in the 1974 squib "The Stone Thing" (*Elric: To Rescue Tanelorn* 321–6).
36. Moorcock, *Corum: The Prince in the Scarlet Robe* 469.
37. Moorcock, *Corum: The Prince in the Scarlet Robe* 470.
38. Moorcock, *Corum: The Prince in the Scarlet Robe* 451.
39. *Elric of Melniboné* was first published in the U.S., with unauthorized edits, under the confusing (and also unauthorized) title *The Dreaming City* (New York: Lancer, 1972); it appeared in a proper edition from DAW in 1977.
40. Michael Moorcock, *Corum: The Prince with the Silver Hand* (London: Gollancz, 2013) 426.
41. Michael Moorcock, *Count Brass* (Clarkston, GA: White Wolf, 2000) ix.
42. Michael Moorcock, *Hawkmoon: Count Brass* (London: Gollancz, 2013) 365.
43. Moorcock, *Hawkmoon: Count Brass* 374.
44. Moorcock, *Hawkmoon: Count Brass* 363, 389.
45. Moorcock, *Hawkmoon: Count Brass* 389; the two brothers, then, can be associated with the "Guardians" of "To Rescue Tanelorn..."
46. Moorcock, *Hawkmoon: Count Brass* 390.
47. Moorcock, *Hawkmoon: Count Brass* 391.
48. Moorcock, *Hawkmoon: Count Brass* 392.
49. Michael Moorcock, Interview with John Picacio, *Locus* 73.6 (December 2014) [36–39, 64] 64. In this Moorcock echoes his friend M. John Harrison, who blogs that "Every moment of a science fiction story must represent the triumph of writing over worldbuilding.... It is the great clomping foot of nerdism. It is the attempt

to exhaustively survey space that isn't there"; "very afraid," *Uncle Zip's Window* (January 27, 2007) <http://web.archive.org/web/20080410181840/http://uzwi.wordpress.com/2007/01/27/very-afraid/>.
50. Greenland, *Death Is No Obstacle* 141.
51. Michael Moorcock, *The Nomad of Time* (London: Gollancz, 2014) 66.
52. Moorcock, *The Nomad of Time* 148.
53. Brian Baker argues usefully that beyond its manifest critique of imperialism, *The Warlord of the Air*, through its very form as pastiche Edwardian "scientific romance" critiques the colonialism inherent in Victorian and Edwardian adventure fiction; see "Witness to the End of the World: Colonialism, the Scientific Romance, and Michael Moorcock's 'Nomad of the Time Streams' Trilogy," *Foundation* 34 (2005): 40–48.
54. Moorcock, *Locus* Interview 39 (quoted from the *LA Times*).
55. Arthur Symons, "The Decadent Movement in Literature," *Literature and Culture at the Fin de Siècle*, ed. Talia Schaffer (New York: Pearson Longman, 2007) 71.
56. Michael Moorcock, *The Dancers at the End of Time* (London: Gollancz, 2013) 42.
57. Moorcock, *The Dancers at the End of Time* 11.
58. Moorcock, *The Dancers at the End of Time* 572.
59. Moorcock, *The Dancers at the End of Time* 582.
60. Moorcock, *The Dancers at the End of Time* 619.
61. In his 1977 essay "Starship Stormtroopers," Moorcock savagely attacks what he sees as the "reactionary," "authoritarian," and "paternalistic" tendencies in much postwar science fiction, especially Heinlein's; *Into the Media Web* 555–65.
62. All of these stories, and "Elric at the End of Time," are collected in Michael Moorcock, *Tales from the End of Time* (London: Gollancz, 2014).
63. Moorcock, "Introduction," *Elric: To Rescue Tanelorn* xix.
64. Michael Moorcock, "Afterword to the 2004 Edition (Haunted Palaces and Poisoned Chalices: The World of Gloriana)," *Gloriana; or, The Unfulfill'd Queen* (London: Gollancz, 2013) 383.
65. Moorcock, *Gloriana* xxi, xix.
66. Moorcock, *Gloriana* 383.
67. Moorcock wrote *The Golden Barge* when he was around seventeen; four chapters (with revisions) appeared in *The Time Dweller* (London: Hart Davis, 1969), and the book a whole was published by Savoy (in the UK) and DAW (in the U.S.) in 1979.
68. Greenland, *Death Is No Obstacle* 121.
69. Michael Moorcock, *Wizardry and Wild Romance: A Study of Epic Fantasy* (Austin, TX: Monkeybrain Books, 2004) 118.
70. Moorcock, *Gloriana* 380–1.
71. Edmund Spenser, *The Faerie Queene*, ed. A. C. Hamilton (London: Longman, 1977) 737.
72. Simon Shepherd, *Spenser (Harvester New Readings)* (Atlantic Highlands, NJ: Humanities Research Press International, 1989) 5; Shepherd quotes with relish Karl Marx's opinion of Spenser: "Elizabeth's arse-kissing poet" (3).
73. Moorcock, *Gloriana* 381.
74. Greenland, *Death Is No Obstacle* 119.
75. The rewritten chapter is the only change to the revised edition of the novel (London: Phoenix, 1993); Moorcock "wrote out" the rape, he explains in a 2003 post on "Moorcock's Miscellany," because "I realised after I'd written the book that that sequence MIGHT be used to justify rape and indeed similar arguments HAD been used to justify rape" (http://www.multiverse.org/fora/showpost.php?p=55843&postcount=7). The original ending, ironically, is far a better piece of writing than the revision; in currently available editions of *Gloriana*, Moorcock has restored the original ending but included the revised chapter as an appendix, along with a note explaining his rationale.
76. Moorcock, *Gloriana* 253, 301.
77. See Greenland, *Death Is No Obstacle* 117.
78. Greenland, *Death Is No Obstacle* 122.

Chapter 4

1. Samuel R. Delany, "About 5.750 Words," *The Jewel-Hinged Jaw: Notes on

Notes—Chapter 4

the Language of Science Fiction (New York: Berkley, 1977) 31–32, italics in original.

2. Kathryn Hume, in her *Fantasy and Mimesis: Responses to Reality in Western Literature* (New York: Methuen, 1984) usefully opposes fantasy to "mimetic" fiction, singling out "realism" as a nineteenth- and twentieth-century dominant.

3. The term "novum" is Darko Suvin's; see his *Metamorphoses of Science Fiction: On the Poetics and History of a Literary Genre* (New Haven: Yale University Press, 1979) 63–84.

4. This was especially true of Moorcock's reputation in the U.S., where genre distinctions seemed more deeply engrained in the literary culture than in the UK, where Moorcock's work had been taken seriously in literary circles from early on. But compare his statements quoted in my Conclusion.

5. Michael Moorcock, *Breakfast in the Ruins and Other Stories* (London: Gollancz, 2014) 165.

6. Moorcock, *Breakfast in the Ruins and Other Stories* 166.

7. See Moorcock's comments on the Multiverse website, http://www.multiverse.org/fora/showthread.php?t=6880.

8. Moorcock, *Breakfast in the Ruins and Other Stories* 122, 93.

9. Moorcock, *Breakfast in the Ruins and Other Stories* 7; this most recent publication encloses "Michael Moorcock" in scare quotes, which are not present in earlier editions.

10. Moorcock in conversation, quoted in Neil Gaiman's semi-autobiographical story, "One Life, Furnished in Early Moorcock," in Michael Moorcock, *Elric in the Dream Realms* (New York: Del Rey, 2009) 400.

11. The four Pyat novels appear under the collective title "Between the Wars" in various lists of Moorcock's works, but in their most recent edition, that of PM Press (2012–2013), their overall title is *The Colonel Pyat Quartet*.

12. There are references to Pyat in currently available editions of *The Final Programme*, but these were added for a 1979 revision; see Chapter 2, note 58.

13. Michael Moorcock, *The Cornelius Quartet* (London: Gollancz, 2013) 985.

14. John Clute, review of *The Laughter of Carthage*, in *Canary Fever: Reviews* (Harold Wood, Essex: Beccon Publications, 2009) 24; Michael Moorcock, "Michael Moorcock, 1939-," *Into the Media Web: Selected Short Non-fiction, 1956–2006*, ed. John Davey (Manchester: Savoy, 2010) 34.

15. Michael Moorcock, *Byzantium Endures* (1981; Oakland, CA: PM Press, 2012) 2, 3.

16. Moorcock, *Byzantium Endures* 1.

17. Moorcock, *Byzantium Endures* 11.

18. Michael Moorcock, *The Vengeance of Rome* (2006; Oakland, CA: PM Press, 2013) 574.

19. Moorcock, *Byzantium Endures* 11.

20. Moorcock, *Byzantium Endures* 2–3.

21. Michael Moorcock, *The Laughter of Carthage* (1984; Oakland, CA: PM Press, 2012) 5.

22. Moorcock, *Byzantium Endures* 190–92.

23. Moorcock, *The Laughter of Carthage* 494–96.

24. Moorcock, *The Laughter of Carthage* 478.

25. Moorcock, *The Laughter of Carthage* 465.

26. According to Max Wilcox on the "Terminal Café" website, the two books were written in tandem, one during the day and the other at night; see http://www.novymir.com.au/terminalcafe/vonbek.html#The%20City%20in%20the%20Autumn%20Stars.

27. The specific episodes described here are the seventeenth ("Ithaca"), the fifteenth ("Circe"), and the fourteenth ("Oxen of the Sun").

28. Colin Greenland, *Michael Moorcock: Death Is No Obstacle* (Manchester: Savoy, 1992) 103.

29. Greenland, *Death Is No Obstacle* 105.

30. Jeff Gardiner, *The Law of Chaos: The Multiverse of Michael Moorcock* (Manchester: Headpress, 2014) 117.

31. Greenland, *Death Is No Obstacle* 104.

32. John Clute, review of *Mother London*, *Look at the Evidence: Essays and Reviews* (Brooklyn: Serconia, 1995) 112.

33. That is, until the publication of *The Whispering Swarm* in 2015.

34. Michael Moorcock, *Mother London* (1988; New York: Harper & Row, 1989) 377, 380.

35. Moorcock, *Mother London* 378.
36. Moorcock, *Mother London* 468–9.
37. Moorcock, *Mother London* 5.
38. Moorcock, *Mother London* 386–7.
39. Michael Moorcock, "Blitz Kid," illustrated by Walter Simonson and Bob Wiacek, *9–11: The World's Finest Comic Book Writers and Artists Tell Stories to Remember*, ed. Paul Levitz (New York: DC Comics, 2002); the full text of "Blitz Kid" is available online at http://www.multiverse.org/wiki/index.php?title=Blitz_Kid.
40. Moorcock, *Mother London* 413.
41. Moorcock, *Mother London* 495–96.
42. Moorcock, *Mother London* 476.
43. Moorcock, *Mother London* 370.
44. Moorcock, *Mother London*, 455.
45. Clute, *Look at the Evidence* 113.
46. Greenland, *Death Is No Obstacle* 98.
47. Greenland, *Death Is No Obstacle* 100.
48. See Chapter Five for further discussion of these works.
49. Greenland, *Death Is No Obstacle* 137.
50. Michael Moorcock, *Jerusalem Commands* (1992; Oakland, CA: PM Press, 2013) 469.
51. John Clute, review of *Jerusalem Commands*, *Canary Fever* 26.
52. The ship shares its name, we recall, with the spaceship in *The Black Corridor*.
53. Moorcock, *Jerusalem Commands* 294.
54. Michael Moorcock, *King of the City* (New York: William Morrow, 2001) 421. Both the UK and American first editions of *King of the City* note Moorcock as "Author of *Mother London*" on their front covers.
55. John Clute, review of *The Vengeance of Rome*, *Canary Fever* 30.
56. For a more extended discussion of the von Bek "family," see Chapter Five.
57. References earlier in the tetralogy make it clear that Pyat was in the UK by 1940; prisoners only began being systematically exterminated in Auschwitz in September 1941, and the Final Solution was not fully set in train until the Wannsee Conference in early 1942.
58. Moorcock, *The Vengeance of Rome* 514, 502.
59. Moorcock, *The Vengeance of Rome* 507–08.
60. Moorcock, *The Vengeance of Rome* 300.
61. Moorcock, *The Vengeance of Rome* 574–75.
62. Moorcock, *The Vengeance of Rome* 576.
63. On the Rose, see Chapter Five.
64. Moorcock, *The Vengeance of Rome* 250–51.
65. Moorcock, *The Vengeance of Rome* 536.
66. Clute, *Canary Fever* 29.

Chapter 5

1. Moorcock recounts this period of his life in "Michael Moorcock, 1939-," *Into the Media Web: Selected Short Non-fiction, 1956–2006*, ed. John Davey (Manchester: Savoy, 2010) 34–38; *Letters from Hollywood* (London: Harrup, 1986) provides a vivid and amusing chronicle of Moorcock's time in California.
2. Moorcock has often expressed his admiration for Hans Jakob Christoffel von Grimmelshausen, whose picaresque novel *Simplicius Simplicissimus* (1668) is set during the Thirty Years War; in his introduction to *Von Bek*, Moorcock calls Grimmelshausen "my literary hero" (*Into the Media Web* 581).
3. Michael Moorcock, *Von Bek* (London: Gollancz, 2013) 5, 8–9. On Magdeburg, see C. V. Wedgwood, *The Thirty Years War* (1938; London: Methuen, 1981) 288–91.
4. So widespread are Grail stories that the British comedy troupe Monty Python could count on an audience's familiarity with the basics of Grail-lore as a precondition for their satirical take in the 1975 film *Monty Python and the Holy Grail*.
5. Moorcock, *Von Bek* 197.
6. Moorcock, *Von Bek* 204–05.
7. Colin Greenland, *Michael Moorcock: Death Is No Obstacle* (Manchester: Savoy, 1992) 110.
8. Greenland, *Death Is No Obstacle* 111.
9. This balloon-based confidence scheme is parallel to the one Colonel Pyat's friend Prince Nikolai (with Pyat's unwitting collusion) mounts in *The Laughter of Carthage*.
10. Moorcock, *Von Bek* 373–74.
11. Michael Moorcock, *The Cornelius Quartet* (London: Gollancz, 2013) 182.

12. Moorcock, *Von Bek* 583.
13. Greenland, *Death Is No Obstacle* 111.
14. Greenland, *Death Is No Obstacle* 114.
15. More tantalizing are Moorcock's abortive plans to use material cut from *The City in the Autumn Stars* in an "oriental fantasy" about "sexuality and gender identity"—*Manfred, or The Gentleman Houri*; see Greenland, *Death Is No Obstacle* 115–16.
16. Michael Moorcock, *The Dragon in the Sword* (New York: Ace, 1986).
17. See Moorcock's introduction to *Elric: To Rescue Tanelorn* (New York: Del Rey, 2008) xv.
18. Howard V. Chaykin, *The Swords of Heaven, The Flowers of Hell* (New York: Heavy Metal, 1979).
19. Moorcock, *Into the Media Web* 571, 573.
20. This is clearest from the novel's placement in the Eternal Champion omnibus editions Moorcock would prepare in the 1990s. In the English omnibus series, "The Tale of the Eternal Champion," *The Dragon in the Sword* appears in the second volume, *The Eternal Champion* (London: Orion/Millennium, 1992), which also collects *The Eternal Champion* and *Phoenix in Obsidian*; in the American series, "The Eternal Champion," the novel appears in the second volume, *Von Bek* (Stone Mountain, GA: White Wolf, 1995).
21. Michael Moorcock, *The Eternal Champion* (London: Gollancz, 2013) 365.
22. Moorcock, *The Eternal Champion* 367.
23. Moorcock, *The Eternal Champion* 395.
24. Moorcock, *The Eternal Champion* 405.
25. Moorcock, *The Eternal Champion* 650.
26. Michael Moorcock, Introduction to *Elric In the Dream Realms* (New York: Del Rey, 2009) xv.
27. Moorcock, *Elric In the Dream Realms* xvii.
28. Moorcock, *Elric In the Dream Realms* xx.
29. Michael Moorcock, *Elric: The Fortress of the Pearl* (London: Gollancz, 2013) 57.
30. Michael Moorcock, *The Stealer of Souls* (New York: Lancer, 1967) 18.
31. Michael Moorcock, *The Weird of the White Wolf* (New York: DAW, 1977) 41. Compare *Elric: The Stealer of Souls* (New York: Del Rey, 2008) 21, which has inserted a reference to the "dream couches" on which Elric has learned his sorcery, explored in the Moonbeam Roads trilogy (2001–2005) and the graphic novel *Elric: The Making of a Sorcerer* (2007); see Chapter Six. While the Del Rey edition—in the first volumes at least—reprints the Elric stories in the order of composition, it does not print their earliest *texts*.
32. Moorcock, *Elric: The Fortress of the Pearl* 225.
33. See the Introduction to *Elric: Swords and Roses* (New York: Del Rey, 2010) xxv–xxvi.
34. Swinburne spent the last three decades of his life in semi-forced retirement in Putney. "Ernest Wheldrake" was an undergraduate invention of Swinburne's: Swinburne reviewed *The Monomaniac's Tragedy, and other poems* in the Oxford magazine *Undergraduate Papers* in 1858, and thrilled Victorian readers with his assessment of this mad poet "who savoured the joys of murder in the last thrilling spasms of his child victim or tore at his mistress's small-clothes with his teeth"; they were no doubt disappointed to find that Wheldrake did not exist. See Donald Thomas, *Swinburne: The Poet and His World* (New York: Oxford University Press, 1979) 44–45.
35. Moorcock, *Elric: The Revenge of the Rose* 44, 111, 122; the latter reference is to the second Hawkmoon novel, *The Mad God's Amulet*.
36. Moorcock, *Elric: The Revenge of the Rose* 49–50.
37. Michael Moorcock, *Corum: The Prince in the Scarlet Robe* (London: Gollancz, 2013) 293.
38. Moorcock, *Elric: The Revenge of the Rose* 41.
39. Moorcock, *Elric: The Revenge of the Rose* 43.
40. Moorcock, *Elric: The Revenge of the Rose* 190.
41. Moorcock, *Elric: The Revenge of the Rose* 225.
42. Moorcock, *Elric: The Revenge of the Rose* 247.
43. Moorcock, *Elric: The Revenge of the Rose* 52.

44. Moorcock, *Elric: The Revenge of the Rose* 89.
45. Moorcock, *Elric: The Revenge of the Rose* 86.
46. See the Appendix for a full listing of the two omnibus series and some brief indications of the differences between the UK (Orion/Millennium) and U.S. (White Wolf) presentations. The first Millennium omnibuses (in hardback and trade paperback) apparently used readily available texts, but saw little revision apart from proofreading. Their mass market paperback reprints some years later, and the far more leisurely publication schedule of the White Wolf volumes, allowed for more comprehensive revision in many volumes. In what follows, I will discuss the texts of the hardcover White Wolf volumes, which seem to be a fair representation (apart from some matters of layout and some typographical errors) of Moorcock's most mature intentions for his texts, circa the second half of the 1990s.

Both John Davey and Michael Moorcock have provided helpful comments on the omnibus editions on the "Moorcock's Miscellany" website; see http://www.multiverse.org/fora/showpost.php?p=22021&postcount=12, http://www.multiverse.org/fora/showpost.php?p=114715&postcount=43, and http://www.multiverse.org/fora/showpost.php?p=27965&postcount=6.

47. *The Wrecks of Time* was first published in book form in 1971 as *The Rituals of Infinity*; *The Winds of Limbo* first appeared as *The Fireclown*; and *The Shores of Death* was first published as *The Twilight Man*.
48. James Joyce, *Ulysses: The Corrected Text*, ed. Hans Walter Gabler et al. (New York: Random House, 1986) 28.
49. See Jane Millgate, *Walter Scott: The Making of the Novelist* (Toronto: University of Toronto Press, 1984) 172–73.
50. Michael Moorcock, Introduction to *Kane of Old Mars* (1998), *Into the Media Web* 590.
51. Michael Moorcock, *Hawkmoon* (Stone Mountain, GA: White Wolf, 1995) vii.
52. Michael Moorcock, *The Roads Between the Worlds* (Stone Mountain, GA: White Wolf, 1996) viii.
53. Alveric from Dunsany's *The King of Elfland's Daughter*; Alfric from *Three Hearts and Three Lions*, Imric from *The Broken Sword*.
54. Lin Carter, *Imaginary Worlds: The Art of Fantasy* (New York: Ballantine, 1973) 200.
55. In *The Whispering Swarm* (New York: Tor, 2015) 150, Moorcock comments that "Cornelius" is "the name I looked for that could not be easily identified with one European nation."
56. Interestingly enough, Jermays the Crooked first appeared *before* the creation of Jerry Cornelius.
57. Moorcock reckons that the first appearance of a von Bek in his fiction, though comparatively unrelated to the rest, is Katinka van Bak in *The Champion of Garathorm* (1973); see his comment on the "Multiverse" website, http://www.multiverse.org/fora/showpost.php?p=53041&postcount=22. I'd suggest an even earlier prehistory for the Bek name: Earl Au*bec*, the protagonist of "Earl Aubec and the Golem" (published in 1964 as "Master of Chaos," *Elric: To Rescue Tanelorn* 161–78) and the hero of "Earl Aubec of Malador," a series of four novels outlined (but never written) in 1966 (*Elric in the Dream Realms* 372–82).
58. Michael Moorcock, *Lunching with the Antichrist, A Family History: 1925–2015* (Shingletown, CA: Mark E. Ziesing, 1995) 3.
59. Moorcock, *Lunching with the Antichrist* 97, 100–01.
60. Neither "A Dead Singer" (1974) or "Dead Singers" (in *Lunching with the Antichrist*) should be confused with the 1971 Jerry Cornelius story "Dead Singers."
61. Moorcock, *Lunching with the Antichrist* 202; compare Michael Moorcock, *My Experiences in the Third World War* (Manchester: Savoy, 1980) 51.
62. This bridge, entitled "Limbo," is on 160 of *The Eternal Champion* (Stone Mountain, GA: White Wolf, 1994).
63. Michael Moorcock, "In Lighter Vein," *Sojan* (Manchester: Savoy, 1977) 137.
64. Michael Moorcock, *The Time Dweller* (New York: Berkley, 1969) 165; *Von Bek* (Stone Mountain, GA: White Wolf, 1996) 693.
65. Michael Moorcock, *The Roads Between the Worlds* (Clarkston, GA: White Wolf, 1996) 1.

66. Moorcock, *The Roads Between the Worlds* 264.
67. Moorcock, *The Roads Between the Worlds* 390.
68. Greenland, *Death Is No Obstacle* 142.
69. See Moorcock's various comments on the novel on the Multiverse site: http://www.multiverse.org/wiki/index.php?title=The_Steel_Tsar.
70. Greenland, *Death Is No Obstacle* 143.
71. Bastable has already appeared briefly as a League member in *The End of All Songs* (1976). The organization seems to toggle between being a "Guild" and a "League": it is the Guild of Temporal Adventurers in the first editions of the Bastable books, then the League in the omnibus revisions and the Cornelius stories; more recently, in the Moonbeam Roads novels, it is once again a Guild. I have attempted no consistency in my own references.
72. Greenland, *Death Is No Obstacle* 143.
73. Michael Moorcock, *The Steel Tsar* (New York: DAW, 1981) 145, 158.
74. The name is a portmanteau of Jerry Cornelius and the *Hope Dempsey*, the spaceship of *The Black Corridor*; it will reappear to name ships commanded by Maurice Quelch (in *Jerusalem Commands*) and Horace Quelch (in the Second Ether books).
75. See Chapter 1, note 34.
76. See Moorcock's comment on the Multiverse site, http://www.multiverse.org/fora/showpost.php?p=3772&postcount=2.
77. Alan Moore, introduction to Michael Moorcock, *Elric: The Stealer of Souls* (New York: Del Rey, 2008) xix; John Clute, "Introduction to The Michael Moorcock Collection" (in all volumes of the 2013–2015 Gollancz collection) xii. Interesting enough, most of the "Bek" name changes of the Orion/millennium-White Wolf omnibus editions have been removed from The Michael Moorcock collection, and the names reverted to their originals.

Chapter 6

1. Michael Moorcock, general introduction to "The Michael Moorcock Collection" xv; this introduction appears at the beginning of each of the 2013–2015 Gollancz volumes.
2. William Sims Bainbridge, *Dimensions of Science Fiction* (Cambridge: Harvard University Press, 1986) 54–55.
3. James Gleick, *Chaos: Making a New Science* (New York: Penguin, 1987) 307.
4. Gleick, *Chaos* 7–8.
5. "Get the Music Right: Michael Moorcock interviewed by Terry Bisson," in Michael Moorcock, *Modem Times 2.0* (Oakland, CA: PM Press, 2011(98.
6. Gleick, *Chaos* 103.
7. Gleick, *Chaos* 228–29; the Mandelbrot set is defined on 223.
8. Michael Moorcock, *London Bone* (London: Scribner, 2001) 235.
9. Michael Moorcock, *Blood: A Southern Fantasy*, in *The War Amongst the Angels* (London: Gollancz, 2014) 62, 61.
10. Moorcock, *The War Amongst the Angels* 9.
11. *Fabulous Harbours* was published in the U.S. as *Fabulous Harbors*.
12. The long story "Lunching With the Antichrist," in fact, appears in both collections.
13. For an overview of Blakiana, see Michael Moorcock, "The Odyssey of Sexton Blake" (1961), *Into the Media Web: Selected Short Non-fiction, 1956–2006*, ed. John Davey (Manchester: Savoy, 2010) 451–58.
14. Rose von Bek, of course, also appears in *Jerusalem Commands*, published four years earlier.
15. Moorcock, *The War Amongst the Angels* 530.
16. Moorcock, *The War Amongst the Angels* 537, 538–49.
17. *Conan the Barbarian* #14, "A Sword Called Stormbringer!" (March 1972) and *Conan the Barbarian* #15, "The Green Empress of Melniboné" (May 1972), script by Roy Thomas, art by Barry Windsor-Smith. These issues have been often reprinted.
18. Michael Moorcock, Walter Simonson, Mark Reeve, and John Ridgway, *Michael Moorcock's Multiverse* (New York: DC Comics, 1999).
19. The script of "Duke Elric" is reprinted in Michael Moorcock, *Duke Elric* (New York: Del Rey, 2009) 165–260.
20. Moorcock, *Duke Elric* 243, 250.
21. Michael Moorcock, "Introduction

to the French Edition of Elric," *Elric: Swords and Roses* (New York: Del Rey, 2010) 407.

22. Michael Moorcock, *Elric: The Moonbeam Roads* (London: Gollancz, 2014) 133. "Duchess Miggea of Dolwic" is a none-too-subtle anagrammatic reference to Baroness Margaret ("Maggie") Thatcher, who lived in a gated community in Dulwich, London, after her retirement.

23. Moorcock, *Elric: The Moonbeam Roads* 188.

24. Moorcock, *Elric: The Moonbeam Roads* 72.

25. Moorcock, *Elric: The Moonbeam Roads* 335–36.

26. In *Stormbringer*, he is tied to the mast; see Michael Moorcock, *Elric: The Stealer of Souls* (New York: Del Rey, 2008) 314–19. In *Destiny's Brother* and *Son of the Wolf*, we are told he has been "crucified to the yardarm" (*Elric: The Moonbeam Roads* 447), echoing the scene in *The English Assassin* where Jerry has been similarly crucified to the "lowest yard of the mizzen" of a yacht (Michael Moorcock, *The Cornelius Quartet* [London: Gollancz, 2013] 503–04)—not to mention the conclusion of *Behold the Man*.

27. Moorcock, *Elric: The Moonbeam Roads* 656.

28. See Paul M. Sammon, *Conan the Phenomenon: The Legacy of Robert E. Howard's Fantasy Icon* (Milwaukie, OR: Dark Horse, 2007) 118–19 on the book series.

29. Michael Moorcock and Walter Simonson, *Michael Moorcock's Elric: The Making of a Sorcerer* (New York: DC Comics, 2007). The script of *Elric: The Making of a Sorcerer* is reprinted in Michael Moorcock, *Elric in the Dream Realms* (New York: Del Rey, 2009) 213–345.

30. Moorcock, *Elric in the Dream Realms* 215–16.

31. Moorcock, *Elric: The Moonbeam Roads* 448.

32. Moorcock, *Elric: The Moonbeam Roads* 889.

33. Moorcock, *Elric: The Moonbeam Roads* 989. 985; Michael Moorcock, *The Eternal Champion* (London: Gollancz, 2013) 7. Moorcock complicates matters by mentioning, *in propria persona*, that he has had most of his stories about Elric from "Mr John D—, that contemporary manifestation of the Eternal Champion," who "married a distant relative of mine and eventually settled in the north" (*Elric: The Moonbeam Roads* 761).

34. Moorcock, *Elric: The Moonbeam Roads* 865.

35. Michael Moorcock, *The Nomad of Time* (London: Gollancz, 2014) 5.

36. Michael Moorcock and Storm Constantine, *Silverheart: A Novel of the Multiverse* (2000; Amherst, MA: Pyr, 2005) 5; Moorcock quoted in Jeff Gardiner, *The Law of Chaos: The Multiverse of Michael Moorcock* (Manchester: Headpress, 2014) 133.

37. Quoted in Gardiner, *The Law of Chaos* 133, bracketed word Gardiner's.

38. Michael Moorcock, "I'm writing the new Doctor Who," *The Guardian* (20 November 2009), http://www.theguardian.com/books/2009/nov/21/michael-moorcock-doctor-who-author.

39. Michael Moorcock, *Tales From the Texas Woods* (Austin, TX: Mojo Press, 1997); Moorcock himself dates "Johnny Lonesome" to 1956.

40. Michael Moorcock, *The Metatemporal Detective* (Amherst, MA: Pyr, 2007). Of all of Moorcock's work, what has been most signally neglected in this book is his large body of short fiction. In addition to the important collections I've mentioned (*Lunching with the Antichrist* and *Fabulous Harbours*), Moorcock has published several other significant collections, including *London Bone* (2001), which assembles (mostly) realistic (mostly) London-related stories. There are three substantial volumes devoted to miscellaneous short fiction in the Gollancz "Michael Moorcock Collection," but they represent only a fraction of his published short stories. A very useful representative collection of his short fiction is *The Best of Michael Moorcock*, ed. John Davey with Ann and Jeff VanderMeer (San Francisco: Tachyon, 2009).

41. Moorcock, "I'm writing the new Doctor Who."

42. Michael Moorcock, *Doctor Who: The Coming of the Terraphiles; or, Pirates of the Second Aether!!* (London: BBC Books, 2010) 324.

43. Douglas A. Anderson, in J. R. R. Tolkien, *The Lord of the Rings: Collector's Edition* (Boston: Houghton Mifflin, 1994) v.

44. Michael Moorcock, *The Whispering Swarm* (New York: Tor, 2015) 137, 173.

45. The sanctuary is more commonly spelled "Alsatia," and as such has figured in a number of literary works, most prominent among them probably Sir Walter Scott's *The Fortunes of Nigel* (1822).

46. One is reminded, though, that Moorcock has presented Duval and Turpin as "tramway-tobymen" in *The War Amongst the Angels*.

47. Alexandre Dumas's *Twenty Years After*, the first sequel to *The Three Musketeers*, similarly features the Musketeers attempting to save Charles I from execution; the plot element of exchanging prisoners seems clearly borrowed from Dickens's *A Tale of Two Cities*, not to mention Dumas's *The Man in the Iron Mask*.

48. Prince Rupert (1619–1682) was Charles I's nephew and perhaps the most capable of his military commanders in the Civil War.

49. See Michael Moorcock, "Michael Moorcock, 1939–," *Into the Media Web: Selected Short Non-fiction, 1956–2006*, ed. John Davey (Manchester: Savoy, 2010) 30–32.

50. I have in mind Joyce's *A Portrait of the Artist as a Young Man* rather than *Ulysses*, though the latter novel has many autobiographical elements.

51. Colin Greenland, *Michael Moorcock: Death Is No Obstacle* (Manchester: Savoy, 1992) 143.

Conclusion

1. See Michel Delville, "The Moorcock/Hawkwind Connection: Science Fiction and Rock 'n' Roll Culture," *Foundation* 62 (1994): 64–69, and Jeff Gardiner, "Hawkwind: Michael Moorcock & Robert Calvert," *The Law of Chaos: The Multiverse of Michael Moorcock* (Manchester: Headpress, 2014) 148–52. There is a substantial section of essays on musical topics, including the liner notes to the 1994 reissue of the Deep Fix album *New World's Fair*, in Moorcock's *London Peculiar and Other Nonfiction*, ed. Michael Moorcock and Allan Kausch (Oakland, CA: PM Press, 2012) 163–83.

2. Michael Moorcock, Julien Blondel, Didier Poli, Robin Recht, Jean Bastide, *Elric, Volume 1: The Ruby Throne* (London: Titan Comics, 2014), and Michael Moorcock, Julien Blondel, Jean-Luc Cano, Julien Telo, Robin Recht, and Didier Poli, *Elric, Volume 2: Stormbringer* (London: Titan Comics, 2014); Chris Roberson and Francesco Biagini, *Elric: The Balance Lost*, 3 volumes (Los Angeles: Boom! Studios, 2012).

3. Neil Gaiman, Foreword to Michael Moorcock, *Elric in the Dream Realms* (New York: Del Rey, 2009) xiii-xiv.

4. "Tributes to Michael Moorcock," *Locus* 73.6 (December 2014): 42–44.

5. Michael Moorcock, *The Golden Barge* (New York: DAW, 1979) 10.

6. Moorcock, *The Golden Barge* 11.

7. Harold Bloom, *The Western Canon: The Books and School of the Ages* (New York: Harcourt Brace, 1994) 548.

8. John Clute, "Introduction to *The Michael Moorcock Collection*" xii; this introduction appears at the beginning of each of the 2013–2015 Gollancz volumes.

Bibliography

Aldiss, Brian W. *The Detached Retina: Aspects of SF and Fantasy.* Syracuse: Syracuse University Press, 1995.

Alpers, Hans Joachim. "Loincloth, Double Ax, and Magic: 'Heroic Fantasy' and Related Genres." Trans Robert Plank. *Science Fiction Studies* 5.1 (March 1978): 19–32.

Anderson, Poul. *The Broken Sword.* 1954; London: Gollancz, 2014.

_____. *Fantasy.* New York: Tor, 1981.

_____. *Three Hearts and Three Lions.* New York: Berkley, 1978.

Attebery, Brian. *Strategies of Fantasy.* Bloomington: Indiana University Press, 1992.

Bainbridge, William Sims. *Dimensions of Science Fiction.* Cambridge: Harvard University Press, 1986.

Baker, Brian. "Witness to the End of the World: Colonialism, the Scientific Romance, and Michael Moorcock's 'Nomad of the Time Streams' Trilogy." *Foundation* 34 (2005): 40–48.

Bilyeu, Richard. *The Tanelorn Archives: A Primary and Secondary Bibliography of the Works of Michael Moorcock 1949–1979.* Manitoba: Pandora's Books, 1981.

Bloom, Harold. *The Western Canon: The Books and School of the Ages.* New York: Harcourt Brace, 1994.

Carpenter, Humphry. *Tolkien: A Biography.* Boston: Houghton Mifflin, 1977.

Carter, Lin. *Imaginary Worlds: The Art of Fantasy.* New York: Ballantine, 1973.

_____, ed. *Flashing Swords! #1.* New York: Dell, 1973.

_____, ed. *Flashing Swords! #2.* New York: Dell, 1973.

Chaykin, Howard V. *The Swords of Heaven, The Flowers of Hell.* New York: Heavy Metal, 1979.

Clute, John. *Canary Fever: Reviews.* Harold Wood, Essex: Beccon Publications, 2009.

_____. *Look at the Evidence: Essays and Reviews.* Brooklyn: Serconia, 1995.

Clute, John, and John Grant, eds. *The Encyclopedia of Fantasy.* New York: St. Martin's P, 1997.

Davey, John. *Michael Moorcock: A Reader's Guide.* London: Jayde Design, 1992.

De Camp, L. Sprague. *Literary Swordsmen and Sorcerers: The Makers of Heroic Fantasy.* Sauk City, WI: Arkham House, 1976.

_____, ed. *The Blade of Conan.* New York: Ace Books, 1979.

Delany, Samuel R. *The Jewel-Hinged Jaw: Notes on the Language of Science Fiction.* New York: Berkley, 1977.

_____. *Silent Interviews: On Language, Race, Sex, Science Fiction, and Some Comics.* Hanover, NH: Wesleyan University Press, 1994.

_____. *Starboard Wine: More Notes on the Language of Science Fiction,* rev. ed. Middletown, CT: Wesleyan University Press, 2012.

Del Rey, Lester. *The World of Science Fiction: 1926–1976, The History of a Subculture.* New York: Ballantine, 1979.

Delville, Michel. "The Moorcock/Hawkwind Connection: Science Fiction and Rock 'n' Roll Culture." *Foundation* 62 (1994): 64–69.

Ellmann, Richard. *James Joyce,* 2d ed. Oxford: Oxford University Press, 1982.

Frost, Robert. *Collected Poems, Prose, and Plays.* Ed. Richard Poirier and Mark Richardson. New York: Library of America, 1995.

Gardiner, Jeff. *The Law of Chaos: The Multiverse of Michael Moorcock.* Manchester: Headpress, 2014.

Gleick, James. *Chaos: Making a New Science.* New York: Penguin, 1987.

Greenland, Colin. *The Entropy Exhibition: Michael Moorcock and the British "New Wave" in Science Fiction.* London: Routledge & Kegan Paul, 1983.

_____. *Michael Moorcock: Death Is No Obstacle.* Manchester: Savoy, 1992.

Harrison, Andrew. "Michael Moorcock: 'I think Tolkien was a crypto-fascist.'" *The New Statesman* (July 25, 2115): http://www.newstatesman.com/culture/2015/07/michael-moorcock-i-think-tolkien-was-crypto-fascist.

Harrison, Harry, ed. *SF: Author's Choice 3.* New York: Berkley, 1971

Harrison, M. John. "very afraid" (blog post). *Uncle Zip's Window* (January 27, 2007) http://web.archive.org/web/20080410181840/http://uzwi.wordpress.com/2007/01/27/very-afraid/.

Hartwell, David G. *Age of Wonders: Exploring the World of Science Fiction.* 1984; rev. ed., New York: Tor, 1996.

Hoey, Michael. "Disguising Doom: A Study of the Linguistic Features of Audience Manipulation in Michael Moorcock's *The Eternal Champion.*" *Imagining Apocalypse: Studies in Cultural Crisis,* ed. David Seed. Basingstoke: Palgrave Macmillan, 2000. 151–65.

Hume, Kathryn. *Fantasy and Mimesis: Responses to Reality in Western Literature.* New York: Methuen, 1984.

James, Edward. *Science Fiction in the Twentieth Century.* Oxford: Oxford University Press, 1994.

_____. "Tolkien, Lewis and the Explosion of Genre Fantasy." *The Cambridge Companion to Fantasy Literature.* Ed. Edward James and Farah Mendlesohn. Cambridge: Cambridge Univeristy Press, 2012. 72–74.

Jones, Langdon, and Michael Moorcock, eds. *The Nature of the Catastrophe.* London: Hutchinson, 1971.

_____. *The New Nature of the Catastrophe.* 1993; London: Orion, 1997.

Joyce, James. *Ulysses: The Corrected Text.* Ed. Hans Walter Gabler et al. New York: Random House, 1986.

Kaplan, Carter. *Tally-Ho, Cornelius!* Hyde Park, NY: Mustard Lid Press, 2008.

Latham, Rob. "*New Worlds* and the New Wave in Fandom: Fan Culture and the Reshaping of Science Fiction in the Sixties." *Extrapolation* 47.2 (2006): 296–315.

Löwy, Michael, and Robert Sayre. *Romanticism Against the Tide of Modernity.* Durham: Duke University Press, 2001.

Mendlesohn, Farah. *Rhetorics of Fantasy.* Middletown, CT: Wesleyan University Press, 2008.

Millgate, Jane. *Walter Scott: The Making of the Novelist.* Toronto: University of Toronto Press, 1984.

Moorcock, Michael. *The Bane of the Black Sword.* New York: DAW, 1977.

_____. *The Best of Michael Moorcock.* Ed. John Davey with Ann and Jeff VanderMeer. San Francisco: Tachyon, 2009.

_____. *Breakfast in the Ruins and Other Stories.* London: Gollancz, 2014.

_____. *Byzantium Endures.* 1981; Oakland, CA: PM Press, 2012.

_____. *Casablanca.* 1989; London: Gollancz, 1993.

_____. *A Cornelius Calendar.* London: Gollancz, 2015.

_____. *The Cornelius Quartet.* London: Gollancz, 2013.

_____. *Corum: The Coming of Chaos.* Clarkston, GA: White Wolf, 1997.

_____. *Corum: The Prince in the Scarlet Robe.* London: Gollancz, 2013.

_____. *Corum: The Prince with the Silver Hand.* London: Gollancz, 2013.

_____. *Count Brass.* Clarkston, GA: White Wolf, 2000.

_____. *The Dancers at the End of Time.* London: Gollancz, 2013.

_____. *Doctor Who: The Coming of the Terraphiles; or, Pirates of the Second Aether!!* London: BBC Books, 2010.

_____. *The Dragon in the Sword.* New York: Ace, 1986.

_____. *The Dreaming City.* New York: Lancer, 1972.

_____. *Duke Elric.* New York: Del Rey, 2009.

_____. *Elric in the Dream Realms.* New York: Del Rey, 2009.

_____. *Elric: The Fortress of the Pearl.* London: Gollanz, 2013.

_____. *Elric: The Moonbeam Roads.* London: Gollancz, 2014.
_____. *Elric: The Revenge of the Rose.* London: Gollancz, 2014.
_____. *Elric: The Sleeping Sorceress and Other Stories.* London: Gollancz, 2013.
_____. *Elric: The Stealer of Souls.* New York: Del Rey, 2008.
_____. *Elric: Swords and Roses.* New York: Del Rey, 2010.
_____. *Elric: To Rescue Tanelorn.* New York: Del Rey, 2008.
_____. *The Eternal Champion.* London: Orion/Millennium, 1992.
_____. *The Eternal Champion.* Stone Mountain, GA: White Wolf, 1994.
_____. *The Eternal Champion.* London: Gollancz, 2013.
_____. *The Final Programme.* New York: Avon, 1968.
_____. *Gloriana; or, The Unfulfill'd Queen.* London: Phoenix, 1993.
_____. *Gloriana; or, The Unfulfill'd Queen.* London: Gollancz, 2013.
_____. *The Golden Barge.* New York: DAW, 1979.
_____. *Hawkmoon.* Stone Mountain, GA: White Wolf, 1995.
_____. *Hawkmoon: Count Brass.* London: Gollancz, 2013.
_____. *Hawkmoon: The History of the Runestaff.* London: Gollancz, 2013.
_____. "I'm writing the new Doctor Who." *The Guardian* (20 November 2009). http://www.theguardian.com/books/2009/nov/21/michael-moorcock-doctor-who-author.
_____. Interview with John Picacio. *Locus* 73.6 (December 2014): 36–39, 64.
_____. *Into the Media Web: Selected Short Non-fiction, 1956–2006.* Ed. John Davey. Manchester: Savoy, 2010.
_____. *Jerry Cornelius: His Lives and His Times.* London: Gollancz, 2014.
_____. *Kane of Old Mars.* London: Gollancz, 2015.
_____. *The Laughter of Carthage.* 1984; Oakland, CA: PM Press, 2012.
_____. *Letters from Hollywood.* London: Harrap, 1986.
_____. *London Blood.* London: Scribner, 2001.
_____. *London Peculiar and Other Nonfiction.* Ed. Michael Moorcock and Allan Kausch. Oakland, CA: PM Press, 2010.
_____. *Lunching with the Antichrist, A Family History: 1925–2015.* Shingletown, CA: Mark V. Ziesing, 1995.
_____. *The Metatemporal Detective.* Amherst, MA: Pyr, 2007.
_____. *Modem Times 2.0.* Oakland, CA: PM Press, 2011.
_____. *My Experiences in the Third World War.* Manchester: Savoy, 1980.
_____. *The Nomad of Time.* London: Gollancz, 2014.
_____. *The Opium General and Other Stories.* 1984; London: Grafton, 1986.
_____. *The Retreat from Liberty: The Erosion of Democracy in Today's Britain.* London: Zomba Books, 1983.
_____. *The Roads Between the Worlds.* Clarkston, GA: White Wolf, 1996.
_____. *The Secret of the Runestaff.* New York: Lancer, 1969.
_____. *Sojan.* Manchester: Savoy, 1977.
_____. *The Stealer of Souls.* New York: Lancer, 1967.
_____. *The Steel Tsar.* New York: DAW, 1981.
_____. *Tales from the End of Time.* London: Gollancz, 2014.
_____. *Tales from the Texas Woods.* Austin, TX: Mojo P, 1997.
_____. *The Time Dweller.* London: Hart Davis, 1969.
_____. *The Time Dweller.* New York: Berkley, 1969.
_____. *Travelling to Utopia.* London; Gollancz, 2014.
_____. *The Vengeance of Rome.* 2006; Oakland, CA: PM Press, 2013.
_____. *Von Bek.* Stone Mountain, GA: White Wolf, 1995.
_____. *Von Bek.* London: Gollancz, 2013.
_____. *The War Amongst the Angels.* London: Gollancz, 2014.
_____. *The Weird of the White Wolf.* New York: DAW, 1977.
_____. *The Whispering Swarm.* New York: Tor, 2015.
_____. *Wizardry and Wild Romance: A Study of Epic Fantasy.* Austin, TX: Monkeybrain Books, 2004.
_____, ed. *New Worlds: An Anthology.* London: Fontana, 1983.
Moorcock, Michael, Julien Blondel, Didier Poli, Robin Recht, and Jean Bastide. *Elric, Volume 1: The Ruby Throne.* London: Titan Comics, 2014.
Moorcock, Michael, Julien Blondel, Jean-Luc Cano, Julien Telo, Robin Recht, and

Didier Poli. *Elric, Volume 2: Stormbringer*. London: Titan Comics, 2014.

Moorcock, Michael, and Storm Constantine. *Silverheart: A Novel of the Multiverse*. 2000; Amherst, MA: Pyr, 2005.

Moorcock, Michael, and Walter Simonson. *Michael Moorcock's Elric: The Making of a Sorcerer*. New York: DC Comics, 2006.

Moorcock, Michael, Walter Simonson, Mark Reeve, and John Ridgway. *Michael Moorcock's Multiverse*. New York: DC Comics, 1999.

Nicholls, Peter, ed. *The Science Fiction Encyclopedia*. Garden City, NY: Doubleday, 1979.

Pater, Walter. *Selected Writings of Walter Pater*. Harold Bloom, ed. 1974; New York: Columbia University Press, 1982.

Pynchon, Thomas. *Slow Learner: Early Stories*. Boston: Little, Brown, 1984.

Roberson, Chris, and Francesco Biagini. *Elric: The Balance Lost*. 3 vols. Los Angeles: Boom! Studios, 2012.

Schaffer, Talia, ed. *Literature and Culture at the Fin de Siècle*. New York: Pearson Longman, 2007.

Sammon, Paul M. *Conan the Phenomenon: The Legacy of Robert E. Howard's Fantasy Icon*. Milwaukie, OR: Dark Horse, 2007.

Shepherd, Simon. *Spenser (Harvester New Readings)*. Atlantic Highlands, NJ: Humanities Research Press International, 1989.

Spenser, Edmund. *The Faerie Queene*. A. C. Hamilton, ed. London: Longman, 1977.

Suvin, Darko. *Metamorphoses of Science Fiction: On the Poetics and History of a Literary Genre*. New Haven: Yale University Press, 1979.

Thomas, Donald. *Swinburne: The Poet and His World*. New York: Oxford University Press, 1979.

Tolkien, J. R. R. *The Lord of the Rings: Collector's Edition*. Boston: Houghton Mifflin, 1994.

_____. *The Tolkien Reader*. New York: Ballantine, 1966.

Veldman, Meredith. *Fantasy, the Bomb, and the Greening of Britain: Romantic Protest, 1945–1980*. Cambridge: Cambridge University Press, 1994.

Wedgwood, C. V. *The Thirty Years War*. 1938; London: Methuen, 1981.

Index

Ackroyd, Peter 103, 168
Adams, Douglas: *The Hitchhiker's Guide to the Galaxy* 81
The Adventures of Jerry Cornelius (Moorcock, Harrison, Dean, and Jones) 149
The Adventures of Una Persson and Catherine Cornelius in the Twentieth Century (Moorcock) 55–56
The Alchemist's Question (Moorcock) 56
Aldiss, Brian 37, 38, 40, 47
An Alien Heat (Moorcock) 78–79
Amazing Stories 36, 143
Amis, Kingsley 48
"Ancient Shadows" (Moorcock) 80–81
Anderson, Poul 134; *The Broken Sword* 24, 25, 27, 31; "A Logical Conclusion" 17–18; *Three Hearts and Three Lions* 17–18, 22, 24, 25, 27, 29
Arioch 28, 114, 126–127, 150
"Aspects of Fantasy" (Moorcock) 31
Astounding Science Fiction 37
Attebery, Brian 31
Atwood, Margaret 168
Austen, Jane 118
The Avengers 97

Bailey, Hilary 38, 113, 161; *see also The Black Corridor*
balance 2, 10, 28–30, 34, 65–66, 118, 126–127, 132, 150, 157–158
Ball, Clifford 24
Ballard, J.G. 36–39, 161; *The Atrocity Exhibition* 40; *The Burning World* 37; *The Drowned World* 37; "The Terminal Beach" 39; *The Wind from Nowhere* 37
Balzac, Honoré: "Comédie Humaine" 131
Bastable, Oswald 6, 22, 75–77, 86, 130, 132, 134, 136, 138–140, 145, 151, 153, 156, 160

Baum, L. Frank 21; *The Wonderful Wizard of Oz* 22
Bayley, Barrington J. 36, 89
Beardsley, Aubrey 78
Beerbohm, Max 78
Behold the Man (Moorcock) 10, 44–45, 63, 81, 87, 99
Benjamin, Walter 34
Bester, Alfred 37
Biagini, Francesco: *Elric: The Balance Lost* (with Roberson) 167
Bierce, Ambrose: "An Occurrence at Owl Creek Bridge" 154
Bismarck, Otto von 137
"The Black Blade's Summoning" (Moorcock) 147
The Black Corridor (Moorcock, with Bailey) 39, 45–46, 130, 132
Blake, Sexton 140, 147, 159; *see also* Sexton Blake Library
"Blitz Kid" (Moorcock, Simonson, and Wiacek) 101
Blood (Moorcock) 138, 142, 145–150, 153
Bloom, Harold 169
Blowup 97
Blue Öyster Cult (band) 8, 166
Borges, Jorge Luis: "The Secret Miracle" 154
Boys' World 89
Bradbury, Ray 37
Breakfast in the Ruins (Moorcock) 12, 50, 88–90
Brecht, Bertolt 34
The Brothel in Rosenstrasse (Moorcock) 10, 96, 99, 113, 117, 135, 148
Brunner, John 38
The Bull and the Spear (Moorcock) 72
Bunyan, John 82
Burroughs, Edgar Rice 5, 15, 21, 31, 61–

62, 159; *The Gods of Mars* 61; *A Princess of Mars* 22, 61; *see also* Carter, John; Tarzan
Burroughs, William 36, 40, 49, 122; *Naked Lunch* 36
Butterworth, Michael 38
Byron, George Gordon, Lord 26
Byzantium Endures (Moorcock) 90–96, 103, 104, 106, 113, 123

Cabell, James Branch 68
Calvert, Robert 166
Calvino, Italo 49
Campbell, John W. 37
Camus, Albert 26; *The Stranger* 24
Carnell, E.J. ("Ted") 24, 35–36, 168
Carter, Angela 168
Carter, John 15, 19, 26, 57, 61, 134
Carter, Lin 23, 30, 72
Casino Royale 97
Cawthorn, James 26, 130, 149, 155, 166; *see also The Distant Suns*
Chabon, Michael 168, 169
The Champion of Garathorm (Moorcock) 73
Chaos 2, 10, 12, 16, 28–29, 34, 40, 44, 66, 68, 71, 74–75, 81, 87, 112, 120–121, 126–127, 132, 142, 144–147, 150, 151, 158, 160, 163
chaos theory 142, 144–145
Chaykin, Howard 119, 149
The Chinese Agent (Moorcock) 134
The City in the Autumn Stars (Moorcock) 62, 96, 107, 112, 114, 115–118, 135, 137–138, 152, 156
City of the Beast, aka *Warriors of Mars* (Moorcock) 61–62
Clute, John 20, 34, 105, 107, 110, 141
Coleridge, Samuel Taylor 81
Conan 11, 19, 23–25, 57, 70, 72, 149, 154–155
"Conan: American Phenomenon" (Moorcock) 26
Conan Doyle, Arthur 11; *see also* Holmes, Sherlock
Conan the Barbarian (film) 23, 149
The Condition of Muzak (Moorcock) 1, 11, 50, 51–54, 55, 90–91, 97, 98, 102, 110, 123, 157
Conrad, Joseph 77
Constant Fire, aka *The Transformation of Miss Mavis Ming* (Moorcock) 62, 81
Cornelius, Jerry 6, 11, 13, 35, 41–44, 46–57, 67, 79, 81, 86–87, 88, 90–91, 96, 110, 122, 130, 131, 134–135, 145, 150, 157, 161

Cornelius, Mrs. 50–51, 54, 90–91, 96, 102, 105, 110
Corum 5, 11, 21, 29, 60, 62, 69–73, 74–75, 120, 121, 128, 131–132, 135, 142, 153, 160, 169
Count Brass (Moorcock) 73
"Count Brass" trilogy (Moorcock) 72–75, 119
"Crossing into Cambodia" (Moorcock) 136
Cunningham, Michael 169
A Cure for Cancer (Moorcock) 43–44, 47–48, 52, 53, 54, 88

Daker, John 16–19, 22, 70, 112, 118–122, 128, 131–132, 136, 137, 151, 156–157; *see also* Erekosë; Urlik Skarsol
The Dancers at the End of Time (Moorcock) 78–81, 125, 139, 160
d'Annunzio, Gabriele 111
Dante Alighieri, *Divine Comedy* 131
Daughter of Dreams, aka *The Dreamthief's Daughter* (Moorcock) 7, 87, 150–153
Davey, John 7, 130, 133
"A Dead Singer," aka "Dead Singers" (Moorcock) 136
decadence 64, 70, 78–79
de Camp, L. Sprague 17, 23, 72
The Deep Fix (band) 8, 107, 166
"The Deep Fix" (Moorcock) 39
Delany, Samuel R. 23, 57, 58–59, 86
"The Delhi Division" (Moorcock) 47
Del Rey, Lester 59
Destiny's Brother, aka *The Skrayling Tree* (Moorcock) 151, 152, 153, 155
Díaz, Junot 169
Dickens, Charles 2, 88, 103
Disch, Thomas M. 38, 40, 58, 161
The Distant Suns (Moorcock, with Cawthorn) 130
Doctor Who 159–160
Doctor Who: The Coming of the Terraphiles (Moorcock) 159–160
Dostoevsky, Fyodor 88
Dowson, Ernest 78
The Dragon in the Sword (Moorcock) 104, 112–113, 118–123, 129, 130, 131, 135, 136, 137, 143, 145, 152, 157
"The Dreaming City" (Moorcock) 24–26, 41–42, 70, 72, 124, 151
Dumas, Alexandre 162–163
Dunsany, Edward Plunkett, Lord 30, 134; *The King of Elfland's Daughter* 27
Duval, Claude 148, 162
Dworkin, Andrea 56

Index

Eddison, E.R. 30
Einstein, Albert 137
Eldren 17–20, 27–28, 70, 120–121, 145, 152; *see also* Melnibonéans; Vadhagh
Eliot, George 88
Eliot, T.S.: *The Waste Land* 114
Ellison, Harlan 167; *Dangerous Visions* 58, 59
Elric 5, 6, 7, 11, 13, 16, 19, 21, 22, 35, 40–42, 56–57, 60, 62, 66, 67, 70–72, 74–75, 81, 86, 104, 113, 119, 121, 123–127, 131–132, 134, 140, 142, 147–148, 150–158, 161–162, 168–169
"Elric at the End of Time" (Moorcock) 81, 119, 125
Elric of Melniboné (Moorcock) 72, 155, 167
Elric: The Making of a Sorcerer (Moorcock and Simonson) 155–156
The End of All Songs (Moorcock) 78
"End of Time" stories (Moorcock) 6, 12, 55, 61, 78–81, 87, 125, 139, 159
The English Assassin (Moorcock) 11, 48–51, 52, 53, 54, 55, 62, 88, 90, 98, 102, 110
entropy 10, 39, 43–44, 48, 52, 80, 143
The Entropy Tango (Moorcock) 55
"Epic Pooh" (Moorcock) 32–33
Erekosë 5, 16–19, 22, 53, 60, 67, 70, 71, 74–75, 104, 112, 118, 119, 121, 131, 151, 157; *see also* Daker, John; Urlik Skarsol
Eternal Champion 2, 5, 6, 11, 12–13, 16–19, 22–23, 29, 61, 62, 66, 68, 71–72, 73–75, 79, 81, 86, 112, 118–122, 128, 130–141, 142, 143, 151, 157–158, 160, 163, 168
The Eternal Champion (Moorcock) 11, 16–19, 22, 27, 67, 70, 76, 136–137, 145, 151, 157

Fabulous Harbours, aka *Fabulous Harbors* (Moorcock) 138, 142, 147–148
Faulkner, William 40
Fielding, Henry, *Tom Jones* 116
The Final Programme (film) 57, 167
The Final Programme (Moorcock) 41–44, 46–48, 49, 52, 53, 54, 56, 96–97, 117, 135, 143, 157
Finch, Jon 57
Firbank, Ronald 78
Firing the Cathedral (Moorcock) 55
"The Flame Bringers" (Moorcock) 26
"Flux" (Moorcock) 137
Ford, Henry 93
The Fortress of the Pearl (Moorcock) 9, 113, 123–125, 130, 152
Fowles, John: *The French Lieutenant's Woman* 122

Fox, Gardner 23
Frazetta, Frank 5, 13, 166
Friedrich Barbarossa 17, 19, 53
Frost, Robert: "Directive" 114
Fuest, Robert 57, 167

Gaiman, Neil 167; *Sandman* 167
Gernsback, Hugo 36, 143
Gillan, Karen 160
"The Girl Who Killed Sylvia Blade" (Moorcock) 148
Gleick, James 144
Gloriana; or, The Unfulfill'd Queen (Moorcock) 12, 61, 81–85, 86, 90, 102, 112, 113, 125, 168
Godard, Jean-Luc 57
The Golden Barge (Moorcock) 19, 82, 84, 132, 168
Gordon, Giles 38
Gould, Robert 155, 166
The Great Rock 'n' Roll Swindle, aka *Gold Diggers of 1977* (Moorcock) 55
Greenland, Colin 38, 39, 75, 139, 165
Guardian Fiction Prize 1, 123
Guild of Temporal Adventurers 55, 129, 139–140, 145, 151, 153

Harrison, M. John 38, 47; "The Ash Circus" 47; "The Nash Circuit" 47; "Running Down" 39
Hartwell, David G. 38–39
Hawkmoon, Duke Dorian 5, 11, 21, 29, 60, 62–67, 70, 73–75, 119, 131–132, 135, 142, 156, 169
Hawkwind (band) 8, 48, 90, 166; *Chronicle of the Black Sword* 166
Heinlein, Robert A.: *Starship Troopers* 80
The History of the Runestaff (Moorcock) 62–66
Hitler, Adolf 109, 137; *Mein Kampf* 92–93
Holger Danske (Ogier Danois) 17, 19, 53
The Hollow Lands (Moorcock) 78
Holmes, Sherlock 11, 57
Holy Grail 6, 114–115, 117, 135, 147, 150
Horace 3
Howard, Robert E. 5, 21–24, 31; "The Phoenix on the Sword" 72; *see also* Conan

The Ice Schooner (Moorcock) 130

"The Jade Man's Eyes" (Moorcock) 118, 135
Jagger, Mick 77
Jakes, John 23
Jakubowski, Maxim 47

James, Henry: "New York Edition" 131, 133
James, William 21
Jerusalem Commands (Moorcock) 91, 104–106
The Jewel in the Skull (Moorcock) 62, 65, 166
Johnson, Lionel 78
Jones, Jeffrey Catherine 166
Jones, Langdon 38, 47; "The Eye of the Lens" 39; *The New SF* 47
Joyce, James 37, 38, 40, 49, 50, 88, 164; *Ulysses* 10, 50, 54, 97–98, 103, 132

Kaluta, Michael William 166
King Arthur 17, 19, 25
King Charles I 162–163
King of the City (Moorcock) 100, 107, 112, 141, 167, 168
The King of the Swords (Moorcock) 69–70, 71, 73, 74
"Kings in Darkness" (Moorcock and Cawthorn) 26
The Knight of the Swords (Moorcock) 27, 70, 72
Kuttner, Henry 24

The Land Leviathan (Moorcock) 77–78, 138, 139
Langland, William, *Piers Plowman* 154
"The Last Enchantment" (Moorcock) 119
The Laughter of Carthage (Moorcock) 91, 93, 95, 96, 103, 104, 106, 116, 123
Law 2, 10, 12, 16, 28–29, 34, 40, 44, 66, 68, 71, 74–75, 87, 112, 126–127, 132, 142, 144, 150, 151, 158, 160, 163
Lawrence, D.H. 38
League of Temporal Adventurers *see* Guild of Temporal Adventurers
Le Guin, Ursula K. 21, 22
Leiber, Fritz 23, 24
Lenin (Vladimir Ilyitch Ulianov) 77
Lessing, Doris 168
Lethem, Jonathan 169
Lewis, C.S. 21, 22, 48
Lewis, Wyndham 37
London Bone (Moorcock) 167
Longfellow, Henry Wadsworth: *The Song of Hiawatha* 152
Lord of the Spiders, aka *Blades of Mars* (Moorcock) 61–62
Lunching with the Antichrist (Moorcock) 135–136, 147, 148

Macdonald, George 30
The Mad God's Amulet, aka *The Sorcerer's Amulet* (Moorcock) 62, 65, 166

Makhno, Nestor 95, 139
Mandelbrot, Benoit 144–145
Marvell, Andrew 163
Masters of the Pit, aka *Barbarians of Mars* (Moorcock) 61–62
Matthews, Rodney 166
McCarthy, Cormac 168–169
Melnibonéans 27–28, 121; *see also* Eldren; Vadhagh
Melville, Herman: *Moby-Dick* 10
Merril, Judith 57–58; *England Swings SF* 58
Métal Hurlant 57
The Metatemporal Detective (Moorcock) 159
Michael Moorcock's Multiverse (Moorcock, Simonson, Reeve, and Ridgway) 56, 149–150
Miéville, China 33
Milton, John: *Paradise Lost* 80, 112
Mirenburg 96, 117, 152
Modem Times 2.0 (Moorcock) 55
Moebius (Jean Giraud): *Le Garage Hermétique* 57
"Moonbeam Roads" trilogy (Moorcock) 9, 13, 143, 150–160
Moorcock, Linda Steele 113
Moorcock, Michael: "abandons" fantasy 81, 85, 112; consolidates his work in omnibus editions 130–141, 142; edits *New Worlds* 35–40; "ends" Eternal Champion sequence 60–61, 73–75, 113, 118–119, 121–122, 143, 151, 157–158; and formal experimentation 49–50, 97–98; on J.R.R. Tolkien 30–34; literary awards and reputation 1, 45, 103, 123, 167–169; and "new wave" SF 57–59, 123; renames characters 134–141; revises work 134, 136–141; on world-building 21–22, 75; youth and early career 15–16
Moore, Alan 141, 167; *The League of Extraordinary Gentlemen* 77, 167; *V for Vendetta* 167; *Watchmen* 167
Moore, C.L. 24
Morris, William 30, 32, 154
Morrison, Grant 167
Mosley, Walter 168
Mother London (Moorcock) 1, 6, 9, 12, 50, 88, 96–104, 107, 111–112, 122–123, 141–142, 167–169
multiverse 2, 16, 20–23, 69, 72, 86, 128–129, 137, 138, 145–146, 158, 160, 163
Mussolini, Benito 108
My Experiences in the Third World War (Moorcock) 136

Index

Nabokov, Vladimir, *Lolita* 164; *Look at the Harlequins!* 164
Nebula Award 45
Nesbit, E. 75; *New Treasure Seekers* 76; *The Story of the Treasure Seekers* 76; *The Wouldbegoods* 76
"new wave" in SF 57–59, 123
New Worlds 2, 11, 35–40, 44, 46, 57–61, 80, 113, 122, 143, 161, 162
"No Ordinary Christian" (Moorcock) 148
"Nomad of the Time Streams" trilogy (Moorcock) 11–12, 22, 75–77, 81, 138–141
nouveau roman 49

The Oak and the Ram (Moorcock) 72

Paolozzi, Eduardo 36
Pater, Walter: *The Renaissance* 52, 64, 78
Peake, Mervyn 12, 30, 61, 82, 84, 113; *Gormenghast* 82; *Gormenghast* trilogy 82–83; *Titus Alone* 82; *Titus Groan* 82
"The Peking Junction" (Moorcock) 47
Persson, Una 50, 53, 55–56, 124, 127, 129, 134, 139–140, 145, 151, 153
Phoenix in Obsidian, aka *The Silver Warriors* (Moorcock) 5, 7, 11, 18, 22, 67–68, 70, 76, 114, 119, 135, 136–137, 145
Picacio, John 166
"The Pleasure Garden of Felipe Sagittarius" (Moorcock) 130, 137
Pound, Ezra 93, 111; *The Cantos* 93
Powell, Enoch 77
Pratchett, Terry: "Discworld" novels 81
Pratt, Fletcher 17
Priest, Christopher 58
Prince Rupert of the Rhine 162–163
Princess Diana 55
The Protocols of the Elders of Zion 92
Proust, Marcel 37, 164; *Time Regained* 54
Pullman, Philip: *His Dark Materials* 152
Pyat, Colonel 12, 90–96, 104–106, 108–111
"The Pyat Quartet," aka "Between the Wars" (Moorcock) 9, 12, 61, 88, 90–96, 101, 103–106, 108–112, 141, 142, 159, 168, 169
Pynchon, Thomas 169; *The Crying of Lot 49* 47; "Entropy" 39

The Queen of the Swords (Moorcock) 70, 126–127
The Quest for Tanelorn (Moorcock) 60–61, 73–75, 81, 113, 114, 118, 119, 121–122, 129, 131, 143, 145, 157

Radcliffe, Ann 118
Raleigh, Sir Walter 83
Reagan, Ronald 77
realistic fiction 86–88, 110–111
Reeve, Mark 150
The Retreat from Liberty (Moorcock) 56
The Revenge of the Rose (Moorcock) 113, 123, 125–129, 143, 146, 148
Riches, Jill 113
Ridgway, John 150, 155
Roberson, Chris: *Elric: The Balance Lost* (with Biagini) 167
Röhm, Ernst 108
Rohmer, Éric 57
"The Romanian Question" (Moorcock) 55
Rowling, J.K. 152
Runacre, Jenny 57
The Runestaff, aka *The Secret of the Runestaff* (Moorcock) 62, 135
Rushdie, Salman 169; *The Satanic Verses* 103
Ruskin, John 32
The Russian Intelligence (Moorcock) 134

The Sailor on the Seas of Fate (Moorcock) 22, 74, 118, 124, 131, 145
Sallis, James: "Jeremiad" 47
Sartre, Jean-Paul 24, 26
Schwarzenegger, Arnold 23
Science Fantasy 24, 26, 31, 35–36, 68
Science Fiction Adventures 20
Science Wonder Stories 143
Scott, Sir Walter: *The Bride of Lammermoor* 133; "Waverley Novels" 131, 133
"Second Ether" stories (Moorcock) 9, 12, 107, 138, 142–143, 145–149, 160
Sex Pistols (band) 55
Sexton Blake Library 15, 147
The Shores of Death, aka *The Twilight Man* (Moorcock) 131, 132, 137
Shrimpton, Jean 97
Silverheart (Moorcock and Constantine) 158–159
Simonson, Walter 150, 155–156
Sinclair, Iain 103, 150, 163, 168
Sladek, John 38, 58
The Sleeping Sorceress (Moorcock) 72
Smith, Matt 160
Smollett, Tobias 116
Sojan 15, 18
Son of the Wolf, aka *The White Wolf's Son* (Moorcock) 143, 151–153, 155–158
"The Spencer Inheritance" (Moorcock) 55
Spender, Stephen 77

Spenser, Edmund: *The Faerie Queene* 82–84
Spinrad, Norman 38, 47, 167; *Bug Jack Baron* 40
Sputnik 38–39
Stalin, Josef 139–140
The Steel Tsar (Moorcock) 77–78, 96, 134, 138–140
Stormbringer 5, 7, 11, 16, 25–26, 42, 67–68, 72, 121, 152, 153, 156
Stormbringer (Moorcock) 25–26, 29, 72, 135, 153, 155, 166, 167
Story, Jack Trevor 48
The Sundered Worlds (Moorcock) 6, 20–21, 131, 136–137, 145, 160
Swinburne, Algernon Charles 111, 125
sword and sorcery 23–24
The Sword and the Stallion (Moorcock) 72–73, 114
The Sword of the Dawn (Moorcock) 62, 166
The Swords of Heaven, the Flowers of Hell (Chaykin and Moorcock) 119, 149
Symons, Arthur 78

Talbot, Bryan: *The Adventures of Luther Arkwright* 57
Tales from the Texas Woods (Moorcock) 159
Tanelorn 68–70, 73–75, 118, 137, 153
Tarzan 15, 26
Tarzan Adventures 15, 19
Tennyson, Alfred Lord: *Idylls of the King* 114
Thatcher, Margaret 107, 126
"Through the Shaving Mirror" (Moorcock) 145
Times (London) 1, 168
"To Rescue Tanelorn…" (Moorcock) 68–69, 136–137
Tolkien, J.R.R. 30–34, 48; *The Lord of the Rings* 9, 21, 27, 30–34, 75, 161; "On Fairy-Stories" 21, 33–34
Tolstoy, Leo 88
Truffaut, François 57
Turpin, Dick 148, 162
Twain, Mark: *A Connecticut Yankee in King Arthur's Court* 17
Twiggy (Lesley Hornby) 97
Tygers of Pan Tang (band) 166

Urlik Skarsol 5, 22, 67–68, 70, 119, 134; *see also* Daker, John; Erekosë

Vadhagh 27–28, 70, 152; *see also* Eldren; Melnibonéans

Vallejo, Boris 166
VanderMeer, Jeff 167
The Vengeance of Rome (Moorcock) 91, 94, 103, 104, 108–111, 159
"Von Bek" novels (Moorcock) 107, 112–118, 135, 137, 152
Vonnegut, Kurt: *Slaughterhouse-Five* 47

Wagner, Richard: *Parsifal* 114
Walpole, Horace: *The Castle of Otranto* 83
The War Amongst the Angels (Moorcock) 7, 138, 142, 143, 147, 148–149, 150, 157
The War Hound and the World's Pain (Moorcock) 9, 96, 107, 112, 113–117, 123, 128, 135, 137, 138, 158
The Warlord of the Air (Moorcock) 50, 61, 62, 75–78, 111, 138, 139, 156, 157
Waugh, Evelyn 111
Weill, Kurt 137
The Weird of the White Wolf (Moorcock) 124
Weird Tales 23–24
Wells, H.G. 2, 61, 75; *The War in the Air* 75
Whelan, Michael 166
Wheldrake, Ernest 85, 111, 125–126, 148
"While the Gods Laugh" (Moorcock) 26, 28–29, 41–42
The Whispering Swarm (Moorcock) 13, 143, 158, 160–165
Whistler, James McNeill 78
Whitbread Prize 1, 103, 123
"The White Pirate" (Moorcock) 148
"White Stars" (Moorcock) 80
Wiener, Norbert 143
Wilde, Oscar 78
Williams, Charles: *War in Heaven* 114
Williams, Tad 168
Wilson, Angus 168
The Winds of Limbo, aka *The Fireclown* (Moorcock) 62, 81, 131, 132, 137
Windsor-Smith, Barry 155
Wodehouse, P.G. 159–160
Woodroffe, Patrick 166
Woolf, Virginia 37, 40; *To the Lighthouse* 10
world-building 21–22, 75
The Wrecks of Time, aka *The Rituals of Infinity* (Moorcock) 131, 132, 137–138, 140–141

Zenith the Albino 140, 147
Zoline, Pamela 38, 58; "The Heat Death of the Universe" 39

www.ingramcontent.com/pod-product-compliance
Ingram Content Group UK Ltd.
Pitfield, Milton Keynes, MK11 3LW, UK
UKHW042004140426
5217IPUK00015B/974